THE DRUM HANDBOOK

THE **DRUM** HANDBOOK

Buying, maintaining, and getting the best from your drum kit

Geoff Nicholls

THE DRUM HANDBOOK

Buying, maintaining, and getting the best from your drum kit

A BACKBEAT BOOK
First edition 2003
Published by Backbeat Books
600 Harrison Street,
San Francisco, CA94107, US
www.backbeatbooks.com

An imprint of The Music Player Network United
Entertainment Media Inc.

Published for Backbeat Books by Outline Press Ltd,
Unit 2a Union Court, 20-22 Union Road, London, SW4 6JP, England.
www.backbeatuk.com

ISBN 0-87930-750-1

ART DIRECTOR: Nigel Osborne
EDITOR: John Morrish
DESIGN: Paul Cooper Design
EDITORIAL DIRECTOR: Tony Bacon
PHOTOGRAPHY: Miki Slingsby

Origination and Print by Colorprint (Hong Kong)

03 04 05 06 07 5 4 3 2 1

CONTENTS

INTRODUCTION
AT THE HEART OF MODERN MUSIC

"Growing up, I thought I was going to be a rock star. I always wanted to play the drums but my dad didn't want me to play. We actually had a drum kit in the house but I was never allowed to play it – it was on top of a wardrobe. Really wanting it means I still get excited when I sit behind the kit. If I'd been given it on a plate maybe it wouldn't have happened. It was a burning desire."

ANDY GANGADEEN (THE BAYS)

The drum kit has been with us for about 100 years. It acquired its modern form in the late 1930s, when Gene Krupa was the only drummer ever to become a matinee idol.

I believe the drum kit was the most important new musical instrument of the 20th century, even more so than the electric guitar or the keyboard synthesiser. OK, I might be a bit biased, but this is how I see it.

The 20th century was the century of rhythm. Although the drums may have been in the background for much of the music, the kit was the one constant instrument throughout all those world–changing musical movements that began in the USA: starting with the early stirrings of jazz in the southern states, through big-band swing and the bebop revolution, on to rhythm and blues and rock'n'roll and thence to soul, funk, heavy metal, disco, punk, and so on.

While the principal instruments changed with fashion, from trumpet and clarinet to piano, saxophone, electric guitar and then synthesiser, the drum kit was always there providing the beat. Admittedly, there was a significant blip in the 1980s as computers and samplers appeared, but now the acoustic drum kit seems firmly re–established for the next century.

Despite this impressive legacy, the drum kit remains a mystery to many people. It looks complicated. Perhaps because it is hidden behind singers and guitarists – with the drummer in turn hiding behind the instrument – it's not obvious what the kit does, and how the drummer goes about it. Then there is the lingering perception that the drum kit is not a 'proper' instrument and that drummers just do their thing with no set method. Nothing could be further from the truth.

Some of this misconception arises because the form of the drum kit is not that obvious. Although there is a standard basic layout, every drummer personalises his or her kit, and the scope for individual design is vast. Some kits are minimal and some are massive. My aim in this book is to explain and demystify as many aspects of the acoustic drum kit as I can manage in the space available. By 'acoustic drum kit' I mean the familiar modern instrument, comprising drums

and cymbals and the hardware necessary to mount them. The drum kit is a big subject that really could occupy several tomes. So I've included a Bibliography to guide you towards further information. There's also a full Glossary to help you find the meaning of any unfamiliar terms.

THE JOY OF DRUMS

I doubt if there's a single person in the world who has not at some time wanted to play the drums. On the face of it, the drums are the easiest instrument to play, and you can get rid of a load of frustration and aggression at the same time.

There is a thriving industry, particularly in California, based on the premise that a group of individuals can reap therapeutic value and experience bonding by sitting in a circle banging on single drums. I have no doubt that this is true. We all have the urge to tap and bash things. As babies, that's exactly what every one of us does. Then in school we all play percussion instruments and sing and dance, activities that are rightly seen as essential to our normal, healthy development. As we grow older, and more self–conscious, most of us let singing, dancing and drumming drop away. We may dance socially and sing in the shower, or even have a go at karaoke. But most of us stop drumming. We never lose the desire, though. It's pretty normal to want to have a go at drumming. So don't feel awkward, don't be shy – have a bash.

But once we've accepted that basic urge and we contemplate the drum kit as a serious proposition, are there any drawbacks? Well, there are the obvious objections: the kit takes up a lot of space and it is noisy. It can also harm your hearing and put your back out – but so can squeezing a violin under your ear and sawing away for several hours every day.

There is, however, one non–injurious yet probably more relevant drawback that you might want to consider. It is that the drum kit is, for the most part, an accompanying instrument. Many full drum kits have been bought, only for the novelty to fade after a month or two when the realisation settles in that it's only fun when you're playing along with other instruments.

Drum solos are great – but there's a limited market for them. And they're not that easy to play unless you really develop your technique. But playing with others in a band – when everyone's having a good time (in more senses than one) – is the best fun ever. I don't have the slightest statistical evidence for this, but I'd lay money on the fact that drummers enjoy their gigs more often and more intensely than anyone else in the band. As well as being a great cardiovascular workout, drumming is a joyous occupation and it spills over into the drummer's personality. Often derided as mad, drummers are more often simply enthusiastic.

> "Luckily, drummers are generally friendly. Drumming is vocational, along the lines of having your hands in wet soil – it's the real stuff."
>
> GARY HUSBAND (ALAN HOLDSWORTH, LEVEL 42)

Drummers just love to play. And drummers love to watch other drummers play. They go to 'drum clinics' where they bond and share. There is an international drumming community that is stronger than that for any other instrument. Come and join us.

DO I NEED A FULL KIT?

Before moving on I want briefly to address a subject that often crops up when thinking about buying your first drums. Is there an alternative? Well, you could think about taking up the marching side drum, which is, of course, another thing altogether. Many top players started off in American school parade bands or the pipe bands of northern Britain and their counterparts in

"I learned to read early on and went through the rudimental period. The first three years without a drum kit – I don't know where I had the discipline to keep on with it when I was only ten."

ANDY NEWMARK (SLY STONE, ROXY MUSIC)

Europe. That involves playing a special sort of snare/side drum: a deep drum with extremely high-tension heads. There are different skills involved here, to do with ensemble playing and stick choreography. The camaraderie and the shared discipline are inspiring and fulfilling. You also learn complicated rudimental beats that you may never acquire if you start out bashing on a full kit. Learning to play the parade side drum is quite different from playing a drum kit, but it could help you a great deal with your hand technique.

But most people reading this book will be thinking about playing in bands and will have the drum kit in mind. Drum kits take up quite a bit of room, and one of the first considerations for young drummers – or more often their parents – is this: do I have to buy the whole thing? Could I buy just a snare drum to start off with? If money is short, this may be unavoidable, but don't forget you'll still need to buy the drum itself, sticks, a snare drum stand and preferably a stool. The snare drum is just one part (albeit a very important part) of the kit. It's a bit like buying a guitar with one string: sure, you'd get a few tunes out of it, but your range would be severely restricted.

Thinking along the same lines, how about starting with just a **practice pad**? Well, a practice pad is a useful tool, but it's not an instrument at all. You sometimes read the story of a top drummer who spent years toiling with just a practice pad before being allowed onto the snare drum and now, as a result, has fabulous hands. Well, bully for them. People with that sort of dedication do sometimes become mega players, but they're rare individuals. For most young drummers, desperate to let loose on a full kit, a practice pad is incredibly frustrating and might even put them off altogether.

All right then, how about a full practice pad kit? It would be cheaper than a real kit and quieter. Once more, practice kits have their place and can be useful for working out moves and practising your strokes. But again, you are not playing an instrument – you're banging on a set of toneless rubber/wood pads, for pity's sake. That is not making music.

Another alternative that often comes up is this: should I buy an **electronic kit** instead of an acoustic kit, so I can practise 'silently' wearing headphones? Well, leaving aside the fact that young people buy drum kits just so they *can* make an appalling racket, it is not quite true to say electronic kits are quiet when they're not being amplified. Most rubber pad kits still make a significant amount of tapping noise. And the kits made by ddrum, Roland and others which use real plastic heads – even when they are fitted over foam pads – make even more sound. Anyone hoping for a quiet night in while you're stamping on the electronic bass drum pad upstairs in your bedroom can forget it. It will cause as much grief as a real bass drum, simply because of the vibrations. Down in the basement, OK, you will probably get away with it.

Having said that, a more recent development is the introduction of woven mesh heads, which are much closer to being silent. Certainly, you could play these in an adjoining room and barely be heard. There are a few different versions of these heads and they are now being fitted to electronic pads, including those by Pintech, Roland and Koby. They are great fun to play and have a nice bouncy feel.

So that is one solution. However, before following that path, you should be aware that the electronic kit is not the same instrument as the acoustic kit. Indeed, there's no reason why it should be. Electronic kits will provide you with a truly fantastic choice of sounds – percussive and tuned – but nothing can prepare you for the experience of playing an acoustic kit except playing an acoustic kit. The gulf in feel between an electronic kit and an acoustic kit is noticeably greater than that between a digitally sampled electronic piano and a real acoustic piano. The nuances of touch and dynamics you get from an acoustic kit are more subtle and extensive than even the best electronic kit can offer. And the best electronic kit is as expensive as a top acoustic drum kit. Then you've got to amplify it, which involves speakers that can handle the full frequency range and power without blowing up every time you slam the kick pedal.

That sounds as if I'm against electronic kits. I'm really not. The modern electronic percussion controller will give you a thousand stored sounds, you'll be able to play chords, use the sequencer as a practice tool to develop your sense of time and groove, play along with pre-set songs, CDs, MP3s and much more.

Yet the fact is you can go to a dozen shows by major acts and the drummer in each of them will inevitably be playing an acoustic kit. There may well be electronics involved, but they will be in the form of add-on pads triggering samples and sequenced percussive loops, etc. I don't know why the acoustic kit has retained this central lynchpin position, but I do have a theory. And, for almost 20 years, I have been expecting the electronic kit to catch up with the acoustic kit and push it into the sidelines, as has happened with the acoustic piano (in commercial music). It hasn't happened yet – but I wouldn't bet against it happening in the future.

My theory? All right, for what it's worth, the sound of an acoustic kit in the flesh is loud and obnoxious and bursting with overtones. Mike that up and put it through a PA system and it still has a lot of presence and edge. The sound of an electronic kit is much safer: it's already processed and the rough edges have been taken off. The dynamic range of sound is much narrower and cleaner. Put that through the PA and the end result is bland.

Some people say electronic drums "don't shift air". I think of it as if the sound has already gone through one generation and now it's gone through a second. It's been diluted. So when you see drummers playing electronic kits live on television, or in concert or at trade shows, they nearly always sound like they're playing plastic trays. There's no depth or power. The nasty edge has gone. Until this is sorted out, most drummers will continue to play acoustic drums live for the fundamental beat.

If noise is a problem you can always muffle the sound of your acoustic kit. This will spoil the feel to a large extent, but it will allow you to practise your beats and fills, maybe with headphones on, playing along to favourite tracks. You can simply put cloths of various thicknesses over your drums, which will cut out half the sound straight away. You can buy rubber practice discs of the correct diameters to cover each of your drums. You can stuff your bass drum with blankets and pillows. There are also muffling devices such as Remo's Muff'ls, which are circular plastic trays with foam inlays that sit beneath the heads so you can play on the batter heads unimpeded. The problem with these is that you have to take the heads off to fit them, and this is unlikely to be something you want to do regularly. Muffling devices for cymbals include elasticised cloth bands that fit around the perimeter of each cymbal and rubber discs that sit on the cymbals and effectively kill the sound. This is an area crying out for your own ingenuity, and it doesn't have to cost much at all.

So now let's turn our attention to the drum kit itself. What exactly is it? Where did it come from? And why does it take the form it does? Later in the book you'll find a short chapter on vintage kits and the kit's evolution. But for now let's just say that the drum kit is a conglomeration of several instruments, with many rhythmic functions, that have come together over the past century to be played by a single seated individual. The kit has been gradually honed to fulfil the functions of today's music; music of almost unlimited variety.

The kit is remarkably versatile and elastic. And the drums will find a place in more styles of music than any other instrument.

SECTION 1 | THE BASICS

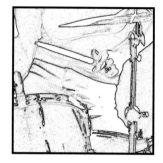

HOW TO BUY DRUMS
AND BUDGET KITS

I come from the generation that was turned on to pop music by The Beatles, and I blame Ringo Starr for awakening my lifelong passion for drums. Then again, I also remember being impressed at an extremely young age by seeing a snare drum in an amateur group, all gleaming white pearl and chrome and making this extraordinary noise.

Many of us spend years slavering over the drums as an object of lust before actually getting our first kit. You will probably already have idols you've seen on the TV and may know the type of drums and cymbals they use. You may have saved enough to start with a budget kit, or you may be looking for a better quality kit secondhand. Whatever the case, you've started to do some market research. And this is essential. Take every opportunity to study the gear, go along to drum stores and trade fairs and gather all the information and brochures you can.

The choices of drums, cymbals and hardware are immense and this book can only tell you so much. It can help you make some valid comparisons and maybe read between the lines, and then it's up to you.

THE RIGHT PRICE

Because of price cutting it's sometimes difficult to see where the budget lines end and the middle lines start. Reductions of up to 40-50 per cent are not unknown in the USA. This can be extremely confusing and drummers have been known to travel huge distances in order to get the best discount. Nowadays, of course, there are great on-line offers as well as magazine adverts that include shipping costs. As with all other commodities dealers juggle their margins and price incentives and a lot depends on the relationships they build up with the manufacturers and distributors.

The big manufacturers hold annual dealer days where the dealers who show up are rewarded with special discounts if they place their orders on the day. This means that one dealer may stock up on a dozen of this season's latest kit, which it can sell cheaper than the store down the road while still chalking up the same profit.

Loyal dealers will also get the chance to buy last year's kits (and last year's colours) at big discounts, so the distributor can clear its warehouse ready for the new lines. This is another way for you to get a bargain. If your dealer has a kit that looks perfectly good but is a lot cheaper it's probably just outstayed its welcome on the shelves. This doesn't mean it's a bad kit, just that the manufacturers are pushing a slightly different line this season.

On the other hand, as with cars and clothes, you can easily get stuck with a colour that will cause you embarrassment a year or two down the line. Don't land yourself with an obviously duff finish just because it's really cheap. Make sure you can live with it and that your band won't disown you.

Competition in the beginner market is fierce and designs are upgraded every year. Dealers vie

> "You have to be a bit of an anorak. You have to read up and know that a double ply head will lower the pitch. You don't have to be a complete trainspotter but you have to know a bit – it's like a carpenter saying I can't be bothered to find out about the right tool so I'll just bang away with a chisel."
>
> *DAVE MATTACKS (PAUL McCARTNEY, XTC, RICHARD THOMPSON, MARY CHAPIN CARPENTER)*

with one another to offer the keenest prices, and are often willing to cut profits to the bone in order to get your first-time custom. Once hooked, a drummer will always need to come back for new sticks, heads and upgrades to better hardware, snare drums and cymbals, etc. It's tempting to go for the cheapest deal, but that is not always the best move.

Remember that these kits may look superficially the same, but a crucial way they can differ is in the hardware package that is attached. So if you see a kit offered which is much cheaper than standard, it will probably have outdated or flimsier hardware.

THE RIGHT SOUND

If you've not played a drum kit before, the big question is how do you know if it sounds any good? Drum kits in the flesh may not sound anything like your preconception. What you hear on recordings, television and live concerts can be very misleading. The drums have been processed through all sorts of studio and PA gear.

In any case, drums sound quite different from a distance than they do when you're sitting right on top of them, behind the kit. This is especially true when you're playing on your own and the ring and resonance of the drums is not being absorbed by the sound of the other instruments. It also hasn't helped that for the last two decades drummers have regularly mimed on TV to tracks that have never been near a real drum kit nor seen a drumstick. They've been programmed on a computer, more often than not by a producer or keyboard player.

The bottom line is this: drums ring and resonate a lot more in the flesh than you may imagine. This is perplexing for new drummers. I remember a young drummer telling me he'd just bought some new drums and they were ringing and how could he stop it? He was genuinely surprised when I told him that was the whole idea. If his drums resonated a long time it probably meant they were good drums and the heads were fresh.

Drummers still regularly plaster their top heads with horrid strips of sticky tape to get a more controlled and shorter sound, which is what they know from their CDs. If they could go into the studio and isolate their favourite drum tracks on the mixing desk they would probably be dumbfounded to hear just how much ringing and ambience were present.

The thing to appreciate is that the ringing overtones of a drum are mostly lost in the overall sound when a band plays. But that ambience and long decay is the way the drums project. If you muffle too much of it, your sound will be dry and dead and you won't cut through. Out front you'll perhaps hear some impact, but no body and tone. There will be times, when you use close miking, when you will need a bit of damping. We'll talk about that later. But for now, don't worry too much about your drums ringing.

BUYING A USED KIT

With drum kits, as with everything else, it's possible to pick up a bargain if you buy secondhand (or used). Just remember that some older kits are undeniably wretched and you should be very careful to inspect every aspect for faults and breakages. If you have a drum teacher, or an experienced drumming friend who will accompany you, so much the better. Failing that take someone – anyone – along for a lay opinion and moral support. Drum kits are simple mechanical devices of wood and metal and you don't need to be a genius to work out that the kit you're being sold is no good. Worn threads, cracked castings, scarred finishes – they're easy to spot if you take the time.

When examining a kit, divide the task into three: the drums, the hardware and the cymbals. First the drums. If the plastic covering is badly scratched or bubbled, then the kit has been knocked about and is probably not worth bothering with. Like cars again, there are plenty out there with good finishes. Look inside each shell and make sure the shell itself is not cracked. It's unusual these days, but who knows? This is obviously unrepairable; leave the building now. It's easy to see inside the shell if the drum has transparent heads. If not then look through the air hole and if it looks at all suspicious take the head off and examine it properly.

The tension brackets and their bolts should ideally all be checked. I know there are dozens of them, and it might be a bit embarrassing, but it only takes a few minutes. Take a couple of drum keys with you. On cheap kits, you may find the odd bolt cross-threaded or even missing. Bolts and damaged lugs can usually be replaced, but if possible check with your local drum store first.

Worse, the metal rims or counter hoops may be bent out of round. You can check this by looking at the shell from directly above. Are the small gaps between head, shell and hoop concentric? The head's own hoop should normally be perfectly circular, so if there are any discrepancies then either the shell or the rim (or both?) is out of round. Rims can be replaced but oval shells are useless. Don't even think about it. And if a rim is bent then someone's probably dropped the drum. Take this as a warning sign and either leave now or check everything else with extra care. If the drums have been used for gigging, have they been transported in proper cases or just thrown in the back of the vehicle?

The moving parts – bass drum pedals in particular, hi-hats and snare drum strainers – are all liable to wear and tear. Try them all out. Starter kits are not built for heavy use. If a kit has been kept at home it can last for years. If it's been left out in the school hall for all to thrash, bits will start to go missing in weeks. You can't expect bullet-proof build for a couple of hundred. And these kits are pounded mercilessly by testosterone-fuelled six-foot 15-year-olds with Slipknot posters on their walls for inspiration.

Finally, the cymbals. If they are the crude items thrown in with the starter kit then don't expect much. They may be dented, bent or have cracks. Accept that they are valueless and that you will have to buy better replacements sooner rather than later.

As a novice to the drum world, you may be better off finding a reputable store that deals in secondhand gear. They may have a cheap trade-in kit that they will let you have at a good price. They will have checked the kit over, can offer you a warranty, and can replace any broken or missing parts. Any good dealer will do a maintenance check and replace small items like worn cymbal felts and sleeves. They'll also do you a good deal on fitting new heads, which will make a world of difference. And, if you can afford it, they'll throw in a better cymbal package.

However, because these cheap kits are not built to last forever, and because some of the old ones really are terrible, you may find that some dealers avoid the secondhand starter market altogether. You can't blame them. But as these kits keep on improving, more and more dealers are realising they cannot afford to ignore a potential starter sale.

BUYING A NEW KIT

Although the drum kit may look complicated at first, the components of all drum kits – large or small – fall into three broad areas. These are drums, cymbals and hardware.

The way these three areas have developed over the years could be treated as three separate stories. First there are the drums themselves: cylinders of wood, metal or synthetic materials with membranes tensioned over one or both ends. The technical term is 'membranophones'. Then there are the cymbals, which are metal plates that have been intensively worked. They are classified as idiophones, meaning instruments that make a sound via their own body. Finally, and of crucial importance, there is the hardware. This comprises the stands that support the drums and cymbals and the pedals that operate the bass drum and hi–hat cymbals.

The point is that the cymbal is a quite different instrument from the drum, with separate origins and evolution. The drum companies make the drums and the hardware, but rarely do they make the cymbals. Crafting a wooden shelled drum is a very different game from hammering out a bronze cymbal. Cymbal companies are quite distinct, and yet drums and cymbals have come to be played in such an integrated manner that the term 'drum kit' or 'drumset' is taken to include

cymbals as well as drums. And although we always refer to drum stores, selling cymbals is as important to the retailer as selling drums.

The 'skins' on the drums are called heads. Nowadays they are nearly always synthetic, mostly made from special plastics. Heads too are usually produced by different companies from either the drum or cymbal makers. So straight away you can see that at least three separate companies will normally be involved in producing your kit. The importance of this for would–be drum kit purchasers will become apparent as we go into greater detail.

The standard drum kit today is – certainly so far as the manufacturers are concerned – the five piece kit. This means there are five drums. Note again that there is no mention of cymbals or stands. However, since the drum companies also manufacture hardware, a basic kit will usually include a snare drum stand and one or two cymbal stands, along with a bass drum pedal and hi–hat pedal. Until recently it would not include any cymbals, since – for the last time – the drum companies don't make them. It can come as a shock to discover that a good set of cymbals can cost almost as much as a good set of drums.

However, as the competition has become increasingly hot, and particularly with more and more incredibly cheap starter kits made in Taiwan, China, and elsewhere, it has become the norm for starter packages to include everything that the beginner needs. That is, as well as the five drums, pedals and stands, there will be a stool (or throne) and three or four rudimentary cymbals. Not only that, they even throw in a pair of sticks and basic set–up and tuning instructions. This is a welcome trend, because previously the newcomer often got an incomplete package. And since the kit consists of so many parts it's easy for a starter to be confused. Lesson number one: if you're a first time buyer wanting a budget kit, make sure you get a deal which includes everything you might possibly need to get you started, sparing you the ignominy, frustration and expense of a return visit to the store the following Saturday.

SIZES

The standard five-piece kit consists of a 22″ (diameter) bass drum, 12″ and 13″ tom toms mounted on the bass drum, a 16″ floor tom tom with its own three legs and a 14″ snare drum, plus the aforementioned hardware – stands and pedals. This configuration is often called the standard 'rock' kit. Many manufacturers also offer an alternative with smaller sizes and call it their 'fusion' kit. A typical fusion kit comprises a 20″ bass drum with 10″ and 12″ mounted toms and a 14″ tom suspended from a floor stand rather than mounted on its own legs. Don't be put off by the terms 'rock' and 'fusion'. They are just convenient marketing terms. Almost any kit can be used to play almost any style of music. Bigger drums are just a little louder and deeper sounding.

Drum	Bass	Bass	Tom tom	Tom tom	Tom tom	Tom tom	Tom tom	Snare (w x d)	Snare (w x d)
Sizes	20	22	10	12	13	14	16	14x5.5	14x6.5
Rock		•		•	•		•		•
Fusion	•		•	•		•		•	

The snare drums provided with starter kits have traditionally had chrome plated steel shells, which are the cheapest and easiest to produce. These are either 6.5″ or 5.5″ in depth, again sometimes referred to respectively as rock or fusion sizes. The trend today however is towards including a wood-shelled drum – the implication being that this is upmarket from the standard steel shell model. This is not always the case in terms of performance. Since rather more craft is required to produce a quality wood snare drum, some may prefer the steel alternative.

The early Pearl Export has long been the model for generic budget kits. Amazingly, this kit is from 1983 but would constitute a top quality budget kit today.

BUDGET KITS

The first thing to say is that today's starter kits are incredible bargains. It seems to be a feature of the Oriental way of doing business that each year the product gets better and has more features while the price is maintained or even reduced. This is something we see in Oriental goods from electronics to cars. Budget and starter kits today are almost all made in Taiwan or China, where labour costs are less. This includes kits bearing the names of the famous American, European and Japanese drum companies. Leaving aside any political or moral considerations, the fact is that Oriental factories churn out drum kits that get better every year, at a fraction of the cost possible in North America, Europe or Japan.

The budget market we have today started very early in the 1980s with the first Pearl Export drum kit. If you study the picture, you'll notice it is very similar to some of the cheaper starter kits available widely under numerous different brand names. Many current starter kits still have the same Pearl–style double-post tom–tom bracket and Pearl-style tension lugs. Pearl has kept the Export name and year-by-year improved its specification. And as Pearl's model has improved so the benefits have passed down the line. Dozens of Export clones have been marketed with all sorts of names worldwide, like Active, Aria, Cannon, CB, DB, Diamond, Dixon, Groove Percussion, Hohner, Peace, Percussion Plus, Performance Percussion, Pulse, Session Pro, Sunlite, Stagg, Thunder and Virtuoso.

Sometimes they bear the names of established musical instrument importers/distributors like

Hohner; at other times the names are just made up to sound appealing. The list can never be complete, as names have continually changed over the years and occasionally dealers have gone out of business. There is always this risk, so if you can locate a kit from an established company, so much the better.

Pearl's Export became the biggest selling drum kit in history while continually being upgraded. Thus it gradually moved away from the beginners' market towards the middle, semi–professional, club bracket. This left the beginners' market open to the generic kits that followed in the Export's wake. The problem for Pearl and the other dedicated drum manufacturers was that they were now losing their important introductory market. So in order to build brand loyalty they introduced starter kits again. At first some of these were simply generic kits emblazoned with the names of the illustrious drum companies. And a rather sad sight they made in some cases…

However, the big names soon started to get their act together, imposing their own characteristics and style on cheap kits made under licence in Taiwan, etc. In doing so they created a new upper end for the beginners' market. Hence in the mid-1990s we welcomed Pearl's Forum kit, which undercut its own Export and placed Pearl in the beginner market once again.

The end result of all this activity is that we still have generic kits with various levels of sophistication, but on top of those are kits like the Forum, bearing the names of the dedicated drum companies. The Forum has, of course, been followed by equivalent kits from the other top names – thus the Gretsch Blackhawk, Ludwig Accent, Mapex V, Peavey Radial Pro 501, Premier Cabria, Remo Bravo, Sonor Force 1001, Tama Swingstar, Yamaha YD and Rydeen, and so on.

LEVEL 1 GENERIC STARTER KITS

Before getting on to the big name starter kits, let's first take a closer look at the generic kits. Untold numbers of drummers have started out with these kits, which continue to evolve and do a great job. However, when they first started to appear in the 1980s, quality was variable to say the least. Gradually the Taiwanese – and lately the Chinese – have become more experienced and expert. At the time of writing you can get a very good drum kit, complete with (very) basic cymbals and stool, etc, for £250 to £300 or maybe $250 to $350. Such a kit should give you few problems over your first few years of playing.

Because these kits are bulky items that have been carted half way around the world, you won't be surprised to find that they are shipped unassembled, like the wardrobes at your local cut–price furniture store. Mind you, since drums are cylindrical, be very suspicious if someone tries to sell you a flat–pack. (Only joking – although folding bass drums were actually manufactured in the 1920s.)

Most kits come in one or two cardboard boxes, with the drums telescoped inside one another. The snare, you'll be pleased to hear, will be fully assembled, but you will have to put the heads on the other drums and tune them up. Likewise, the hardware will be collapsed and you will have to put the various sections together. This is no bad thing, since that way the kit arrives with less chance of breakages. In any case, it is good to learn from day one how the kit is assembled and tuned. A pamphlet with minimal written instructions and diagrams will guide you through the process.

Depending on how busy the drum store is, and how sweet–tongued you are, you may be able to get them to help you construct the kit before taking it away. This way, if there are any defects the store will put them right before you leave. They may well want to charge you for their time, but it's money well spent. You'll undoubtedly pick up tips, and the help they'll give you to tune the kit for the first time will be a big bonus.

In my experience as a drum reviewer for magazines, I've had to put together dozens of brand new kits and I have come across the occasional defect. This seems inevitable with even the most expensive equipment. After all, people have been known to buy a Rolls Royce motor car and find faults. At least with drum kits the problems are usually straightforward. The commonest problem I've encountered with cheap kits is finding the occasional cross–threaded or stiff tension bolt. I have to say there's usually only one, and there are 54 tensioners on even the cheapest starter kit.

Sometimes the problem is with a lug nut that has got dislodged inside its casing. Less often, metal rims have bent in transit. In days past shells would be poorly finished with internal blemishes or cracks and the outer plastic wrap might be faulty. Chrome plating could be poor and you'd have to watch out for chrome splinters. I've even encountered cracked castings on the hardware. But there's no doubt that matters have improved greatly. Dealers assure me that these days serious faults are almost unknown.

SHELLS LEVEL 1

Generic kits all have similar, mid-thickness shells, usually straight-sided (see p.46) and made from semi-hardwoods sourced in the Far East. They are often six- or nine-ply and are described vaguely as 'Philippines mahogany' or lauan.

Lauan is not really the same wood as brown or red African or red European mahogany. It is, unsurprisingly, a cheaper, softer substitute that is easier to bend and cheaper to buy. Just be

The Hohner LEX is a typical, good value, recent generic budget kit. It is obviously derived from the early Pearl Export, but note that there are only six brackets on the floor tom and old-fashioned straight-out spurs on the bass drum.

aware that the mahogany used in vintage American drums and in modern high-end drums is a superior timber.

Never mind, the hardwood shells of cheap kits are now relatively well made. They're quite smoothly finished and they're round, which is the important thing. You will inevitably find small blemishes, and since the wood is relatively soft (in comparison with top quality woods) it's a little flaky. So it is inclined to minor splintering around the holes drilled for the hardware: the tom mounts and lugs, etc. This really doesn't matter; it has a negligible effect on sound and stability. You're unlikely to find a shell with an actual crack, but if you do you must return it immediately.

Imperfections are a little more bothersome around the bearing edges, meaning the shell edges over which the heads are stretched. These usually have a 45-degree cut towards the inside of the shell with a smaller 45-degree round-over from the outside. This creates a sharp edge (the equivalent of a violin's bridge) that facilitates accurate tuning and a clean sound.

However, shaping the shell to a narrow edge like this makes the wood fragile around the rim. You may therefore encounter slight unevenness here. Again, nowadays, even the cheapest drum will have a pretty impressive bearing edge and at this level you will hardly be upset by the lack of fine-tuning. That is only likely to bother you once you've been playing a few years, and certainly if you enter a recording studio. By that time you will likely have upgraded to a more professional set anyway.

The shells will be covered in plastic wrap, which will be glued on or possibly held in place by double backed tape. The wrap will usually be in a limited choice of plain colours such as black, silver, deep red or blue. Covering the shells this way means that the outer ply of the shell need not be finely finished and the timber need not be of the highest quality. Again, this is fair enough: what do you expect at the price?

Because life is never simple, there is an exception to the above pattern. A relatively new phenomenon is the maple wood kit from China. Marketed under various names, such as Pulse, Stagg and Virtuoso, and costing only a little more, this is a new generation of generic kit with maple ply shells and natural wood finishes. Maple is usually associated only with expensive drums. It's early days and I don't know enough to comment on the quality of 'Chinese maple', but already the increasing presence of Chinese percussion products at low-low prices is having a big effect on the market.

Remember, the sound of the kit is altered vastly by tuning. Each drum has a plastic 'head' (skin) which is stretched (tensioned) over the shell by turning the tension bolts using a drum key. It's hard to believe at first, but it's the head that generates the sound, not the shells. Cheap kits come fitted with low-cost, inferior heads – it's another way of keeping the price down. These heads have poor tone and they are thin so that they soon get pitted and lose their elasticity. When that happens replace them with a good set of top (batter) heads and revel in what you've been missing.

SNARE DRUMS LEVEL 1

As for the snare drum, it always used to be the case that the snare drum was the weakest link in the beginner package. It would have a steel shell with an ugly internal vertical butt-weld and turned-over bearing edges that were ragged and did not inspire confidence in the overall quality of construction.

The steel would be thin, and the chroming poor so that the sound would be dark and ringy. These might strike you as admirable sonic properties for a tom tom but they're not so hot for a snare drum. You generally want your snare drum to be high pitched and bright with a fastish decay: a sort of short, sharp, shock.

The bottom line is it's probably impossible to make a really good metal-shelled snare drum at this sort of price. The most recent examples are better but will never be great. The trend in any case is towards including a matching wood-shelled snare drum. These are slightly less of a problem in as much as they are less ringy with fewer nasty overtones.

SHELL FITTINGS: RIMS, LUGS AND BRACKETS LEVEL 1

By shell fittings we mean the metal rims, the tension brackets (also called 'lugs'), the tom mounting brackets and floor tom leg brackets. That is, any item of hardware – usually metal – secured to the shell. While separate stands and pedals can be replaced and upgraded, the actual shell fittings are not so easy to change.

In particular you're most unlikely ever to change the tension brackets, and this is an area of concern. One way manufacturers can reduce costs is by fitting fewer brackets/lugs to each shell. This is still seen on the very cheapest starter kits, which are actually a step back from the earliest Export blueprint. So, on a 22″ bass drum, you get just six brackets per head, whereas I really think the minimum requirement is eight. (Pro drums usually have ten.) The pattern will be copied across the whole kit. The snare and floor tom will have six where they should have at least eight. Small toms will have four or five, where they need five or six, etc.

Six brackets on a full size bass drum or snare drum is not really enough. It makes it virtually impossible to get a decent sound. The snare drum in particular will always sound crude and uncontrollable. The drums will still be playable, but the gap between each tuning point is too big to allow you to establish accurate and even tension. You'll still get plenty of volume, but as soon as you try an eight-lug drum you'll realise how much easier it is then to get a controlled and evenly tuned sound.

Now, I do believe there is a place for these bare-necessity kits, which offer a start where money is tight. They are available for less then £200/$200, and sometimes much less. So don't get me wrong, the cheapest kits work and they are amazing value: try buying a flute for that price. But they're definitely for youngsters testing the water.

(And talking of youngsters, there are also 'junior' kits, which are undersized versions of the same type of kit. These obviously have fewer tension brackets and primitive hardware, but in this case they are fully justified. These kits are designed for children and are great fun. You're never too young to start.)

For me the serious beginner market starts with the next level of kit, which has eight tension brackets on the bass drum, snare drum and large tom and five or six on the mounted toms. This level of kit may only be around 25 per cent more expensive: say, £250/$250 upwards. And the good news is that, as standards are steadily driven upwards, six-bracket kits are becoming increasingly scarce. However, there are still lots of them around on the secondhand market. You have been warned.

Earlier examples of the starter kit will have separate brackets with a similar design to the early Pearl oblong lug. By the 1990s some kits sported 'high-tension' brackets, ie, single brackets that spanned the full depth of the shell. Now the fashion has moved back towards smaller top and bottom 'low mass' lugs. To some extent you can date kits by their lug/bracket style.

There is one other shell fitting which is very vulnerable on cheap kits. This is the snare drum strainer and throw-off. Because this is a moving mechanical part it takes a lot of pounding. The mechanism itself is often quite rudimentary and stiff. They have been known to fall to bits. However, they are not expensive and replacing only involves a couple of small screw bolts.

The next thing to consider is the tom tom mount. This is the chunky centrally mounted receiving block whereby the two small toms are mounted on the bass drum. The mount has one or two holes to accommodate the tom mounting posts. These posts support each of the two small toms and allow you to position them within reach.

The tom mounts should also have small 'memory lock' clamps fitted where the posts disappear into the bass drum receiving block and where the horizontal arms disappear into the tom brackets. Once you have decided on your optimum set-up positions, you tighten these clamps with a drum key and the positions are 'memorised' for next time. At the same time the toms are prevented from swivelling on their tubular mounting arms.

The bass drum, meanwhile, is held upright and prevented from sliding forward by two spurs, mounted on either side of the drum towards the lower front. Nowadays these also usually follow the Pearl fold-out design, which means they can be folded flush with the side of the drum for transport/storage. They have spike-tipped extensions, covered with rubber feet, which point forward and down and prevent forward movement when you strike the drum.

Some older and cheaper generic kits have 'disappearing' spurs. These are simply straight rods that project directly out at right angles from the lower side of the drum and can be pushed back inside the drum for storage. They belong to a much earlier and gentler era and are useless for the average modern player. They will stop the drum from rolling over but will do little to prevent forward movement.

One final shell point. Beginner kits nearly always have steel rims on the bass drum. There is nothing wrong with this except that from the next level up bass drums generally have wooden hoops. Steel rims are strong and do the job perfectly well. And they don't scratch so easily as wooden hoops.

HARDWARE: STANDS, PEDALS AND STOOL LEVEL 1

The standard starter kit hardware should include a bass drum pedal, a hi-hat pedal, a snare drum stand, a stool, a straight cymbal stand and probably a boom cymbal stand. With a boom cymbal stand you are able to angle the top section like the boom arm of a crane, so you can position your cymbal within easier reach.

The stands will have fold-out tripod legs. These are referred to as single-braced or double-braced, depending on whether each leg is constructed using single or double lengths of strip steel. Generally the latter are stronger and more stable. Beginner and budget kits customarily had single-braced tripods while double-braced stands were reserved for professional kits. However, double-braced stands have now found their way down to the beginner level, except for the cheapest kits.

However, there is nothing intrinsically wrong with single-braced stands. It all depends on the gauge of the metal and the quality of the construction. Some single braced stands are perfectly adequate, although the type of stand used in the cheapest kits can definitely be flimsy. Assuming the stands are OK though, you may prefer them single braced, particularly if the kit stays put in your bedroom or garage. Cheap kits are often assembled using whatever hardware the manufacturer/supplier needs to shift at the time, and so you often find a mixture of single-braced and double-braced stands. Again this can be perfectly acceptable. Many starter kits are offered with a choice of hardware packages and you simply have to examine what's available and assess if it's strong enough for your needs.

Another thing to look out for is the quality of tilter on the top of your cymbal stands. On the cheapest stands these can be feeble and you may feel it's better to get better stands from the start. This is doubly true if the stands do not have nylon inserts at each telescopic height-extension joint. Like memory locks, these have become universal musts and are one of the smallest, simplest and most useful hardware innovations ever. They stop slippage and prevent over-tightening of stands leading to stripped threads. A godsend.

When it comes to snare drum stands, beginner kits are sometimes lumbered again with outdated designs you really should avoid. All good snare drum stands have tripod cradles that screw up from beneath to form an inverted 'V' shaped basket that cradles the drum. There are some old-fashioned designs which have two fixed-length flat metal strip arms and a third arm, adjustable in length, that slides through a central housing until it grips the snare drum's shell. In order to picture how this works, imagine that the three arms take the form of the CND badge logo.

This design has long been superseded by the basket type. It has a tendency to come loose and there is even the danger of the centre housing of the stand making contact with the underside of the drum if you play hard over a long period. This design is best consigned to history.

The bass drum pedal or 'kick' pedal is probably the most vulnerable item in the kit. It gets stamped on furiously and has to be well made if it is to last. Cheap pedals have thin base plate castings, which can and do crack. The tension spring can fail, the chain drive can also snap. The kick pedal is often the first item you will need to upgrade. The hi-hat is similarly vulnerable although it is not subjected to quite such violence.

A welcome trend in the beginner market is the truly complete package, which at last includes a stool. A proper stool (throne, in the US) is vital. Since you're using all four limbs you must be able to attain the right height and balance. A kitchen bar stool will probably be too high, while an ordinary chair will be too low. In schools and youth centres, etc, I've often seen young drummers resorting to stacking chairs to get the right height. This is uncomfortable, unstable and, worse, will immediately lead you into bad posture. That's no way to start your drumming career. Back problems are a major source of trouble for drummers. If your starter kit does not include a proper height-adjustable stool, you can get one for as little as £15 or $15.

CYMBALS LEVEL 1

The cymbals thrown in with starter kits are crude. They're there to make up a complete package and are just about adequate for getting going. But they won't resonate or project much. They certainly won't sing. And you can't tune a cymbal – what you buy is what you get. Dealers will suggest an upgrade cymbal pack and if you can afford it you will be better off starting with that. Then your first cymbals will be more in keeping with the quality of your first kit.

NAME BRAND KITS LEVEL 1

The next level of drum kit consists of those bearing the familiar names of the dedicated drum companies. These budget kits are also made in the Far East, and if you go back a few years they didn't look much different from the generic brands. Some were pretty indifferent, despite the

Tama's entry level kit is the Swingstar. The generic tom brackets and lugs have been replaced by Tama's own distinctive name-brand designs. Note also the wood shell snare drum.

illustrious labels. But as the market has evolved, kits have taken on more and more of the features of their parent brands, so that now you can get kits by Sonor, Premier, Tama, Mapex and all the other big names, displaying the identity of those companies in their lug designs and tom mounts, etc. As for price, we're talking around £400 upwards in Britain and $400 upwards in the USA. These are street prices, which are sometimes way below the manufacturer's listed prices. You will see discounts of 10 to 20 per cent in Britain and double that or even better in the States.

For example, I've seen Pearl Forums advertised in the USA at $600, which is barely more than half the list price of $950. Yes, pricing and competition are fierce, but it's often difficult to compare like-for-like since there are so many different packages offered by stores and on-line dealers. If you're starting at this level look out for an all-in package, including stool, sticks and cymbals. The Forum even includes a video with advice on setting up and tuning.

The 'designer' companies do not necessarily have their own factories in the Far East. But they have gradually established production shops using their own tools, dies, moulds and quality control procedures, so that they can reproduce their own designs economically. Over the years there have been instances where the shells and items of hardware of one brand are the same as those used by another. But as time goes on each company is gradually producing its own completely individual kits.

Obviously it's nice to move up to the drum world's equivalent of the designer label. The companies want you to get hooked on their product and hope that you will eventually trade up to their more expensive lines. To do this they will try to persuade you of the merits of their particular design solutions. The big difference is that you're moving away from the generic look and buying into the particular style of the big-name company. You'll find that items like the tom mounts, tension lugs, snare throw-offs and pedal foot board castings all have the particular company's look and feel, but are budget versions of the company's pro lines. For example, Pearl's Forum has its famous double post tom mount while Yamaha's YD has its equally illustrious ball and clamp design. You need to get down to the drum store and decide which works best for you – or failing that, which look you prefer.

Shells will still be made from between six and nine plies of semi-hardwood and again you'll see woods like Philippines mahogany, basswood, meranti, falkata and so on. For example, both the Mapex V and Sonor's Force 1001 have nine-ply basswood shells, while the Gretsch Blackhawk has six-ply and Premier's Cabria Lite seven-ply mahogany. The latter two companies have always preferred slightly thinner shells, and you can see them trying to carry that philosophy right through to their cheapest line. Pearl's Forum shells are made using the heat compression moulding system (HCMS) it always uses. Likewise Yamaha's nine-ply Philippine mahogany YD shells benefit from the company's air seal technique.

In terms of finish, most of these kits still have plastic wraps, but the choice of colours is considerably wider and the wrap is hopefully secured a bit better. Many of the features that once made high-end kits more attractive have filtered down to the budget level. Wooden rather than metal bass drum hoops are often fitted.

And in a few cases your toms will have resonance isolation mounts, which were a major selling point of the most expensive kits just a few years ago. By isolation mounts we mean tom tom mounts that do not penetrate the shells of the toms as do the older tom arms. Instead they suspend the toms via a bracket attached to the top metal rim of each drum. The idea is that the tom is left free to resonate rather than being tightly gripped and stifled.

Wood shell snare drums are gradually replacing the previously ubiquitous steel shelled models, and these will give you a warmer, crisper sound. The snare throw-off will be a simple, side-lever affair, which should be sturdy enough under moderate use. And one thing you can be sure of is that there will be no stinting on tension lugs. Snare drums, bass drums and floor toms will all have eight tuning points per head.

NAME BRAND HEADS AND HARDWARE LEVEL 1

Many kits are today fitted with budget heads made by Remo, the leading American professional drumhead company. Remo has a factory in Taiwan that uses American made polyester Mylar film to produce a cheaper version of its own industry standard Weatherking heads. This is a great improvement on the past when, because most of the big name drum companies don't produce their own heads, they would throw on frankly dire heads to keep the cost down. This did the drums no favours. Now that the budget kits are themselves of a better standard the heads are getting better too. Pearl, incidentally, has gone its own way and produces its own ProTone Mylar heads, which also sound pretty good.

As for hardware, nearly all packages now have double braced stands. You will have to look closely at the specifications to see whether you get one or two cymbal stands. If there are two, the second is nearly always a boom stand. The hi-hat and bass drum pedals should be of an adequate standard, which will give you good service until you can afford heftier and more flexible models. Since so many new drummers want to play heavy, their first upgrade is often to a stronger pedal, or even a double pedal, followed by a better snare drum and cymbals.

NAME BRAND CYMBALS LEVEL 1

Like the drum companies, the big name cymbal companies recognise the need to attract new players to their brands, and so they offer boxed starter sets of their budget lines. A set will usually comprise a 16″ crash, 20″ ride and pair of 14″ hi-hats. Dealers will be keen to put drum and cymbal packages together and usually offer two or three basic options. If you've suffered with unbranded starter cymbals up till now then these sets will be a great step forward. Budget cymbals lack some of the body

and shimmering sustain of a professional set, but they're still a big improvement. Popular choices include Sabian Solar, B8, Pro and Sonix, Zildjian ZBT and ZXT, Paiste 101, 302-Plus, 402-Plus and 502-Plus and Meinl MCS and Classics. Dealers will entice you with offers to throw in a cymbal bag or stick bag, a towel with a logo, or whatever.

MID-RANGE KITS LEVEL 2

Once you get beyond the budget area you arrive at the middle bracket of kits, the province of the Pearl Export. This is probably the most hotly contested area of the market, and if you can afford it these kits are the best value of all. They are aimed at the keen amateur, or the semi-professional weekend club player; someone who wants a good reliable kit but can't yet afford a top line outfit. As with the budget level, the present market can be traced back to the appearance of the first Pearl Export around 1982. But things have moved on a lot since then and the latest kits with the Export name bear very little relationship to those early models. You can hardly blame Pearl for hanging on to the Export name since it's such a strong brand, but it does cause confusion in the second hand market. If you see a used Pearl Export advertised, it could be two years old or 20 years old. Try to ascertain the facts before wasting a journey.

The transition from budget to middle range is a little hazy. The middle range kits start just above the budget prices, nominally around £450 or $500, bearing in mind once again that $500 may be half the list price. And note that the price may include hardware but will normally be minus cymbals. There are several levels within the middle bracket, as more and more refinements are added to the basic specification. So, for example, the basic Export has a plastic wrap finish while the Export Select has a lacquered exterior. Other common refinements include additional plies of quality hardwoods, resonance mounting rather than standard tom mounts and wood snare drums instead of steel.

So we have kits with plastic wraps, like the basic Ludwig Rocker, Mapex M, Pearl Export and Tama Rockstar. But even here the standard of wrap is better: Tama points out that its wraps are not stuck on with adhesive tape and neither are they glued just in patches. They are impact glued and bonded over the entire shell. There will also be more colours beyond the plain options of the budget kits. DW's Pacific CX, for example, has superb retro onyx pearl.

SHELLS LEVEL 2

Nowadays you can expect the shells to be perfectly round, devoid of blemishes on the inside, and finished with clean bearing edges for more accurate tuning. The shells are essentially the same as those on the budget kits, also manufactured in Taiwan or China, except that they often have a single ply of top quality hardwood bonded to the inside, for improved projection and tone, or to the outside, to enable a decent lacquered finish with a nice grain.

This trend started with the Export some years ago when a single ply of birch was added to the inside of the shells. Another example would be Yamaha's Stage Custom Standard series, which has the same nine-ply Philippines mahogany shells as the budget YD, except that the outer ply is replaced with a single ply of birch. This is then given a natural matt finish to show off the grain. Then, going up one more level, the Stage Custom Advantage has an additional inner ply of Falkata wood with the grain running vertically to help projection. Plus the shells feature special coloured metallic finishes.

I must mention the special case of the Californian company Drum Workshop, which combines

With mid range 'level two' kits like this Yamaha Stage Custom Advantage you get better shells and hardware, plus a wider choice of finishes and set-ups.

the best of both worlds with its Pacific drums by getting its hardware made in Taiwan but its shells made down the Pacific coast in Mexico, again using a cheaper labour force. Pacific also manages to include 100 percent eight-ply maple and birch shells for the first time in the middle bracket.

There are plenty more types of shell and finish to choose from. They include Ludwig's Rocker, which has a choice of plastic finishes over nine-ply shells with an inner ply of maple, while the Rocker Elite has lacquered finishes. Mapex's M, meanwhile, has seven-ply basswood shells with an outer lacquered ply of maple, while the Pro M has thinner basswood/maple shells and hand-rubbed lacquer finishes.

Pearl's Export Select (ELX) has nine-ply mahogany shells with a UV-lacquered exterior, while Sonor's 2001 has mahogany shells with a wax stained finish and metal bass drum hoops, powder coated with a colour inlay. Premier, meanwhile, uses lacquered finishes on its Cabria Exclusive, as does Pacific on the LX.

Six-ply mahogany shells with UV lacquer finishes and natural maple bass drum hoops feature on Gretsch's Catalina Elite, while Tama's Rockstar Custom has one inner ply of basswood with seven of Philippines mahogany, a choice of eight gloss lacquered finishes and rather tasty Accu-Tune bass drum hoops made from glass fibre reinforced plastic.

Middle range kits usually include stands and pedals, but not cymbals or a stool/throne. However, they are also sometimes available as a so-called 'shell pack': usually a five shell kit including a snare drum, but minus stands and pedals. Be careful to ascertain what's being offered: photographs may include stands and cymbals, but the price may be just for the shell pack. 'Rock' and 'fusion' formats are the most common. They might also be advertised as 'stage' and 'studio' formats, which are more or less the same thing.

If you see a 'jazz' kit mentioned this will probably be a 20″ bass drum with a single mounted 12″ tom and a 14″ floor tom, with or without a matching wood snare drum. Optional extra add-on

DW's budget brand Pacific CX has resonance isolation tom mounts and a double bass drum pedal as standard.

sizes may also be available if you want to extend your kit. Choice is greater than with the budget ranges, but not so wide as with the top lines.

SNARE DRUMS LEVEL 2

The trend is towards wood shell drums, as noted with the budget kits. These will still be basic models, generally with the same shells as the rest of the kit. Where metal shell drums are still available they will benefit from better chroming, which cuts down on some of the excessive ringing of the older, cheaper models. Improvements have been made on the snare strainers too. Cheap, wonky snare strainers with too-small tension knobs and feeble levers have caused untold grief over the years. Frustrated with the stiff, noisy action, drummers would yank on them, leading to sheared rivets and eventual disintegration. Hopefully those days have largely passed.

HARDWARE LEVEL 2

Once you get to the middle range there should be no question of the hardware letting you down. The moving parts, in particular the foot pedals, should now be well engineered and strong enough for serious gigging. They will serve you until you can afford to upgrade to the truly pro quality. Stands are mostly double braced but there are some lighter, single braced stands still available which you may actually prefer.

In fact, your choice of kit may well rest on your personal taste in hardware and on any other incentives the manufacturers or dealers can cook up. DW Pacific has the clever idea of including a double kick pedal as standard with its CX and LX kits. The 402 pedal is a budget version of its class-leading pedals and obviously reflects the fashion for monster double kick chops amongst the young drummers of America today. Incidentally, Pacific also includes a bass drum muffler and a Tommy Igoe video with useful tuning tips.

I've no doubt that we will see more and more incentives like these over the next year or two. The competition is that hot. But don't forget that your local store also wants your custom and it's a good idea, if you have particular preferences, to discuss things with them. They will undoubtedly do their best to accommodate you and offer you a tempting package.

Until recently, what marked the final jump from mid to top line drums was the inclusion of special resonance isolation mounting hardware. But with all the major companies producing their own resonance mounts for several years now, the development costs have been absorbed and we're starting to see resonance mounts on virtually all mid-price drums.

CYMBALS LEVEL 2

While budget kits may have cheap cymbals thrown in with the package, mid range kits usually come without cymbals. And by now you will want a set of pretty good cymbals. If you spend

£1,000 or $1,000 on a kit you will have to spend at least half that to get comparable cymbals. This is where the reality of the drum and cymbal companies being completely separate finally catches up with us.

It's unlikely you will want to keep any of your starter or low budget cymbals. You'll probably be heartily sick of them and ready for something rather more refined. You'll want at least the appropriate mid-price bronze cymbals from one of the proper manufacturers. These cymbals tend to be what's known as B8, sheet or rolled cymbals (see Chapter 12). As with mid-price kits these mid-price cymbals are improving in quality all the time and the choice of ranges is steadily expanding. Some to look out for are Meinl Classic, Raker and Lightning, Paiste 802 and Alpha, Sabian B8, Pro, Pro-Sonix and XS-20, Zildjian ZBT and (for the hard hitters) ZXT, etc. They all have their strengths and weaknesses and characteristic timbres.

While the various different makes of drum sound pretty similar (given the same heads and tuning), you will quickly discover that different makes and types of cymbal all sound quite different. It's up to you to test them out and decide which you prefer. Your dealer will have boxed sets of many of these cymbals, which will come with extra goodies like bags/cases, towels and even videos.

HIGH-END KITS LEVEL 3

Some while ago I was at a major drum manufacturer's annual dealer day. The star endorsees lined up and took it in turns to blast us with the new products. Endorsee 'A' played the budget kit and endorsee 'B' played the expensive one. A dealer sitting next to me leaned over and said, "They've shot themselves in the foot there then ..." Why's that, I asked? "Well, the cheaper kit sounds better than the expensive one."

Oh dear. This is a peculiar thing about drums, and a puzzle for many drummers. The sound of a kit relies on many variables, not least the expertise and touch of the player. I've always felt that, while it's possible to recognize a clear difference between, say, the sound of a Fender Stratocaster guitar and a Gibson Les Paul, it's impossible to listen to a record and say that's a Gretsch drum kit, or that's a Mapex drum kit. But it is possible to say, with some certainty, that's Max Roach, Ginger Baker, Stewart Copeland or Tony Williams.

A player's sound is his or her trademark and is as distinctive as a singer's voice. This is true of all good instrumentalists. So if a cheap kit can sound as good as an expensive kit, is there any point in shelling out all that extra money? Quite definitely, yes. There is a difference in sound between a good budget kit and a massively expensive kit, although it's actually quite small. (It's not just drums: how many classical music buffs can really tell the difference between a Stradivarius and a modern good quality violin?) Great musicians have their own sound, irrespective of what brand instrument they play. But buying the best possible instrument enables that performer to realise his or her own sound to its fullest. Like driving a car, it's when you get behind the wheel that you really appreciate the difference.

I would humbly suggest that today's professional drums are characterised more by the similarities in their sound than the differences. This is meant as a compliment. What I'm really saying is that they've all got their acts together and there are no real duds. They all make accurately rounded shells with decent bearing edges and they all use birch or maple.

You can argue that one make is a little better than the next, but frankly no one is going to know except, possibly, you the player, and only when you've been on intimate terms with the drums for a while. Certainly if you go to a concert it won't make the slightest difference whether the drummer's playing Sonor, Pearl, Brady or Orange County. What will make a difference is whether the drummer's any good. (And whether you can hear him through the wall of PA gear.)

So what are you spending your money on? How do you make a choice? And crucially, how does each manufacturer go about persuading you their product is, after all, the best? Well, lest I appear too cynical, I certainly do think sound comes into the equation when we're making our decision.

The problem is that until you've taken the drums out on half a dozen gigs in different rooms it's very difficult to make a valid assessment, to know whether you're going to be happy with them in the long term. Which is not to say that you can't infer from the design and build quality which make has the best chance of sounding good, of being easy to tune, of being reliable and of offering maximum resonance with a convivial timbre.

In the end, my belief is that choice mostly comes down to which kit you like the look of best, which kit has the coolest image, and which is played by the drummers you most admire. And ultimately, which kit you can afford. After all this, you can only hope that it will sound as good as your fervent expectations. I don't think there's anything wrong with that, either. The most expensive kits may not sound that much different, but they look a million dollars. And this is not to be sniffed at. In the entertainment world, image counts for a great deal. And when you are contemplating forking out a large wad for a new instrument, the way it looks is extremely important.

Time was when drum companies made two lines: student and professional. Today the choice is much greater, with different gradations within each of the main classifications: beginner, middle and top. Now we have reached the top end of the scale and we find the same spread we've seen in the starter and middle ranges. If anything, the top end is the broadest, in the sense that it starts at under £1,000/$1,000 and goes up to four or five times that amount just for a five piece kit.

The reason for this is that at the lower top-end the companies want to minimise the leap from their increasingly good, and ever cheaper, budget lines. While at the very top end, the only way they can differentiate is to make ever more exclusive and luxurious kits. Somewhere in the middle are the top line kits for the 'average' punter. So we have at least three levels again.

As an illustration, Mapex has the Saturn Pro series as its first 'top' line, then the Orion Classic, which in turn is topped by the Deep Forest series, in 100 percent cherry or walnut. Tama has its Starclassic Performer, Starclassic Maple and limited edition Exotix. Sonor has its S Class Pro, Delite and Designer.

Traditionally the big difference between middle and top levels would be that the top line kit had 100 percent premium hardwood shells with a choice of stunning finishes. And to set the kit off there would be a third, top, level of hardware which would usually be the heaviest, ensuring that it could withstand the most demanding touring schedule.

But, as we've seen, no sooner are any refinements added to the top line than the pressure is on to introduce them in the budget lines. Pacific, the budget arm of DW, has 100 per cent maple and birch shells, while many other middle bracket kits already have resonance-enhancing

Top lines like Premier's beautifully crafted 'Series' drums offer enormous variety in size, set-up and finish.

mounted tom toms and lacquered finishes rather than wraps. These luxuries are possible because the manufacturing base, for the metalwork at least, has moved out of America, Europe and Japan to Taiwan and China. This is the pattern we've seen throughout all the lower ranges and it is now also true of the top ranges. The product designers in the USA, Japan and Europe make up 3D CAD (computer aided design) models of every part, and simply wire them over to the Far East where the parts are made. I'm told there's no need any more even to make up prototypes.

The Far Eastern workshops send the parts back for assembly in the home country, where they're bunged on to the shells. Increasingly, manufacturing trades are being lost in the first world countries, but the result is that we drummers are getting better drums at cheaper prices every year.

SHELLS LEVEL 3

So when it comes to the top line drums, assembly takes place back in the home factory. This gives the company direct control over all the finishing, at least for their top line product. The 'raw' shells themselves are either made on site (European and Oriental companies) or bought in from specialist manufacturers (American companies).

Those manufacturers who construct their own shells generally use the same method for all their ranges, cheap or expensive. But the top-level shells will generally be thinner. The reason for this is that thinner shells resonate better and have a deeper, richer timbre. In order to make them thinner, though, they must use the best quality, densest hardwoods. In recent decades that has generally meant birch or maple, but there are signs the companies are exploring other timbers such as beech, oak, walnut and 'real' mahogany: woods which, by the way, have all been used previously in the history of drum making. By the time you're ready to move up to a top class kit you may well have opinions about the sound of particular woods which will dictate whether you plump for a maple, birch, or other kit.

As with some middle bracket kits, the drum makers sell top-line 'shell packs' rather than traditional complete kits. The shell pack concept recognises that, whereas at the lower levels it's handy to buy a complete package, maybe even including cymbals, by the time drummers are ready to buy a first-rate kit they have a pretty exact idea of what they want. So there has to be flexibility in the layout and sizes, etc. A shell pack is just a convenient deal on a set of drums incorporating the toms and a bass drum, together with the mounting hardware but excluding stands and pedals. Often, minus a snare drum too.

The reason for this is that when you upgrade your kit you may not want a complete hardware package. A lot of drummers have a favourite bass drum pedal that they want to hang on to. Or they may actually have set their sights on a particular pedal by another manufacturer. As for the snare drum, there are now so many types and varieties the companies leave that for you to decide. You might even have a lovely old vintage snare that you always play and you really don't want the standard model that comes with the toms you've chosen. In short, drum companies realise they are far more likely to sell you a top end kit if you're free to choose the items you really want and not have to buy loads of bits you don't need.

So shell packs are a liberation. But they're only the start. When it comes to the top level the word now is customisation. Manufacturers have gradually been pressured to offer a much greater range of choice. Sonor started the ball rolling with its Designer Series a decade ago: the idea being that you, the drummer, would be your own kit designer.

This is now the pattern and increasingly customers are given the opportunity to plan their own kit from a multiplicity of choices. The prospective DW buyer, for example, can go on-line and devise the ideal set-up using DW's 'Kit Builder' software: a bit like those kitchen design templates down at your local furniture store.

With the designer concept, choice of shell sizes is almost unlimited. You make up your own kit from however many toms, with sizes ranging in diameter from 8″ to 18″, plus bass drums ranging from 18″ to 24″. Not only that but all the shells are offered in a choice of two, three or even four depths. These may be given names like Standard/Regular/Traditional, Universal/Accel, Power/Deep/X-tra, Square and – for super deep bass drums – Turbo.

You can also choose the type of shell material. Buy a Yamaha Absolute kit and you can specify any drum in maple, birch, beech or oak, because they all have the same price and finishes. Pearl goes further with its Masters Custom Series, allowing you to mix individual plies of maple, birch or mahogany in each single drum.

Then there's shell construction. Some companies, including Premier and Tama, offer you the choice of 'supported' or 'unsupported' shells. Supported shells have a smaller number of plies and are extremely thin but have reinforcing rings. Unsupported shells are a little thicker but have no supporting rings. So, for example, with Premier's Series drums you can have four-ply with support rings or six-ply without, constructed in birch, maple or the Gen-X mix of 50/50 maple and birch. Tama does a similar thing with its supported Starclassic shell with 'Sound Focus Rings'. Sonor offers the choice of two thicknesses of unsupported shell in its Designer series, Maple Light (6.5mm) and Maple Heavy (9.5mm).

Whatever you choose, with a company's top line kit you can be sure that special care has been taken with the bearing edges of the drums. This is a skilled and labour intensive task, but is crucial to the sound and projection of the drums.

The same huge range of choice applies even more in the area of finish. Walk into any large drum store today and you're overwhelmed by the dazzling display of new kits. Drums have never been this beautiful. The manufacturers are falling over themselves to come up with ever more gorgeous finishes. And this tells us a lot. Looks sell. Today you can have a tasteful 1980s-style natural lacquer, or you can have a 1970s-style psychedelic 'moiré' wrap. You can have a 1960s-style classic pearl or glitter, or you can have a new millennium environmentally friendly water-based custom paint job. Many top companies offer several dozen off-the-peg choices and some of them unlimited custom finishes.

Pearl's 50th Anniversary solid maple shell snare drum features 24-carat gold-plated fittings, including 1920s-style tubular lugs and clips and flat section rims.

Yet even beyond these professional lines, manufacturers occasionally come up with truly magnificent specials. Tama's Starclassic Exotix II Materials is a limited edition kit made from African quilted sapele veneered over eight plies of African bubinga. Tama says it will only ever make 100 of these unique kits, each accompanied by its own authentication certificate. Drums like these are very expensive and are aimed as much at wealthy collectors as they are at regular players.

Some of them are so beautiful it's hard to imagine the average drummer would risk taking them out on everyday gigs. The veneering materials and expertise are adapted from the high-end furniture industry, and it's as glorified furniture that some of these kits are destined to spend their lives. DW has Exotic Wood finish kits in such materials as Quilted Cherry, Claro Walnut, Tamo Ash and Zebrawood. The mere names make your mouth water.

Anniversaries also provide good excuses for a touch of excess. Yamaha celebrated its centenary in 1988 (that's a 100 years of pianos, not drums), with extraordinary, RC-9000-style kits in Birdseye Maple, Sapele, Curicote (a rich, extravagantly patterned chocolate brown in case you're wondering) plus hi-tech Carbon. Pearl gave us a 50th anniversary, gold plated, vintage style, solid shell snare drum in 1996, complete with its own presentation case. And as I write, Gretsch is celebrating its 120th anniversary (1883 – 2003) with a limited reissue tribute to its 1950s Round Badge drums, for long the studio drummer's favourite weapon.

When it comes to money-no-object kits, the big boys don't have it all their own way. There is always a place for the individual craftsman to produce small numbers of custom designs. Over the past decade this has been a growth industry – albeit on a cottage scale – particularly in North America. And following the remarkable success of DW there are encouraging signs for smaller emerging American companies like Orange County, Spaun, GMS, Pork Pie and Taye. These and several others are gaining recognition and picking up occasional big name endorsees, which is essential to credibility. Over here in Britain interest in American Orange County drums, for example, has been awakened entirely because Travis Barker of Blink 182 was spotted playing them. There is also a loyal market for Australian-made drums by Brady and Sleishman, which utilise extremely hard native timbers like Wandoo and Jarrah. And in Britain we have a number of specialist custom drum makers, including Noonan, Jalapeno and Richmo. (The Reference section lists website addresses for some of these smaller companies and individuals and they really do make interesting viewing.)

SHELL FITTINGS: LUGS, RIMS AND BRACKETS LEVEL 3

One place where there is still a quantifiable difference between middle and top line kits is in the number of tension brackets employed. In particular it is still usual for middle level kits to have eight lugs per head on a 22″ bass drum and 16″ floor tom while the top line drums have ten. Likewise, top level 14″ snare drums have ten lugs rather than eight, except perhaps when the snare has a heavy die cast rim in which case there might be eight.

Lugs, or tension brackets, are a very important design element in drum making. Ever since the 1930s the design of the lug has been the main identifying trademark of the drum maker. Sometimes they haven't changed for years and are central to the company's image. This is particularly true of the American companies, which have heritage on their side. Hence the lugs of Gretsch, Ludwig and DW are designs that have been around for decades – upwards of 50 years. You can see Ludwig's art deco Imperial lug casing in catalogues from the 1930s, and it looks just as good today.

Meanwhile the European and particularly the Japanese companies change their lug designs quite frequently. The result is that middle and lower ranges may well be lumbered with tension casings (and, incidentally, other mounting hardware like tom brackets) that are previous year's designs. And you'll notice that when DW created Pacific drums as its budget line it came up with a different tension bracket – the point being that you don't get the famous turret lug unless you buy the top line drums.

Since everything in drum design today is expected to minimise the damping effect on the shells, the trend has been towards smaller brackets with a lower mass. These are isolated from the shell by a rubber or nylon/plastic gasket and attached by two small bolts, or in some cases (eg, Spaun's small, round solid brass lug) by a single bolt, which is perhaps even better. Noble and Cooley initiated this trend back in the early 1980s when they started to produce drums with lugs mounted at what they called the 'Nodal Point' of the shell, this being the area of least resonance and therefore least interference with the shell's vibration. With its Absolute Nouveau series Yamaha has taken a completely new turn with a removable lug that hooks on to a bolt positioned in the nodal area. By partially de-tuning the tension bolts, each lug can be slipped off its bolt, allowing the rim and head to be removed while the bolts are still attached to the lugs. This makes head changing quicker and simpler.

Interestingly though, Yamaha is hedging its bets by allowing you to specify either this new type of lug or the earlier, conventional design. The reason for this may be that the idea is not new. It's been tried before, on several occasions, with varying degrees of success: drummers, like other acoustic instrumentalists, are conservative in their preferences. Remo tried a similar principle in the 1980s with its Powersnap latched lugs, and then abandoned it. The Canadian company Ayotte has had more success with its TuneLock lugs (see snare drum on p.33, Ayotte 7-lug), which have an easy release flip-over 'T' hook design, which, by the way, dates back to the 1930s when it was used by Premier in Britain.

The other metal part mounted on each shell is, of course, the rim. Metal rims are nearly always described as either triple flanged or die cast. Top line drums are often fitted with a heftier gauge

Noble and Cooley use a single stud bolt to mount each tubular lug at the nodal area of the shell, thus minimising any damping.

This Ayotte snare drum features unique TuneLock flip-off lugs and hardwood hoops rather than metal rims.

of triple flanged rim than budget and middle range kits. Die cast rims are thicker yet than the heaviest triple flanged rims. They are more stable and less inclined to distort under severe tensioning and brutal rim shot assault. They are therefore sometimes supplied on snare drums even when the rest of the rims are flanged.

HARDWARE: STANDS AND PEDALS LEVEL 3

Just as shell finish is a crucial attraction of top line drums so is the appearance of the metalwork. And this brings us to another way in which top line drums are sometimes made to look more desirable.

Flawless chrome plating is taken for granted, but if you want something more striking you can sometimes get a choice of different platings. The most luxurious is gold, but a popular alternative is powder coating, which is usually black but can be in any colour. How far you extend the special plating is down to your aesthetic sensibility and the depth of your pocket. You may just include the rims or just the lugs, or you could go the whole hog and have all the hardware plated, including the stands.

Top line drums come with top line hardware. This will be the heaviest hardware the company makes, and will have the greatest degree of sophistication, stability, range of extension and adjustability, etc.

Hardware packs, however, are optional, recognising the fact that some drummers may already have hardware they wish to keep. Whereas drums may all sound somewhat similar, the different companies' hardware solutions really are quite variable. Most drummers have a preference for one type over another, particularly as regards tom mounting and bass drum pedals, and this can be a major factor in the final choice of gear. However, there's nothing stopping you buying a set of shells from one manufacturer and accompanying it with a different manufacturer's stands and pedals. You may even decide to use a rack system made by an independent manufacturer such as Gibraltar or Dixon.

Most small drum makers do not make their own hardware. They sometimes go as far as making their own lug because, as we've seen, this gives strong brand identity. But the cost of tooling up to make the metalwork for a drum kit is prohibitive, so small-scale operations will buy it in from generic stock.

This has been a drawback in the past and a major reason why drummers were reluctant to buy from smaller outfits. Occasionally the individual craftsman would be able to obtain good quality parts from one of the major manufacturers. But obviously there are times when the big names don't want their easily identifiable parts stuck on someone else's drums. But these days the generic hardware available from the Far East is of much better quality and the perceived drawback is considerably lessened.

Just about every top line kit made today is fitted with some type of resonance enhancing isolation mount for the toms-toms. Very often this means that the small toms are mounted off floor stands rather than off brackets attached to the bass drum.

The advantage of this is that the bass drum no longer has a heavy base plate restricting its resonance. The disadvantage is that many drummers have actually grown up enjoying the sound the toms make in conjunction with the bass drum, since the two inevitably resonate together when either is struck. It's a matter of taste, but the writing has been on the wall for old style tom mounts for several years now.

The original Gauger RIMS (Resonance Isolation Mounting System) is still hugely popular and used by many drummers. However, most of the top drum companies have now developed their own version of this type of mount. The idea of enhancing resonance wherever possible has become such a big selling point that companies have attempted to apply it wherever they can: to floor tom legs, snare drum stands, snare strainers and so on.

COMPACT KITS

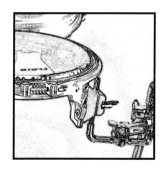

If you have restricted storage or transport problems, there are now quite a few funky compact kits in the budget to middle range. Remo got things rolling a decade ago with the Legero, a full set of standard diameter drums with shallow, single-headed shells. Since all the shells telescoped inside one another it was easy to transport. The Legero was later used by Roland when it introduced its ground breaking V-Drum electronic drums. More recently, the Pearl Rhythm Traveler came along with single-heads again, this time based on cut-down Forum shells. The kick drum is just eight inches deep. Shallow shelled drums like these are actually about as loud as normal drums: remember, it's the heads that produce the sound.

The really new thing about the Rhythm Traveler, though, was the introduction of alternative 'Muffle Heads'. These are made from a fine black fabric mesh which tensions and responds pretty much as a normal plastic head, but is almost silent, producing just a soft ping, rather like an extremely quiet steel pan. There is however a definite pitch difference between drums so you can work out parts realistically. When normal heads are fitted to the kit it can be used for live gigging, and it is particularly handy for clubs where stage depth is minimal.

The mid to late 1990s saw the compact trend extended, with kits like Premier's Club, which also has shallow shells but this time double headed. The Club has a 20″ diameter bass drum with 8″ deep shell, a 10″ mounted and 13″ floor tom with a 13″ snare drum. Sonorís 'Jungle' kit, based

Arbiter's Flats Lite kit features single bolt Advanced Tuning (AT) lugs on featherweight ABS plastic rims for extreme portability. And it's surprisingly loud.

Ideal for the jungle, drum 'n' bass and small group player, Sonor's Jungle kit is typical of the modern, easily portable compact mini-kit.

on the 3001 series, takes the compact kit further with a 16x16 bass drum, 10x9 (US: 9x10) and 13x11 (US: 11x9) toms and special 10x2 (US: 2x10) snare. With its sharp and fast sound it is particularly suited to jazz and drum'n'bass players.

More recently Pacific launched the Chameleon, which also has double headed shallow drums, but comes fitted with normal heads on the top and mesh heads on the bottom. So now you can flip the drums over without having to change heads if you want to have a silent practice session.

Taking the idea of shallow shelled drums to its extreme we come to the Arbiter Flats Pro and Flats Lite kits. These are offshoots of Arbiter's Advanced Tuning (AT) drums. The AT drums have a special rim with a heavy 'V' clamp that allows the head to be tensioned perfectly evenly by turning a single tuning bolt. The Flats Pro and Flats Lite kits have a 'shell' that is just one inch deep and is basically just there to provide a bearing edge for the head. The drums have typical fusion kit diameters of 20″, 10″, 12″; 14″ and are surprisingly loud but supremely transportable. The Lite version is made using very tough plastics and weighs just a few pounds. Once you get over the psychological problem of not having shells to hide behind it's quite possible to do most gigs using either of these kits.

Yamaha has gone a step further with its ingenious HipGig series, though at a rather higher, professional-level price. The HipGig also has a 16″ diameter kick but it is 20″ deep for more bottom end and is accompanied by rather shallower toms: 10x6 (US: 6x10) and 13x7 (US: 7x13). The snare is a more normal 12x5 (US: 5x12). Other comparable kits include Groove Percussion's bargain Travel kit, which has a 16x16 bass drum with small toms and a 12x5 (US: 5x12) snare all in maple. And Mapex's Voyager, which has an 18″ diameter bass drum with 8″, 10″ and 12″ toms and once more a 12x5 (US: 5x12) snare.

VINTAGE DRUMS & CYMBALS

Interest in vintage drums has increased a great deal during the last 20 years or so. Vintage drums do not yet – with a few rare exceptions – attract the sort of prices associated with, say, classic guitars, but their value is rising all the time.

DRUMS THAT MADE HISTORY

There are several sides to the vintage scene. You can have old drums that sound great but are not necessarily rare, or old drums that are very rare, and therefore collectable, but may not always sound that good. Fashion, aesthetics and even snobbery come into the equation. Some drums are scarce and collectable but never get played, which is a pity. Then there are drums that are collectable as memorabilia because they were played by a famous drummer, like Buddy Rich, John Bonham or Tony Williams. Those are often in the hands of the auction houses and we won't trouble ourselves with them.

Some old drums are passed over at sales and vintage fairs, yet may sound great. It largely depends on your own ears and taste. Occasionally, for whatever reason, a collector appreciates cheaper models, eg, Ludwig Acrolytes, Slingerland Students or Premier Olympics. It's worth keeping an eye open for less fashionable drums that are cheap and may reward you with a unique sound. There's always something gratifying about owning a bit of history, regardless of its value.

Some collectors concentrate on a single make of drums and track down every model ever made by that company. Others just pick up whatever they find that takes their fancy. Then there are professional hoarders who see valuable drums as long-term investments.

The drums that interest us all, though, are the drums that made history. There have been two particular occasions in drum kit history when a drummer has been so popular that he's revolutionised the manufacturing world. The first occasion was the reign of Gene Krupa in the 1930/40s, when Slingerland came virtually from nowhere to sell thousands of Radio King drum sets. The second was when Ringo Starr and the Beatles turned Ludwig into a household name and set the Chicago factory on a 24-hour non-stop frenzy of production.

> **"The old stuff looks better – you just need a 20, a 12, a 14. When you're playing for the music you can get by with a small kit."**
>
> *ALAN WHITE (OASIS)*

Krupa's Radio King has become an icon – the epitome of a classy, wood shelled snare drum. Radio Kings were made from the 1930s through to the 1970s. They were mostly made from a single plank of maple and they continued to be made from solid wood long after all the other drum companies had turned to the 'superior' ply construction.

However, single ply drums have a nasty habit of going out of round and there are cases of internal reinforcing rings coming adrift. Any Radio King, therefore, requires careful inspection before parting with a large sum of money. Still, vintage enthusiasts have a special affection for RK snares: more so than for the rest of the Radio King toms and kicks, although they too are great sounding drums. The toms and bass drums were made from three-ply mahogany with reinforcing rings. You might be shocked the first time you look inside to discover they are not finished to anything like the standard of a modern kit.

At the height of Beatlemania, in the mid-1960s, Ludwig massively upped production to churn out 600 Super Classic sets a week. How did they do this? It's almost certain that the quality could not have been maintained. I know for a fact that at least one shipment that turned up in rock mad 1960s Britain ("If Ringo can do it, so can I.") contained bass drums that were decidedly oval. This means that if you come across a mid-1960s Super Classic kit it will certainly be collectable. But it may not be a good drum kit.

> "If you can get a Ludwig kit before 1963/64 the quality control was good – more often than not you'll find care was taken putting it together, because they had more time (before Beatlemania)."
>
> GARY NOONAN (MASTER DRUM-MAKER)

Kits made before 1964, when the Beatles hit America, have, on the other hand, every chance of being fine instruments. As, too, do 'after the goldrush' Ludwigs, up to the middle 1970s. Like the Radio Kings, so many were made that they are not rare. The problem is that in the last few years they've all been snapped up and anyone who has a good one is hanging on, watching its value increase.

Ringo always played a wood shelled Jazz Festival snare drum, but the Ludwig Super Classic kits came with the Supraphonic '400' metal shelled snare drum. The earliest 400s have brass shells, and usually have no serial number on the gold 'keystone' badges. Find one of those and you have a very desirable and collectable drum. Most 400s were made of 'Ludalloy' from around 1964 to the mid-1970s, when they started to use brass again. Ludalloy is actually aluminium. If you don't believe me just check how light these drums are compared to a steel or brass drum. It's the aluminium that gives the drums their characteristic bright yet dry and controllable sound. Supraphonics are common, although many have appallingly bad chrome (aluminium is not easy to plate). They are always worth collecting. Ringo-style Jazz Festivals are much more rare and quite valuable. Those finished in Oyster Black Pearl – like Ringo's – fetch large sums. If someone offers you one you'd be advised to check that it didn't start off a different colour before being conveniently recovered.

> "I need to get an old Ludwig Super Sensitive or Supraphonic 400, cos I think that just about any drummer should have one."
>
> CHAD SMITH (RED HOT CHILI PEPPERS)

In the last decade there has been considerable interest in the drums from the classic rock period of the 1960s. Good quality sets and individual drums from that era now routinely fetch the same sort of prices as decent new drums. It's often claimed that Rogers drums from the 1960s and early 1970s were the best vintage production drums the Americans ever made. They certainly had the best hardware available at the time (Swiv-O-Matic) and they had excellent three or five ply maple shells. Then there was the Rogers DynaSonic snare drum, the most advanced snare drum of its time – a chromed brass beauty with an ingenious, if flawed, parallel snare mechanism. But despite the acclaim, Rogers drums are, for most drummers, simply less desirable than Ludwigs or Gretsches. People don't talk about the Rogers sound the way they do about the Ludwig or Gretsch sound. Having said that, DynaSonic snare drums with *wood* shells are extremely rare and now change hands for many thousands.

SHELLS

Time after time when talking to greying old bores (Whaddya mean, like me?) you'll hear it said that vintage drums sound better. The main explanation that's offered is to do with the wood of the shells.

In relation to old Radio King snare drums, to take the obvious example, the contention is they were made from solid boards of first quality maple, that the wood was steam bent by the sort of

craftsmen who barely exist today and that the drums have had another 60 or 70 years to mature and dry even further. If you think back to the 1930s, you'll realise that there were a lot more craftsmen about who really knew their timbers than there are today, when most furniture, for example, is turned out using extremely efficient and accurate machinery. The result, the bores insist, is that vintage drums produce a crack and a warmth that are unmistakable, priceless, simply the best. Despite being something of a sceptic, I have to say that there's probably some truth in this. When you hear a good old Radio King in the flesh – or a Leedy Broadway or a Super Ludwig – they do have a certain something. There's a sort of hollow ring of wood on wood, like you're playing the shell directly with no metallic intervention. It's very attractive, and you immediately start to hear those old Gene Krupa solos and fills.

Mind you, this raises an important question: is that really the sound you want in the modern era of sequenced electronic backings? Although there is a vintage sound, it may not be an appropriate sound for all circumstances. Times change. In fact, despite not getting any younger myself, I confess I like the sound of modern drums just as much as that of vintage drums.

Nonetheless, it's well known that many recording drummers continue to use vintage drums in the studio, despite endorsing modern makes. It's a cliché that many famous session drummers have a 1950s 'round badge' Gretsch as a studio failsafe. This is not a poor reflection on modern gear. It's just a fact that drums – like any other instrument – mature with age. You simply cannot duplicate the sound of a very old instrument with a new one. Most drummers who use vintage instruments in the studio do not go on the road with them. Occasionally they might take an old

snare drum. Neil Peart of Rush favoured a Slingerland, Jeff Porcaro played a Radio King and Ginger Baker used a Leedy Broadway. The Rolling Stones' Charlie Watts is the only stadium-filling artist I can think of who steadfastly uses a beat up old Gretsch kit. That's because that's the sound he likes, when, of all people, he could have anything he asked for.

Vintage wooden drums nearly always have internal reinforcing hoops or 'glue' rings. The construction of a single ply shell requires support. And although plywood became familiar in the later 1920s, shells continued to have glue rings right up to the 1970s. There are several reasons for this, the main one being that shells were still thin, three-ply shells being common. Once rock players started to get seriously heavy in the late 1960s and early 1970s, the need for thicker shells became apparent and with these the requirement for reinforcing rings disappeared.

Prototypes for the thin, glue-ring supported type of shell include the Ludwig (mahogany/poplar with maple glue rings), Rogers (maple with maple rings) and Premier (birch with beech rings) shells of the 1950 and 1960s. The one company that pioneered straight-sided shells without glue rings right from the 1940s was Gretsch. Gretsch perfected the compromise between making a shell thin and yet sturdy enough not to require glue rings. It has stuck with this type of shell ever since. It's graduated from three-ply to six-ply maple, with the latter becoming the model for the majority of shells around today, both up-market and budget. It's a happy medium that works for most purposes: if it ain't broke there's no reason to mess with it.

> **"Rogers and Camco were the best made drums in the 1960s – the early Rogers Cleveland-made drums were miles ahead of anyone else. The hardware was really good. Oakland-made Camco drums weren't far behind – maybe it was because they didn't sell anywhere near as much, so they had more time to concentrate on making them well."**
>
> *GARY NOONAN (MASTER DRUM-MAKER)*

The bearing edges on vintage drums are often rather different from the sharply angled edges of today. You will often find, for example, a rounded bearing edge, or a shallow angle cut straight to the outer edge.

There are even old Gretsch drums that have bearing edges cut 'the wrong way', ie, sloping downwards towards the outer edge of the shell. The glue rings are also generally a lot chunkier than the slim line versions that appear on a few modern lines today. The more rounded bearing edge profile gives more contact between the head and the shell, softens the attack and projection, and warms the sound. Many drummers have been faced with the dilemma of picking up a vintage drum and wondering whether to have the bearing edges modernised. You have to make a decision about whether to update the drum or whether it should be kept in original condition for historical accuracy. If you do decide to modify the drum the only advice must be to take it to a highly skilled and experienced drum workshop.

Before the 1920s, drums were painted or stained and varnished. Then in the 1920s along came plastic wraps in glorious finishes and colours. The original plastic wrap material is called Pyralin, a name derived from pyroxylin, which is partially nitrated cellulose. Pyralin had already been used in all sorts of instruments, for example as an ivory substitute for piano keys. Now, on the drumset, drummers were introduced to pearls and glitters and the drum companies really went to town. Glitter finishes often had extra diamonds and stripes of different coloured glitters added to make the drums look even more splendid. Drums in these unique early finishes are another big attraction for collectors.

Bass drums (and some snare drums) in the 1920s and 1930s were also fitted with internal lights to warm up the calf heads. Then the front heads of the bass drums were hand painted by artists specially employed by the drum companies. The internal bass drum lights would, of course, shine through the oil paintings, illuminating scenes of idyllic rustic charm: log cabins, mountain ranges, waterfalls and the like. As well as wood drums, the other great collectables from the early days are the Black Beauty brass shelled snare drums made by Ludwig and Slingerland and the Black Elite made by Leedy. The shells were plated in black nickel and then hand engraved, contrasting superbly with the polished brass fittings and rims. Needless to say these drums are quite rare, highly prized and extremely valuable. They sound great too.

HARDWARE

Vintage hardware may be collectable and of historic interest but it's generally not held in such high esteem as the wooden and metal drum shells. This is not because the metal workers were any less skilled than the wood workers, but because much of drum kit hardware had yet to be invented as the kit evolved.

In the 1930s, kits often had 'console' frames on wheels with traps trays and cymbal holders mounted off them. The traps included all sorts of sound effects, from woodblocks to whistles, from klaxons to bird calls. Consoles, although rather different, can be seen as the forerunners of today's rack systems. Gradually they were replaced by individual stands.

The hi-hat pedal came along in the mid 1920s and bass drum pedals were slowly improved. Once rock music took over in the 1960s, drummers started to play two or three times harder than their predecessors and, as we've seen with shells, it was necessary to beef things up. The earlier mounting hardware and stands simply weren't up to the job. Rogers began the revolution from around 1959 with its Swiv-O-Matics, but by the 1970s the historic American drum companies were in decline and it was the emerging Japanese companies who took on the job of modernising the hardware. This they did with unforeseen brilliance and we are today eternally grateful to Tama, Pearl and Yamaha for the way they approached the situation with fresh eyes to initiate the modern era of strong, reliable hardware.

> "There's a myth about anything that's old is great and the truth is that it might be good but it might not be. I've seen some dreadful old things. Same with the old 'K' Zildjians. Tony (Williams) and Max (Roach) and those guys would go through buckets before they found a good one. Modern gear is much more consistent."
>
> DAVE MATTACKS (PAUL McCARTNEY, XTC, RICHARD THOMPSON)

What this means in relation to playing vintage drums today is that very often old drums are lovingly cradled by modern hardware. You may see the Chili Peppers' Chad Smith or Vital Information's Steve Smith playing vintage snare drums in their videos, but they will be mounted on modern stands. Charlie Watts loves his old Gretsch kit, but his hardware is all new. His small tom is mounted on a modern snare drum stand rather than the original Gretsch bass drum mount, which was frankly tragic. Many players of 1960s drum kits mount their toms on Purecussion RIMS™ mounts rather than risk the old hardware.

When it comes to the hardware fixed to the shells of vintage drums you may have a problem. Early tension brackets – like Rogers' so-called 'bread and butter' lugs from the 1950s – are liable to crack, as are many early snare strainers and throw offs.

For a drum to be of prime value it must have its original fittings intact. There are occasions when replacement parts of the same vintage can be found, and for this I refer you to the various vintage societies, dealers and their websites. Original snare drum strainers and original tom mounts, etc, should always be kept untouched (even when they are removed for safe keeping) if the drums are to be of any historical or collectable value.

And this, of course, highlights a problem with buying so-called vintage drums. They have quite often been doctored over the years. Many drums from the 1960s, in particular, have been fitted with new tom tom mounts or even completely refinished, perhaps 10 or 20 years ago before it was realised that the drums might one day become collectable. The only way to be sure of what has happened is to consult the original, dated catalogues (which themselves are increasingly valuable). You should also refer to the steadily growing library of well-researched books on the vintage companies: see Chapter 14.

VINTAGE CYMBALS

When it comes to cymbals the most mystique surrounds vintage 'K' Zildjians, which are sought after by drummers who love their warm, dark, soft quality. They are often quite unsuited to modern playing, which is so much louder. The fact that they were hand made under primitive conditions means that quality is variable in the extreme. It's entirely down to personal taste and usage as to whether an old K is a great cymbal or not.

The Zildjian family crafted cymbals back in Turkey from at least 1623. A secret manufacturing formula was handed down from father to eldest son over the centuries. At the beginning of the last century Zildjian cymbals were commonly used by military and orchestral percussionists, and found their way into the new jazz music from the start. These early Zildjians were often heavy and high pitched.

However, when the new Avedis Zildjian company was started in the USA in 1929, it was able to work closely with the new jazz drummers who were looking for something rather different. As the jazz rhythm was transferred from the hi-hat to the ride cymbal, Avedis Zildjian began to produce thinner and larger cymbals.

Meanwhile, back in Turkey, K Zildjian was still making heavy cymbals. However, by the 1950s it had started to produce thinner modern cymbals. Also at this time, the new small group jazz was catching on and these drummers were targeted by the Gretsch drum company, which was the first to make small 20″ bass drums. Now it so happens that Gretsch was also the sole importers of K Zildjian cymbals at this time. So the combination of Gretsch drums, and hand hammered, relatively thin Ks, became the classic sound of the bebop drummers like Kenny Clarke, Max Roach and Art Blakey, and later Elvin Jones, Tony Williams and so on.

The Ks were genuinely hand made at this time, and the processes were those that had been handed down for centuries. Being entirely hand crafted, they were variable – many were of average quality and the occasional one was a corker.

The cymbals tended to be dark and quite soft, with less of a ping and more of a spread or 'wash' – right on the edge of trashy. This sound suited the small group, where the cymbal did not have to be too loud, but certainly had to be interesting and evocative. So, to be clear, very old K Zildjians tend to be heavy. The thin ones start to appear in the 1940s and 1950s. They are variable and by no means all of them sound that good. They have been treasured in recent years because modern cymbals tend to be brighter and heavier. This is the inevitable result of modern music being much brasher and louder.

Although Ks have the mystique, old Avedis Zildjians from the 1930s onwards are also vintage instruments, and the be-bop drummers and swing drummers also played these. So old Avedis Zildjians are also collectable.

Nowadays some drummers even like the really heavy Ks from the 1920s. Other drummers have an affection for the early Paiste cymbals of the 1960s and 1970s. The companies refine and modify their processes and sounds year by year, so there are always going to be drummers who have a particular affection for an earlier type of cymbal that is no longer in production.

CURRENT COLLECTABLES

So what's actually collectable? The following is a very basic starting point, by no means comprehensive. Some of these drums are worth thousands, others very little. But who knows? Remember, eventually today's kits will be vintage and collectable.

1920s:

- Solid wood snare drums in walnut, mahogany, maple, etc, by Leedy, Ludwig & Ludwig and Slingerland.
- Also, early kits by these manufacturers with colourful Pyralin finishes, painted bass drum heads and internal lights.
- Black Beauty snare drums (brass shelled, black nickel plated and engraved) by Ludwig & Ludwig and Slingerland. Likewise, Leedy Black Elites.
- Early British drums by Premier.

1930/40s:

- Slingerland Radio King snare drums and kits.
- Leedy solid wood snare drums.
- Gretsch Gladstone and Broadcaster kits.
- Duplex aluminium drums.
- European British pre-War Premier and Carlton drums.
- Early K and A Zildjian cymbals.

1950s:

- Gretsch 'round badge' kits with three-ply maple shells.
- George Way 'Aristocrat' drums (forerunners of Camco, in turn forerunners of DW). These have the same turret lugs used today by DW.
- Leedy drum kits.
- K and A Zildjian cymbals.
- Early Paiste cymbals (post 1957).

1960s:

- Slingerland, Rogers, Leedy, Camco, Ludwig and Gretsch kits in good original condition.
- Ringo-style Oyster Black Pearl Ludwigs with matching Jazz Festival snare drums.
- Brass shelled Ludwig Supraphonic snare drums.
- Wood shelled Rogers Dynasonic snare drums.
- Oddities like German Trixon kits (known as Vox in the USA), 'Telstar' (conical) and 'Speedfire' (egg-shaped) drums.
- British Ajax Pipper and Snapper, Premier Royal Ace and 2000 snare drums with kits in good condition.

1970s:

- Ludwig Vistalite, Fibes Crystalite and other rare Plexiglas/Perspex/Acrylic kits such as Zickos (the original), Sonor, Pearl, Asba, Orange (Capelle), Shaftesbury and Hayman.
- Fibreglass drums from Fibes, North, Staccato, Arbiter Autotune and Pearl.
- Early 1970s American Rogers, Slingerland and Ludwig drums with maple ply shells.
- Good examples of post-1975 Japanese kits by Pearl, Yamaha and Tama.
- Premier Resonator, Hayman Vibrasonic and Sonor drums in good original condition.

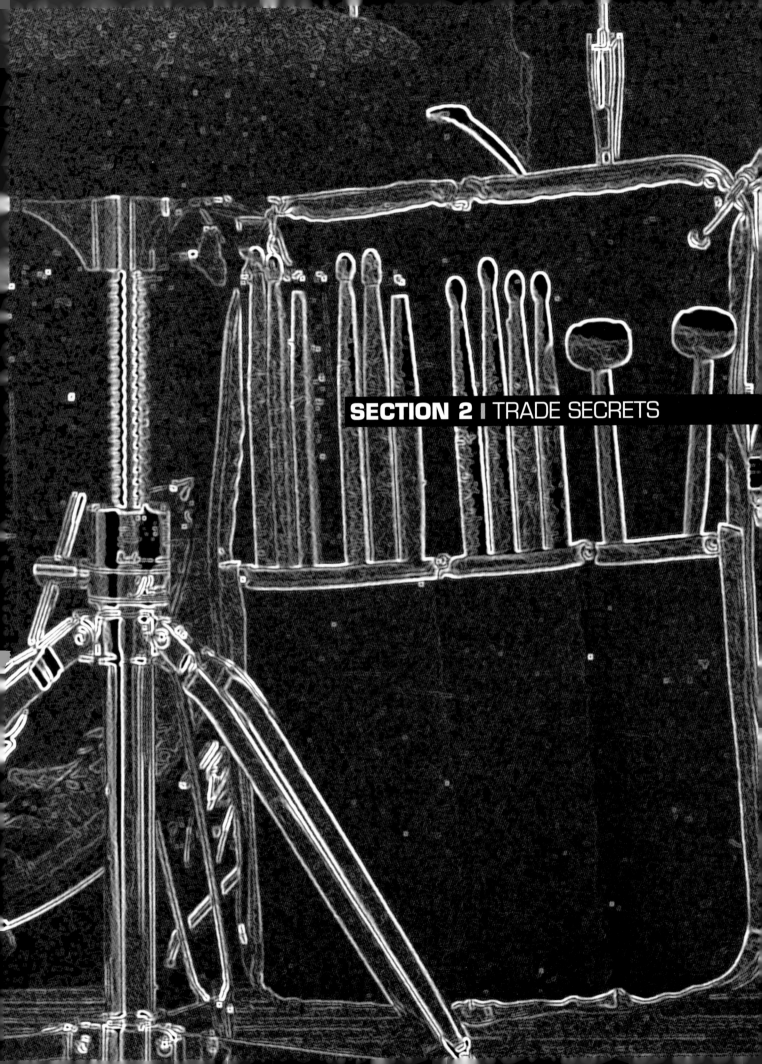

SECTION 2 | TRADE SECRETS

DRUM SHELLS

CONSTRUCTION

Most drum shells, with the exception of snare drums, are made from wood. Snare drums are often made from metal, and very occasionally the toms and bass drum are made from metal too.

For example, every now and then someone comes up with a steel kit. Steel is loud and resonant but it is also heavy. Aluminium drums are a lot lighter, with a somewhat drier tone, and they are currently made by the Trick company in America, which uses sheets of 1/8″ (3.175mm) 'certified grade' aluminium. The word 'certified' highlights one of the advantages of inorganic materials. They are much more consistent than an organic material like wood. Trick says it chose aluminium because of its pureness of tone, sustain and durability. The ultimate in metal shells, though, are the titanium drums made by the Japanese company Kitano. Kitano claims that titanium gives you the best of everything – warmth, projection, sensitivity, power, you name it. But then so it should, since we're talking around $12,000 for a standard five piece kit.

As well as metal, there are synthetic shells made from Plexiglas/Perspex or fibreglass. These were plentiful in the 1970s but are rarely made nowadays. Ludwig made a large number of colourful Plexiglas 'Vistalite' drums in the mid-1970s and they are great favourites with collectors. Fibes, the original maker of fibreglass drums, is still producing both fibreglass and acrylic 'Crystallite' shells today. Then there's the Rocket drum company, which makes carbon-fibre kits. But by far the most successful (semi) synthetic shell material is Remo's 'Acousticon', which is made from hardwood fibres impregnated with resins. Remo use Acousticon for all their drum kit and percussion shells.

MULTI-PLY HARDWOOD SHELLS

There are several different ways of making a wooden cylinder, but today the great majority of shells are made from multi-ply hardwood. The multi-ply lamination process was perfected on drums, so it's claimed, by Fred Gretsch Snr in 1927.

Sonor plywood shell with inner reinforcing hoops. This was the commonest type of shell until the late 1960s, and it has made a partial comeback in recent years.

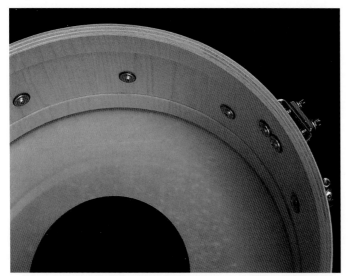

Until that time, shells were made by steam bending a single plank or board of wood and then holding it in the round by fixing 'reinforcing hoops', or 'glue rings', inside the top and bottom edges. The introduction of plywood was seen as a great advance over the single ply 'solid shells' of the day. Ludwig and Ludwig ran a famous advertising campaign for their so-called Aero-Kraft laminated bass drum shell, dropping it out of an aircraft into a cornfield to demonstrate that it would not break. And, I believe, it didn't.

During the 1940s, Gretsch improved their ply shells by cross laminating them. This involved arranging alternating plies in opposing directions, vertically and horizontally, making the resulting shell much stronger. Cross lamination meant the shells no longer needed reinforcing rings, so the straight sided 'unsupported' shell was born. Straight sided, cross-laminated plywood shells are the commonest type available today. Shells are further strengthened and kept in the round by staggering the seams where the plies join so that there isn't just a single butt join at one point around the shell's circumference. They also occasionally have scarfed joins, rather than butt joins: a scarf joint is a smoothly graduated, overlapping join covering a greater contact area.

The thickness and number of plies in a shell generally varies from around 3mm (1/8″) three-ply to 12mm (1/2″) twelve-ply. The thickness of plies can vary though, so a six-ply shell might be 6mm, or it might be 5.5mm or 7.5mm. Thinner shells are traditionally favoured, as they are with other acoustic wooden instruments, the shell being the resonance chamber that gives the drum its particular flavour or timbre.

It has always been the goal of the drum maker to construct a drum that's both light and strong. In far off times this was because drummers had to march into battle carrying their drums slung around their necks. Then in the early days of jazz, portability was still prized – first because the early jazz bands were also marching bands, then later because most drummers didn't have their own transport. They would drag their kit around on public transport. We still want lightweight drums today, but this has to be offset against the fact they must be strong to withstand the rigours of much louder contemporary drumming.

A thin shell is fragile and liable to deform from the circular and go oval. So reinforcing hoops, or glue rings, are still sometimes fixed to the inside top and bottom edges for stability. This is something you will find with some of the professional level drums made by companies like DW, Premier, Pearl and Tama. It's a matter of personal taste whether you feel the advantage of having a very thin and resonant shell is negated by the cramping effect of the glue ring.

Tama, for example, offer glue ring shells as an option on their Starclassic drums and they say that top endorsee Simon Phillips prefers them because he likes the slight "mellowing or muting effect" they have on the sound. DW says that its reinforcing hoops both strengthen the shell at its weakest point and raise the shell's pitch. DW uses reinforcing hoops of maple, which are 'graduated': ie, they get bigger as the drum diameter gets bigger. Premier do a similar thing with their Series Maple and Birch drums. A tom tom with a diameter of 8″ has a glue ring of around 7/8″ deep, while a 22″ diameter bass drum has a glue ring of around 1.5″ depth. Noble and Cooley, uniquely I believe, fix their reinforcement rings at what they call the 'nodal' points of the shell. These are areas an inch or two in from the top and bottom edges where there is minimum interference with the shell's natural resonance. The effect of these rings is to create a "clean and dense sound", according to N&C.

Thicker shells don't need this strengthening and so they are termed straight sided, or 'unsupported'. The thicker the shell the higher the pitch and the shorter the sustain. So a thick shell will be very stable, with a bright sound, while a thin shell will have a deeper sound and more resonance.

If the shell is very thick (rare these days except with occasional snare drums) the shell tends more towards becoming a passive chamber and the head does most of the talking. That is, the drum will be loud, while the character of the head will be less coloured by the material of the shell. But with a thin shell the wood resonates more and absorbs more of the energy and overtones of the head. So in this case the type of wood the shell is made from will colour the sound more noticeably.

The table below shows the directions in which these various sound parameters tend roughly to move as the shell gets thicker or thinner.

> "The thicker the shell the higher the pitch, which is what you want from a snare drum. If you want a snare with more middle or bottom end we make it deeper shelled, not thinner."
> *GARY NOONAN*

Thick shell	=	higher pitch, shorter sustain, louder
Thin shell	=	deeper pitch, longer sustain, softer
Thick shell	=	passive chamber – head type dominates sound
Thin shell	=	resonant chamber – shell material dominates sound
Thin shell with reinforcing rings	=	compromise between two types

Pretty well all budget and middle price drums have straight sided, medium thickness shells with six to nine plies. The Pearl Export's shells are six-ply and 7.5mm. Top line drums are also mostly straight sided, but the fact they are made from harder, denser woods means they can afford to be a little thinner while being as strong or stronger. You'll notice also that the plies themselves can vary in thickness, so, for example, Spaun's maple shells are eight-ply and 5.5 mm thick while Premier's Birch and Maple Series drums are six-ply and about 5.9mm thick. Sometimes the bass drums and larger floor toms are thicker than the smaller toms. Noble and Cooley's CD Maples small tom shells are six-ply and 1/8″ (3.2mm) thick, whereas their bass drums are eight plies and 1/4″ (6.4mm) thick. DW calls this 'proportionate-ply' configuration. Thus their small drums are thinner five-ply, medium drums are six-ply and larger drums eight-ply.

Occasionally snare drums are also made with a large number of plies since thicker shells give a higher, brighter attack. British custom drum builder Jalapeno makes 1″ thick snare drums with 45 plies, while Peavey's unique Radial Bridge design snare drum is 1.75″ (45mm) thick. These drums really do have a loud, piercing attack and they are very sensitive. But they weigh a ton. Incidentally, by complete contrast, Peavey uses the thinnest three-ply 1/10″ (2.5mm) thick maple shells for its tom-toms.

Straight-sided, unsupported shell by Sonor, who unusually have the inner grain running vertically. The other shell is a solid, 1990s single-ply Slingerland Radio King, with supporting glue rings.

For mainstream multi-ply drums, it seems to be the pattern that the European and Oriental drum companies largely make their own shells while many American companies buy in their shells ready-made. American companies buy plywood tubes in all the diameters they need from large-scale specialist manufacturers like Keller and Jasper. The various diameter tubes are then sliced into individual shell lengths (depths). Each drum company takes these 'blanks', cuts bearing edges, drills them and finishes them as necessary. So although many companies may share the same supplier this certainly does not mean you get the same result from each.

The Europeans, like Premier and Sonor, and Orientals, like Pearl and Yamaha, have traditionally made their own shells, often using their own patented processes. For example, Yamaha's Air Seal System (also used by Premier) and Sonor's 'Cross Laminated Tension Free' (CLTF) system. These involve cutting sections of plywood and layering them up inside circular moulds. Each section must be an exact length so that it lines up correctly inside the mould.

Sometimes you'll see cheaper shells which have butt-joined plies with tiny gaps where the plies don't quite reach around the circle. These gaps may have filler to disguise them. High-end shells overcome this problem by using sloping butt joins, angled rather than vertical. The plies are 'spiraled' into the fibreglass former moulds and microwaved, ensuring a very tight join. An alternative method is to use a scarf joint, as does Pearl with its Heat Compression Moulding System (HCMS). The scarf joint also eliminates the gap problem, but again, the cutting of the long overlapping scarf must be very accurate or the shell will not be flat. It will have a lump or depression in the area of the join. You can safely assume that problems such as these have been eliminated in the shells of the major companies, which these days are excellent in their appearance and finish.

The plywood itself often starts out as two- or three-ply board, which is already cross-laminated. Layering up two or three lots of three-ply gives us the six-ply and nine-ply shells we're familiar with. As we've seen with budget kits, sometimes a single ply of better wood is put on the inside of a six-ply shell making seven-ply. And sometimes an extra outer veneer is applied for finishing, making eight-ply. Some companies, the most prominent of which is Sonor, have the outer veneer and innermost ply running vertically top to bottom of the shell, which they say helps the projection of sound up and down the shell. Most other companies have the inner and outer plies applied with the grain running horizontally.

The more plies there are in the shell the more layers of adhesive glue. Glue is an insulating material and it's a major reason why solid shells with no glue except for the single join are said to resonate better. However, the process of gluing the multi-ply shells and then curing them is usually done by microwave heating. This process bakes the wood and the adhesive together so they fuse as one and thus – in theory – resonate as one. However, there are those who say it's better to construct the shell without baking it. I have to confess I have no opinion on this point. If you can hear a difference, your ears are better than mine.

SOLID SHELLS

Solid shells are today highly prized, but they are difficult and expensive to make and are usually reserved for snare drums. It's most unusual for a complete drum kit to be made from solid timber, although at least one major company, Noble and Cooley, has offered a full range of solid sizes in the recent past.

A solid 'single ply' shell with reinforcing rings. Below: a modern shell with 45 degree bearing edges.

Another way of achieving what is almost a solid shell is via the ancient technique of stave construction. This is the same method used to make barrels – and some congas and bongos – where vertical sections of wood are joined into a circle. This type of construction produces a shell that is free from the 'wanting-to-straighten-out' tension of bent wood. The Italian company Tamburo constructs complete kits in this manner, using maple and mahogany. The staves have interlocking zigzag cuts so that they slot together precisely. Each different diameter of drum requires the staves to be cut at a different angle, which means a large investment in special machinery. Tamburo drums are, however, left with multi-flat-faced exteriors. Although this looks rather attractive it creates a problem with the bearing edge. Rather than sanding the edge into a round, Tamburo has chosen to attach a circular edge sleeve made from a tough black plastic material called ABS. This strengthens the shell but insulates the head from direct contact with the wood. Still, when I tried them, they certainly projected very well.

BEARING EDGES

Whichever type of construction is used to make the shell, the bearing edges are crucial to the sound, projection and tuning of the drum. Modern bearing edges are usually routed to an almost sharp point, typically cut to a 45 degree angle on the inside of the shell, while the outer cut will also be 45 degrees or rounded over so that the head transfers vibration to the shell when it's tightened over the edge. The inner cut will usually be deeper than the outer cut, thus maximising the diameter of the drum. The fact the bearing edge is sharp means the attack and projection of the head are increased. This has not always been the case. Vintage drums often have much more rounded edges so that considerably more of the head is in contact with the shell. This gives a warmer, less attacking sound and theoretically imparts more of the character of the shell.

Other shells have different routed angles. Gretsch toms, for example, have 30 degree inner edges for a warmer sound, while Gretsch snare drums have 60 degree edges for attack. Specialist manufacturers Pork Pie Percussion use a 60 degree inner cut with a rounded-over outer edge to achieve maximum vibration of the shell. Spaun drums have an equal 45 degree cut both inside and outside, rising to a central, sharp 'peak'. Spaun say this means the edge makes contact with the flat part of the head rather than the rounded collar, improving tuning and head resonance.

Another way of ensuring the bearing edge contacts the flat of the head and not the collar is to make the shell slightly undersized. So although a shell may have a nominal diameter of, say, 12", in fact the shell is slightly less than that. The Premier Series shells, for example, are all 3mm undersized. This way a gap is opened up between the standard sized metal rim and the shell so that when the standard sized head is fitted it cannot be cramped between shell and metal rim. A sort of bridge is created which should aid the free resonance of the head – and shell. There's always an opposing philosophy, though, and I remember once reading a handout from the Slingerland company claiming that the fact that its vintage Radio King shells were tight against the hoops was one factor in the unique sound of these sought after old drums.

Whatever the shell size, the bearing edge must be perfectly true all round so that the head can be tensioned evenly, achieving the same pitch at each tension point. This is one of the most crucial aspects of shell construction. Any slight dip or irregularity in the bearing edge will result in a dead spot in the head, which will have to be accommodated in tuning. This distorts the head and messes with the overtones. If you have a problem drum in your kit, which is always infuriatingly difficult to tune, then it might be worth inspecting the bearing edges for irregularities (see Tuning, Chapter 11).

Note, however, that the bottom edge of your snare drum is an exception. It should have two slight dips – one on each side – where the snares are attached to the shell. These dips are known as snare beds and their purpose is to help the snares lie flat, reducing snare buzz. On old drums the beds may be quite pronounced while on modern drums they are more likely to be very gradual depressions spanning several inches. They may only be noticeable on careful inspection. Since resonant snare heads are very thin they mould easily to the slight dip. You will, though, have to give the tension rods on each side an extra tweak to smooth out the wrinkles.

AIR HOLES

Air holes are typically incorporated within the drum maker's badge as in this example on a late 1970s Gretsch 'octagonal badge' drum.

It's normal for most double-headed drums to have a small hole (maybe 3/8" or 10mm) drilled through the side of the shell to allow the escape of air. When the drum is struck the batter head is depressed and air is forced out through the hole. The hole is often disguised within the company's badge, the plate being held in place by a grommet that is fixed into the air hole.

In some older shells, like Gretsch round badge drums from the 1950s, there was no air hole. Striking the drum increases the pressure inside the shell and elevates the tone and slightly compresses it. Since these Gretsches were closely associated with bebop jazz, and bebop drummers tuned their drums high and played fast and light, this suited the drums. It may indeed be part of 'That Great Gretsch Sound'.

With today's harder hitters, air holes are generally considered necessary. In fact some drums have several holes. Yamaha's Birch Absolute bass drums have four extra holes. The extra holes are even more useful now that so many drummers are returning to bass drums with no port hole in the front head.

SINGLE HEADED DRUMS

Single headed 'concert' toms were all the rage in the 1970s but are rarely seen today. No doubt the fashion will return again some day. When you strike a single headed tom, the stimulated air column travels down the shell and straight out the end with no barrier to stop it. It projects well enough, although mostly towards the ground. The synthetic shell North and Staccato drums of the

1970s both twisted round, so that the mouth projected forward in an attempt to overcome this situation.

The single headed drum will have good attack followed by swift decay. When you strike the top head of a double-headed tom, the top head vibrates and sends energy down the drum where it collides with the bottom head and partially reflects back up the tube. The sound is therefore sustained and made more complex. There is less escape and so the walls of the drum are involved more. The sound must project through the walls rather than simply dissipating through the open bottom. All this adds to the colour and sustain of the drum, though it detracts a little from the initial attack.

To sum up, then: single headed toms have more attack, but less tone and faster decay. Double-headed toms, on the other hand, have less attack, but more tone and slower decay.

NO-SHELL DRUMS

The British inventor Marcus de Mowbray makes drums that are basically frames with a top and a bottom rim and head but with no shell in between – and they still sound remarkably like other drums. The diameter of the head and the distance between the top and bottom head seems to be enough to do the trick. Marcus also makes timpani with just a top head and no massive copper bowl. And they sound like timpani.

Other drums, like Arbiter's Flats and Remo's Roto-toms, which have just top heads but no shells, also project loads of sound. The sound, though, is more open and spread-out, which is perhaps what you'd expect. When it comes to normal, wood shelled drums, the size of drum, how it's tuned and played and the type of head all have a bigger impact on the perceived sound than the shell itself. What the shell does though is to change the timbre slightly – it's the icing on the cake for the high budget buyer.

If you want proof that the shell affects the sound you only have to think of the difference in timbre between a steel shell and a wood shell snare drum. Most drummers can hear such a difference very easily, though they might not always recognise it on a recording. Obviously the shell acts as a resonating chamber absorbing and reflecting, reducing and amplifying various frequencies – acting like a combination of amplifier and graphic equaliser – and so the sound is coloured and altered in subtle ways. But never forget that the generating source is the head.

WOODS

When it comes to buying a professional kit, the first decision you probably make is whether to buy birch or maple drums, since most high-end kits are described as 'maple this' or 'birch that'. This was not always so. Growing up during the 1960s and 1970s, I really don't remember much talk about the type of wood employed in making shells. The catalogues glossed over the question and often didn't let on.

In any case most drums were covered in plastic wraps – pearls and glitters – and given exciting names like Rogers Starlighter, Ludwig Super Classic and, erm, Premier 303 (why there was never a Premier Keith Moon I'll never know). Nowadays the type of wood is often included in the name, eg, Gretsch Renown Maple, Ludwig Classic Birch, Sonor Force Maple, or Yamaha Oak Custom, etc. So presumably it must be very important.

MAPLE AND BIRCH

The great interest in wood choice began at the end of the 1970s, when lacquered finishes began to catch on. For a decade, plastic wrap finishes became almost obsolete on top-end drums. The often translucent finishes made the type and quality of wood much more apparent. In particular, Yamaha made the Recording Custom kit for Steve Gadd, and stressed the fact that it was a birch kit. Gadd was also the first great session superstar, and of course close attention to sound is essential in the studio. Birch, it was claimed, was the perfect wood for recording. It was a masterstroke of marketing and we all fell for it. This despite the fact that virtually every great record in the previous history of recorded drumming had been made on maple or mahogany Gretsches, Ludwigs, Slingerlands and Rogers.

Throughout the 1980s, lacquered kits with natural grain were all the rage. They were nearly all birch, and were made by the emerging Japanese companies, which put many of the historic American companies out of business. Then, during the 1990s, North American maple became popular again and coincided with the resurgence of American companies like Noble and Cooley and, in particular, Drum Workshop. Birch drums had been cheaper for the Oriental companies to make than maple and this added to their popularity.

But by 1997, Pearl, for example, found birch had become as expensive as maple. So, with sales dropping off, it stopped producing its 100 per cent birch drums. The perception was that birch should be cheaper than maple. Yamaha tackled the same problem by coming up with its Absolute series where birch and maple drums are the same price and you can mix them in the same kit. Quite a few Yamaha drummers now use a combination of maple bass drums for low-end power with birch small toms for added cut. This seems to be an emerging trend.

Premier's new Series drums are available in maple, birch or Gen-X birch/maple hybrid, all at the same price. Pearl, meanwhile, has its Masters Custom series in which you can specify any combination of maple, birch or mahogany in the ply make-up of each individual drum. So if you want your toms to have birch outer plies, mahogany inners and maple in the middle, you can.

You may have heard birch described as sounding quieter and more focused, mahogany as warm, while maple is the unruly American cousin. As I mentioned above, maple and mahogany were the most popular woods of classic American drums and suited the era before miking-up where you needed the warmest, loudest, most open sounding kit possible. And maple drums became popular again in the 1990s when there was a return to 1960s-influenced retro-rock bands alongside a fashion for playing vintage drums. Birch is often said to be more controlled, and was perfect for the tight and punchy sound of the computerised and fusion-mad days of the 1980s. Interestingly, birch is once more making something of a return today with the popularity of tighter dance/R&B grooves. So we can see there is a loose logic in the swinging fortunes of maple and birch under the influence of fashion and musical trends.

The importance attached to choice of wood today reflects the intense scrutiny that modern recording and close miking places on your drums. But a word of warning: I've heard many completely contradictory statements about birch and maple from highly respected drummers. The same words are sometimes used to describe them both. The sound a wood imparts is subtle, and different drummers hear it in different ways. I'm afraid there's no clear-cut formula.

> **"The hoops, heads, snare wires and sticks make a huge difference to the drum – more so than if you change from maple to birch or beech."**
>
> *GARY NOONAN*

What I would say is that however small an effect the type of wood has, you can hear a difference in sound between a birch and maple kit, particularly when you're in the driver's seat. Different people characterise it in different ways but for what it's worth, my feeling is that maple is slightly warmer, louder and more open – 'bangier' – while birch is slightly more 'focused' and harder. This is the distinct impression I got many years ago when I first played my Yamaha RC 9000 birch kit, following several years of playing my Gretsch maple kit. I've still got both, and the longer I've had the Yamaha the warmer it sounds. In fact both kits are maturing very nicely, and this points up another factor. Age is a major reason why vintage drums always seem to sound so good.

I've also often heard birch described as brighter, with more cut, attack and projection, but slightly less resonance. However, not wanting to confuse the issue even more, it's important to remember that the sound is hugely affected by the type of head you choose. When birch was most popular, in the 1980s, many drummers used double-ply Pinstripe heads, which themselves have a dark, controlled, attacking sound. Then when maple resurged in the 1990s the trend was back to single-ply Ambassador heads, which have a much brighter, more resonant sound. Heh ho…

It's not unusual for shells to be made from a mixture of woods. In particular, budget shells often have cheap wood in the middle with a single, better ply on the inside and/or outside. But professional drums also sometimes have interesting hybrids. Mapex's Saturn Pro Studio series is made up from four plies of maple on the outside with two plies of walnut on the inside. And as we've seen, with Pearl's Masters Custom series you can specify any combination of maple, birch and mahogany. This may point up another way forward for the manufacturers to tempt us in the near future.

> **"I don't consider birch dark. I think it has more characteristics in the studio than maple."**
>
> *J R ROBINSON (MICHAEL JACKSON)*

One final word on this admittedly complicated subject. Changing head types will have a greater effect on your sound than the type of wood used for your shells. Yet while you can always change your heads, once you've bought your drums you can't change the wood. The type of wood acts like a subtle EQ on your sound, imparting a flavour or fragrance, and like an expensive perfume it's much prized and talked about. How you choose to bring out this flavour depends very much on your heads and tuning. This may be the main reason why different drummers seem to say contradictory things about these two fine woods. If it's any consolation, either wood will give you a great drum kit.

EXOTIC WOODS

Many hardwoods have been used in the history of drum making. In fact you can make a drum out of virtually any wood and it will have its own sound. Examples include mahogany, beech, ash, walnut, oak, poplar, rosewood, cherry, ebony and numerous others.

Recently the big companies have turned to different woods, having done just about all they can with maple and birch. The problem for most drummers is that we are so used to being told maple or birch are the best that we are frightened to risk serious investment in any other wood. I think the choice of heads, how you tune them and how you play them are always going to be the biggest factors in determining your sound, so the actual species of wood is less important than is made out. But since the wood shells are the most prominent, expensive and gorgeous aspect of the kit a disproportionate importance is placed on their type. Please feel free to disagree.

If you like the look of a particular wood (and you can afford it), at least try it out in the store. For example, speaking as someone who regularly reviews drum kits, I was pleasantly surprised when Yamaha's Beech Custom kit turned up one day. The beech wood seemed to straddle maple and birch and if anything, had the best of both of them. And it was cheaper. Sonor made beech wood drums between the 1960s and the 1980s and I always thought they sounded great. Yamaha now also makes an Oak Custom kit, while Mapex offers its Deep Forest snare drums in both walnut and cherry.

These are all traditional drum-making woods and it would be good to see more experiments with viable alternatives in the future. Using unusual timbers is also perfect for the smaller scale specialist drum maker. The RMV company, for example, makes drums from Brazilian Bapeva, which it says is 30 per cent harder than birch. Now that has to be worth hearing.

One other I must mention is Pearl's limited edition Masters Classic in genuine four-ply African mahogany. All those great Ludwig Super Classics of the 1950 and 1960s had three-ply mahogany/poplar/mahogany shells, while the vintage Slingerland Radio King sets with the fabulous Gene Krupa tom tom sound were also mahogany ply. Mahogany is renowned for its deep, rich, warm and rounded sound. I've no doubt mahogany kits would be popular today were it not that real mahogany, from Africa, Honduras and North America, is a rare and expensive wood.

SUSTAINABLE WOODS

The mention of real mahogany leads us to another question. How damaging is drum making to the world's shrinking rainforests? Whenever I've asked drum companies they have, of course, all said they only use hardwoods for their regular lines from sustainable, managed and replenishable stocks. They're well aware of the problem. But this is a hot political issue and despite – or because of – many hours looking around on the web I don't feel qualified to make any binding judgments. There are surprisingly labyrinthine issues and arguments, which are far too abstruse and involved to explore here.

Most people accept, however, that deforestation of old growth timbers is detrimental to the world's eco-systems. Many species are under threat and some trees take hundreds of years to grow to maturity. But is the world going to stop using hard wood products? It's a similar dilemma we face every time we fill up the car with petrol. Are we suddenly going to stop driving? I don't think so. Luckily the impact of the drum industry on timber resources is minute compared with that of the construction and furniture industries. But it's still an issue that drummers might want to take time to consider.

You can divide hardwoods into two categories. Those which are managed, replanted and harvested; and those from tropical forests, mainly in the Far East, Africa, Central and South America, etc, which are to a large extent irreplaceable. I think we've all heard something of the rain forest issues. The managed forests, on the other hand, are mostly in the northern hemisphere and include relatively fast growing species like maple, birch and beech. These are what most high-end kits are made from. My guess is that if you buy a typical professional set made of maple or birch, etc, you're on pretty safe ground. Phew.

But what about the truly exotic woods which increasingly appear on mouthwateringly beautiful, limited edition drums? You may need to ask some searching questions of the manufacturers. There may be a perfectly reasonable explanation, for instance that the wood is from trees which have fallen through natural causes, storms or earthquakes, or that the timber has been salvaged from ancient wooden buildings, etc. There are reputable timber companies that deal in small quantities of exotic timbers that have come through these relatively blameless routes. A good example is the Exotic Finish series from DW, which scours wood yards for rare, one-off logs that may have been lying around for decades. And then there are DW's Lake Superior Timeless Timber drums. These are veneered with timber made from logs that had been submerged at the bottom of Lake Superior for a century.

The reason genuinely old timbers are so prized is that they come from ancient trees from deep in the forest, where there is little light and the growth rings are exceptionally densely packed. This means the wood is extra hard and resonant. It is impossible to get that sort of wood from regularly harvested, sustainable, new growth forests. So modern hardwood drums, while being beautifully made and finished, lack that extra something that comes from truly old wood. And this, of course, is the argument for vintage wood shells. Drums from the 1920s and 1930s, for example, were made at a time when old growth timber was more readily available. The longer you keep your modern kit though, the more the wood will dry and increase in resonance. If you've got a well-made modern kit, just remember it will one day be a vintage kit too.

CHEAP MAHOGANY

The area that is probably the most questionable regarding conservation is the low-end market where large numbers of cheap kits are churned out using fairly non-specific hardwoods. To get to the bottom of this you will have to trawl through the many websites that deal with the issues surrounding depletion of timber species. All I can say is that they don't make pretty reading. The rainforests of Indonesia, the Philippines, Malaysia, Korea and elsewhere have been heavily exploited and it would be naive to think the situation is totally under control. We can't be smug either, as we in the northern hemisphere have already done irreversible damage to our own forests, and the situation is not exactly hunky-dory here.

Most beginner, budget and middle range kits are said to be made from mahogany. Other woods that you will encounter are basswood and falkata, which tend to be used more in the middle market as cheap substitutes for maple. The mahogany used in budget kits is not the same wood you see in period furniture, which is a deep red colour, nor the genuine mahogany that was used in vintage drums and today in, for example, Pearl's Masters limited edition series. No, this is so-called Philippines mahogany, a rather loose term for a different wood, otherwise known as lauan, ramin or meranti. It's a pale whitish wood that is smooth and easy to work and stains nicely. The DIYers among you may recognise it from hardwood mouldings and picture frames, etc. It's also used extensively for furniture and flooring.

As with so many things in the West, we want ever cheaper, better quality products and we turn a blind eye to the origins and means. I'm aware that this whole subject is controversial and I have no easy answers. Indeed, I hesitated to bring the subject up at all. But I do believe it's something we should think about. Remo makes all its drum shells from its own semi-synthetic material called Acousticon. This uses wood fibres from various species of recycled hardwood, impregnated with resins, making it a relatively conservation-aware material.

Acousticon is close to wood in look and sound but is harder and has a more consistent density. Remo drums are loud and bright and work well with any type of head combination. Acousticon is also used very successfully in the construction of Remo's extensive range of percussion instruments. So far as I'm aware, no other company has really investigated viable wood-related alternatives. As I mentioned at the beginning of this chapter, there have been many experiments with synthetic materials – like Plexiglas – and various metals over the years, particularly in the 1970s. However, wood shelled drums are today more popular than they have ever been. It seems we want the real thing and more earth-friendly alternatives are a long way from dominating the market.

FINISHES

The finish that is applied to wooden drums is a major selling point. Shells are either 'wrapped' with a plastic covering or they are finished with stains, lacquers, acrylic paints, oils and waxes, or even, very rarely, French polish. Wraps or covers have the advantage over natural finishes that they are often harder wearing and less likely to scratch. They also involve less labour and specialist equipment since the outer veneer of the shell need not be finished to anything like the standard required by a sealed wood or paint finish. For this reason the cheapest drums are always covered in single coloured wraps. The more decorative wraps like pearls and, in particular, sparkles can themselves be quite expensive. Most of the up-market plastic finishes are made in Italy and imported into the USA by the Delmar company based in Berlin, Connecticut. Cheaper plastic finishes are also made in the Far East.

The process by which pearl finishes are produced involves casting a big block of plastic, which starts in a liquid state with the flakes of pattern running right through it. This block is then sliced into thin layers, like wood veneers, which are laminated onto a plain coloured backing, usually black, white or blue. The backing colours the pearl and strengthens it. A clear protective sheet is also applied to the surface. Sparkle or glitter finishes are produced in a similar way with real metallic specks floating in the material. Vintage Champagne Sparkle is the most luxurious and expensive, with very fine specks of real silver and copper mixed in together. Other coloured wraps include flames, swirls and moiré finishes, which are made from polycarbonates, which hold little prisms of light giving a 3D effect.

When a plastic wrap is applied to the drum shell, it acts as an insulating outer coat. It would seem likely that it must dampen the shell to some extent, although the general consensus is the effect is negligible if the wrap is applied properly. On cheap drums the wrap is stuck on with double-sided tape or with patches of adhesive. This can leave air pockets, which further insulate the shell. With better drums the wrap has adhesive applied over the entire area and the wrap is heat rolled onto the shell, so there is no chance of any air pockets and bubbles. In fact, as Sonor state, if you were to try to remove the wrap you would destroy the shell first.

Natural and lacquered finishes became very popular during the 1980s, while covered finishes were almost totally absent from high-end drums. But in the past decade the pearl and sparkle wraps have returned, while stained, lacquered and painted finishes have become ever more exotic and hi-tech. Applying many layers of paint or lacquer, etc, to the outside of the shell must also affect the shell's resonance, though perhaps to a lesser extent. Pearl says its Masters drums go through a 31-stage finishing process. But, as with other companies, it maintains this actually enhances the resonant and timbral qualities of the drums rather than diminishing them.

One major reason for buying a top class kit is to get a beautiful finish. Lacquers in satin or high-gloss lustres that enhance the grain of the wood are extremely hard-wearing and easy to keep clean. Polyurethane lacquers are sprayed onto the shell resulting in a transparent finish that dries very hard, giving extra depth to the colour when polished. As well as plastic wraps with sparkle finishes, some drum companies use sparkle finishes which are lacquer or non-lacquer urethane. Again the actual sparkles are metal flakes and the finish may involve a dozen or more layers. This is a difficult and painstaking process that is unsurprisingly expensive. Oil and wax finishes are also popular, though not so common. The oil seals the shell, which is then waxed and buffed to a rich, satiny sheen.

As you will have noticed if you've done any home decorating lately, there is a major movement towards water-based stains, paints and lacquers and away from pungent solvent-based materials. Environmental legislation is getting stricter in the West and the drum world has benefited. Water based finishes are clearer and more resistant to yellowing and cracking. Some finishes are also dried using an ultra-violet light process that is incredibly fast, completed in a matter of seconds rather than hours.

The technology of wood finishing is evolving constantly, and there are literally hundreds of different materials, processes, paints, lacquers and stains, both water- and solvent-based. During the 1980s and early 1990s, most top-end drums had natural finishes showing off the wood grain. These have a natural appeal, but sometimes drumsets looked more like suites of furniture than instruments of rock and roll glamour. It's heartening today to see at least a partial return to the lack of taste epitomised in the 1970s, with gaudy, colourful and brash finishes more widespread again.

INTERIOR FINISH

While the exterior finish has little if any effect on the drum's sound, this is not the case with the interior. Since the sound generated by the head travels down the interior of the shell and then bounces around inside, it seems reasonable to assume the inner surface of the drum has an effect. Pearl has recently tested out many different combinations of wood plies in its Masters Custom series. It found that the inner ply is crucial and that mahogany, for example, has a marked effect, making the sound noticeably warmer.

Most modern shell interiors are very lightly sealed, just enough to keep out moisture. But this has not always been the case. Until the 1970s many shells had heavily lacquered interiors. Others were painted on the inside with a thick coating of white paint (Ludwig, Camco, Hayman) or grey paint (Rogers, Tama). I think the only company that still does this is Gretsch, whose drums have a thin silver paint on the inside. This is in line with the Gretsch philosophy not to change the sound for which it is so famous. Any hard, reflective inner surface will produce a brighter sound. Conversely, a porous inner surface will produce a softer, warmer sound.

Many budget shells, as noted previously, have an inner ply of harder wood for better projection.

I once read an interview with Buddy Rich in which he said something to the effect that he didn't much mind what snare drum he played so long as it had several coats of varnish on the interior to brighten up the sound. Buddy was obviously out of step with today's thinking. Evidently, this is another factor in drum sound that is under the influence of fashion. Today's requirement is for as natural an interior as is practical.

SIZES

Bigger drums are louder. The greater the diameter and depth, the louder and deeper the sound. Snare drums have always been available in different depths. If you wanted a higher pitched, faster responding drum you'd get a shallow snare, say 5″ or 4″. If you wanted a more powerful drum you'd get a 6.5″, 8″, or even deeper. Over the past two decades this flexibility of choice has gradually extended to tom toms. Up till the end of the 1970s, we had the standard sizes that had been around since the 1930s. A 13″ diameter tom would be 9″ deep, a 12″ would be 8″ deep. Floor toms would be square sizes for that big fat sound: 14x14 and 16x16, Just occasionally floor toms would actually be deeper, so a 16″ tom might be 20″ deep. Bass drums, from 18″ right the way up to 28″ in diameter, would all be 14″ deep.

Then in the 1980s things started to get interesting. First we were introduced to 'power' sizes. So a couple of inches of depth were added to the standard mounted toms – now the 12″ tom was 10″ deep and the 13″ became 11″ deep. At the same time the 14″ deep bass drum become 16″ deep. These power sizes took over as standard, the direct result of the fatter sounds on records coming from the new Linn drum machines, plus the massive success of big-hair stadium rock.

The other big influence during this period was the rise of the star session drummer personified by Steve Gadd. As is typical in the studio, Gadd favoured smaller drums and he started to use a 10″ diameter tom. At the same time he popularised floor stands and shallower floor toms. So now we had the opposite concept – the 14″ tom became 12″ or even 10″ deep, while the 16″ became 14″ deep. Since then we've had the in-between size 15″ floor tom, which can be either 13″ or 12″ deep, and at the other end, 8″ toms which are usually 8″, though occasionally 7″ or even 6″, deep.

> "Big drums are not necessarily bigger sounding. With the 24″ kick you have to play it harder. I've been debating whether to go back to the 22 but I like the way the 24 looks. I use a felt beater – I don't like wooden beaters, they seem to kill the drum."
>
> *ANDY NEWMARK (SLY STONE, ROXY MUSIC)*

So now we can see a pattern emerging. By the middle of the 1980s the choice in tom depth was becoming almost as wide as that which we'd enjoyed with snare drums for decades, while the choice of diameters was also steadily expanding.

It was inevitable, following this progression, that someone would try all 'square sized' small toms – thus 10x10, 12x12, 13x13. These sizes have not really caught on though. More successful has been the compromise between the traditional and power sizes, so now we have 12″ toms that are 9″ deep and 13″ toms that are 10″ deep. This does seem like a happy medium between the traditional attacking sound of the old sizes and the fat sound of the power sizes.

Finally there are the so-called 'quick' sizes. These are extra shallow toms that have a very fast response. These were first tried by Noble and Cooley, who maintained their drums had such depth of tone they didn't need deep shells. N&C toms might, for example, have a diameter of 14″ with a depth of 7″, or a diameter of 12″ with a depth of 6″ etc. Several other companies have followed suit. Orange County call their shallow toms 'compact' sizes. They have 22″ and 20″ bass drums which are just 12″ deep, while their 10″ tom, for example, is just 4″ deep. As with so many other concepts, shallow toms are not a new idea. Louie Bellson famously used shallow Gretsch mounted toms in the late 1940s with Duke Ellington's orchestra, and the idea was copied here in Britain in the 1950s by Eric Delaney and Basil Kirchin among others. During the 1960s Premier drums featured a unique 14″ tom that was only 8″ deep. Mounted in triplicate, these unique toms featured loudly on numerous great hits by The Who, as pummelled by Keith Moon.

Shallow depth drums have the further advantage of being easily transportable and for that reason extra shallow toms and bass drums are also a feature of so-called portable kits like Pacific's Chameleon and Pearl's Traveler. Other portable kits, like Sonor's Jungle and Yamaha's Hipgig, have shallow toms with small diameters mounted on deep bass drums.

And talking of which, the current trend is more and more for 18″ deep bass drums following almost 20 years when 16″ was standard. Occasionally you'll even see 20″ deep monsters. For the ultimate in low end, DW make add-on 'Woofers', which are 8″ deep shell extensions for their 22″ or 24″ diameter bass drums. The idea is to enhance the low end even further. Woofers are also fitted with May internal microphones.

Most budget and mid priced kits are available in two configurations, often called 'rock' and 'fusion'. The rock kit will be 22″, 12″, 13″ and 16″ while the fusion kit will be 20″, 10″, and 12″ and 14″, each with an added snare drum. Occasionally you might see the term 'jazz kit'. This will usually indicate a four-piece kit consisting of 20″, 12″ and 14″ in traditional depths with a shallow snare drum.

The actual sizes that make up so-called 'fusion', 'rock' and 'jazz' kits are really an accident of history. Before wide choice came along a small group jazz kit would have an 18″ or 20″ bass drum with 12″ and 14″ toms. A rock or big-band kit would have 22″ or 24″ bass drum with 13″ and 16″ toms. So when, in the late 1960s, manufacturers first began to sell kits with *two* mounted toms there were only 12″ and 13″ sizes available. When these were added to the rock kit we got the familiar 12″, 13″ and 16″ configuration... spot the imbalance.

Countless drummers over the decades have struggled to get decent melodic intervals out of this badly matched set. If you think about it, you'd probably be better off with 10″, 13″ and 16″. Even 20″, 12″, 13″, 14″, with the extra tom added to the 'jazz' set makes more sense. Meanwhile, the 20″, 10″, 12″, 14″ of the fusion set-up is perfect if you like smaller sized drums.

Once you get to the professional level, of course, you don't have to go along with the shell sizes offered in standard kits. These days you are invited to configure your own shell pack choosing from a much greater variety of sizes. You might though have to wait several months for a special or unusual order. To give just one example, Tama offers Starclassic Maple toms in diameters ranging from 8″ to 18″, each with a choice of three or four depths. So a 12″ tom is available in depths of 8″, 9″, 10″ or 11″, stopping one inch short of 'square'.

SNARE DRUMS

A top-level kit deserves a top-level snare drum. While budget and middle level kits can sound fine, budget snare drums are usually disappointing. The characteristically clean and precise nature of the snare drum calls for quality shells of the best hardwoods or metals. And the added complication of the snare mechanism itself – which must be set up just right – means that only the best will do.

For the majority of drummers the snare drum is the most important part of their kit, and in all types of music the sound of the snare drum is a crucial ingredient in defining the feel. This has always been true, but the emphasis on snare sound has become even more pronounced since drum machines and samplers came along during the 1980s. These allowed the pitch of any snare drum sample to be stretched over a couple of octaves or more, which in turn led to producers

using all sorts of improbable sounds to represent the backbeat. In particular, the typical snare drum sound changed during the 1980s from the deep, fat, reverbed Linn-type snare to the opposite extreme of a thin metal-shelled piccolo. Every drum manufacturer launched a piccolo snare, and it became commonplace for drummers to mount a second snare on the side of their kit, to the left of the hi-hat. This initiated an explosion in snare drum variations that shows no sign of abating today.

Most drummers who have just one kit will gradually collect several snare drums. Session drummers on major commercial projects may well turn up to the studio with a flight case containing 10 or 15 snare drums, all of different sizes, different materials – wood, metal or synthetic – and different vintages, from new to anything up to 80 years old. This just illustrates the importance placed on the snare drum in recording. Although the snare is usually employed to knock out a relentless two and four backbeat, the sound of the drum goes a long way to determining the type of record you're listening to. That's true whether it's the bell like clang of HM, the smooth 'tick' of a breathy R&B hit, or the fat, woody thump of a rock ballad.

> "I've got quite a collection. Even on the road I take 25 snares. Sometimes in a real ambient arena I might use an even darker sounding wood drum, or in a real dead atmosphere, sometimes out of doors, I may use a brass drum – for extra crack. 6.5″ is OK and 8″ is a little deep; 7″ is right about in the middle – you can tune it high or low."
>
> *GUNS'N'ROSES, MATT SORUM (THE CULT)*

In the 1970s the recording of an album would begin by getting a good drum sound and the whole vibe of the album would revolve around that. But nowadays the sound of the drums may well change on every track. Snare drums reflect this huge range of dynamics, timbre and pitch. Whatever else, it's great news for the manufacturers because now they can flog the average drummer three snare drums, whereas in the old days you'd have one and maybe a spare if you were lucky.

Because the snare has become so important to an individual's sound, the Oriental drum-makers in particular have turned to producing 'signature' model snare drums. Often the star drummer will have two or more signature drums – a wood shell and a metal shell. It can be quite instructive to see what various players go for. Concentrating just on metal shell drums, jazz drummers Marvin 'Smitty' Smith (Pearl) and the legendary Roy Haynes (Yamaha) both choose copper, which is warm and responsive. Rockers Chad Smith and Ian Paice (both Pearl) are happy with the clean power of steel. Stewart Copeland, Kenny Aronoff (both Tama) and David Garibaldi (Yamaha) – a stylistically varied trio – all favour classic brass shells, while Simon Phillips (Tama) chooses black nickel-plated bronze. Fusionist Dave Weckl (Yamaha) uses a dry and bright aluminium for his main snare drum, while rocker Tico Torres (Pearl) goes for a heavier cast aluminium. Finally, metal monster Lars Ulrich (Tama) goes for a bell bronze clanger.

While the bass drum and tom toms in any drummer's kit are nearly always made from wood, the snare drum is just as often made from metal. Evidently, then, it's not always meant to match up in timbre with the toms and bass drum. If you think about it, you normally want your tom toms to have depth and warmth, to resonate as much as possible and to have a long note decay. But with your snare drum you generally want a rather shorter note – more of a staccato stab – and, more often than not, less body than your toms. Snare drums are usually tuned higher than toms to achieve a razor-sharp attack and definition. For this reason, the snare drum is usually comparatively shallow, so that the sound waves can travel more rapidly from the top to the bottom head.

Snare drums range in diameter from 10″ to 15″ and from as little as a couple of inches to 12″ in depth. Most snare drums, however, are 14″ in diameter and between 4″ and 8″ in depth with a standard depth of 5.5″ or 5″. The 5.5″ drum is a good all rounder, both quick responding and with a certain amount of body. For extra body and volume, 6.5″ or 7″ deep drums are also popular.

But, as with toms and kicks, snare drum sizes change with fashion. In the 1970s and 1980s deeper drums were popular. This was a time when stadium rock acts wanted big deep sounds. Later in the late 1980s, the fashion went to the opposite extreme and piccolo drums – nominally 13″ diameter and 3″ deep – became all the rage. Obviously piccolos are perky, but they also record well (as do smaller toms, bass drums and cymbals). The problem with piccolos is that the high pitched 'pop' can get a bit tiring.

One way round this is to use a drum that has a smaller diameter but which is a little deeper. So nowadays you might see a 12″ diameter drum with a depth of 5″. Such drums are less piercing than a piccolo, but are still incisive, with a bit more punch. For a similar effect, but with more power, try a 12″ that is 7″ deep. In the past few years we've seen just about every size of small drum – there are even mini snare drums just 10″ across that are ideal for ultra-fast tempo drum'n'bass styles. It's quite normal now for a drummer to have two or even three snare drums mounted about the kit.

METAL SHELLS

Snare drums are often made from steel, which is a relatively cheap and convenient material to work with. Other metals include brass, aluminium, bronze, copper and even titanium. The latter is used by the Japanese company Kitano.

The easiest way to make a metal shell is to roll out a flat strip, bend it into a circle and weld it at the join. Concentric ribs are pressed into the side of the shell to strengthen it and keep it circular. Bearing edges are created by bending over the top and bottom edges into a slightly rounded profile, and these also add to the shell's stability. Cheaper metal drums are all made using this method.

The disadvantage is that the vertical butt weld breaks up the vibration of the shell, reducing the shell's resonance. A better method of construction therefore is to spin a seamless shell from a single sheet of metal so that there is no join. Actually, many spun shells are made in two parts, a top half and bottom half, joined around the centre by a bead channel. This works fine since there is still no vertical butt join.

A third method of making a metal shell is via casting. Whereas spun shells tend to be around 1mm to 1.6mm thick, cast shells may be three or four time this. The result is sometimes a stupendously heavy drum which rings like a bell and may require a specially strengthened snare drum stand to support it.

Mapex has a 5mm bronze monster in its Precious Metals series, while Tama makes Power Metal series snare drums in 3mm bell brass, with rims in the same material. Since bronze is the alloy that cymbals are made from, it made sense when Noble and Cooley designed a drum in collaboration with Zildjian, using the latter's cast bell bronze. More recently, the drum specialist Jeff Ocheltree has made a similar drum using Paiste Signature Bronze cymbal alloy. Noble and Cooley also make snare drums in cast aluminium, which are somewhat lighter.

Among the metals, brass has long been highly prized. This goes back to the days of the black nickel-plated Black Beauty brass snare drums of the 1920s and 1930s. Brass is renowned for its musicality. It cuts through well, but is darker, deeper and warmer than steel. It's also likely to be slightly less ringy and brash, making it a great all rounder that suits every type of player.

Sheet bronze (as opposed to the heavyweight cast stuff) is similar to brass, although brass is more popular. Copper is darker still and has an even warmer timbre. The shells of these metal drums are sometimes hammered to give a dimpled effect, similar to the hammerings that increase the timbral complexity of cymbals. I've also heard it said that the hammering acts like a studio baffle, reducing unwanted harmonics. I'm not sure if these two claims don't cancel each other out. Mapex's Precious Metals series includes snare drums in phosphor bronze and stainless steel,

This vintage Ludwig Supraphonic 400 snare drum, with its Ludalloy shell, is perhaps the most popular metal shell snare drum of all time.

Many drummers have a high regard for brass-shelled snare drums. Here's a Noonan custom model with a two-piece spun brass shell beaded together in the centre.

61

while DW combines the attack of brass with the warmth of maple wood in its Edge series, which combines a maple shell with brass bearing edges.

Still, for loud rock, steel is often the best solution. There is a bit of a prejudice against steel. It's sometimes characterised as being crude and vulgar, largely due to its being used in the cheapest snare drums – which can indeed be that. But a good steel drum, with heavy chrome plating that cuts down some of the more riotous overtones, makes a perfect rock drum.

> "For me the more obnoxious and ringy the snare drum sound the better, because you need it once all the other stuff gets on top of it. It's nice to have some cut to it. I just like to have my head torn off by the snare drum."
>
> *CHAD SMITH (RED HOT CHILI PEPPERS)*

Signature steel drums by rock giants like Chad Smith (Red Hot Chili Peppers) and Ian Paice (Deep Purple) are very popular buys at attainable prices. Steel is not just for loud players, though. It has a great tuning range and is actually very sensitive.

Despite this, the most successful snare drum of all time – the Ludwig Supraphonic '400' – has an aluminium alloy shell known as 'Ludalloy'. A lot of people think old 400s are steel, but if you pick one up you'll see it is significantly lighter than a steel drum. The aluminium has the bite of steel, but it also has a certain dryness. It's almost impossible to get a bad sound from a 400, which is why they are still so popular.

WOOD SHELLS

The fashion for wood or metal drums comes and goes, and at the moment wood drums seem to be 'in'. Metal drums are usually thought of as slightly louder, while wood drums are warmer. This is a simplification and for me the most important difference is in timbre. Wood seems to have a more 'hollow' sound, while metal drums are more 'dense'. Both can be equally resonant, and a good wood drum will still have a shrill, almost metallic, clave-like ping when you play a rim shot. The centre response will often be drier, usually with a faster decay. These are subjective feelings though – you'll have to go out and try a few.

This Pearl Masters Custom snare drum is very unusual in that it has a single ply solid maple shell but no internal reinforcing rings.

MULTI-PLY AND SINGLE PLY

The thicker the shell, the higher the ping, and for this reason your snare drum won't necessarily have the same shell construction as your tom toms. The most sought after toms generally have thin shells, but a good snare shell may well be thicker and heavier, with extra plies for that extra top end. Everyday experience tells you that low frequencies travel through walls and floors better than high frequencies. So a thicker shell with lots of plies will filter out more of the deeper frequencies than a shell with just a few plies. Thus a multi-ply drum will effectively sound brighter than a thin-ply drum. Conversely, if you want a darker sounding snare drum seek out one with fewer, thinner plies.

While most wooden snare drums are made from plywood, a small but significant proportion are made using other, older methods. The commonest of these is to take a single plank of solid timber and steam bend it into a circle. This is known as a solid, or single ply shell, and usually requires reinforcing rings to be glued into the inner top and bottom to hold the wood in the round. This is the traditional way drums were made before plywood came along in the 1920s.

It's generally accepted that solid shells project better, with a purer tone than ply shells. Multiple layers increase insulation (in the same way that several layers of clothing are advisable in cold climates – ie, they retain the energy inside). Also, the more plies, the more adhesive holding them together, which again adds to the insulating effect, restricting resonance. However, the hi-tech adhesives used today cut this detrimental effect to a minimum.

And in any case, they fuse the whole shell together so well that the shell comes pretty close to being solid anyway. Still, I always think you can tell when you have a solid drum – there's a special purity of sound (or am I deluding myself here?).

Solid wood shells have the advantage of not having layers of glue. But there's a bit of a Catch-22 here. The solid shell resonates and projects better than ply, but unfortunately it usually requires strengthening glue rings, which tend to 'restrict', or – let's be positive – 'focus' the sound.

Noble and Cooley solid maple shell snare drums are constructed from "steam bent New England green maple" and have solid maple reinforcing rings. But N&C's rings are mounted at the nodal points of the shell (an inch or so in from the edge) rather than right on the bearing edges. This allows the shell to vibrate with the least possible interference.

Ludwig 1990s reissue Jazz Festival snare drum, in the Oyster Black finish made famous by Ringo Starr and The Beatles. However, Ringo's 1960s drums had supported shells while this version has a straight-sided shell.

STAVE AND SOLID

As well as bending single plies there are other methods of constructing a cylindrical drum. You can turn to the ancient craft of stave construction, which is the method used to make barrels, not to mention congas and bongos.

Or you can stack up several horizontal sections – like pineapple segments in a can. Or, if you're really extravagant, you could carve a cylinder from a massive solid block. All of these methods result in a drum that has none of the inherent tensions of a steam bent shell, where the wood forever wants to unwrap itself – although it must be said stave shells have been known to 'explode' under duress. Staves and segments can actually be less expensive than single ply construction, and you get the chance to mix different woods together in one drum, which can be attractive and may result in a unique timbre.

The Spaun drum company makes stave snares in maple, cherry, walnut, oak, and birch. It also offers three shell thicknesses – 5/16″ (7.9mm), 7/16″ (11mm) and 9/16″ (14mm). British master drum builder Gary Noonan has made stave drums from timbers like Canadian rock maple, rosita and flame sycamore (the slightly softer European relation of maple). The process is similar to 'coopering' a barrel. Noonan starts off with a plank of timber and – whatever size the drum – cuts out 24 stave wedges, which are butted together with space-age anti-creep glue to form the 360 degrees. Each shell is made oversize and then repeatedly turned (shaved) into a perfectly smooth circle.

Noonan has also hewn drums from a solid block of mahogany, turned inside and outside, the modern equivalent of hollowing out a log. The finished shells are 15mm thick. It's expensive and wasteful, but the result is a completely stress-free (and glue-free) shell – the only genuinely, truly one-piece shell you can have.

The snare bed (above) is a shallow graduated dip cut into the bearing edge in the area where the snares are attached.

An added attraction of small companies run by individual craftsmen is that, since they tend to make one-off drums, they are not limited in their choice of woods. They'll try anything once. They also tend to be eco-friendly, only using timbers whose provenance they trust.

Such a company is Drum Solo, which lists an amazing selection of hardwoods, such as hickory, banara, barn oak, peroba, grenadillo and chokte kok, whatever that might be. Similarly, the Head drum company makes stave construction snares from dozens of attractive species, including birds eye maple, wenge, purpleheart, African rosewood, red African padouk, zebrawood and Gabon ebony. It even, unusually, offers softwoods, such as Colorado spruce, heart birch, Philippine mahogany, Douglas Fir and Australian lacewood.

Over in Australia, both Sleishman and Brady make stave shells using indigenous Australian timbers. Brady works with native Australian eucalyptus species called wandoo and the extraordinarily hard jarrah. Sleishman uses pidouk, jarrah and she-oak.

SHELLS WITH GAPS

Back in the 1980s, Ludwig made a snare drum called the Classic Slotted Coliseum. This was 8″ deep, but the shell was split in two round the centre leaving a yawning hole or slot. Spaun has recently resurrected this idea with its Split Snare, which has a one-inch gap running round its centre. To understand the effect of the gaping midriff, think what happens to your bass drum when you cut a hole in the front head. The drum immediately has more punch with less boom. Shell resonance is obviously reduced, because much of the air shoots straight out – and this reduces the sustain, making the sound drier, sharper and louder.

Orange County has come up with a rather more novel version with its 'vented' snare drums, which have large circular holes cut in the sides rather than a single horizontal gash. The effect is quite similar, in that volume and sensitivity are increased while shell resonance is decreased. The lack of shell resonance produces a fast decay.

The British drum maker and inventor Marcus De Mowbray goes even further with his snare drums, which have top and bottom rims but nothing in between, ie, no shells whatsoever. The interesting thing is that these drums are also loud. Perhaps more surprisingly, they're not noticeably lacking in tone.

Most of today's drums have either triple flanged (top) or die-cast (middle) metal rims. The rim on the snare drum (bottom) is a vintage double flanged 'stick chopper' rim, of a type that was common until the late 1930s.

RIMS AND HOOPS

The interaction of the rim with the head and shell is another factor in the sound of your snare drums, particularly when it comes to playing rim shots and cross sticks. Up until the 1960s, rims were very often made from brass, but steel took over and has been the norm ever since. Steel is stronger and better able to withstand modern levels of playing. However, many drummers believe that brass rims produce a warmer and more musical sound. This is another reason why vintage snare drums are often thought to be superior in timbre.

Most rims are pressed and triple flanged. They are available in two standard gauges, 1.6mm and 2.3mm, the latter being reserved largely for more expensive drums and labelled Power Hoops or some such. Die cast rims are usually made from aluminium or zinc, and are heavier and more stable, being less likely to deform. They produce great rim shots and cross stick sounds. But because they are more rigid, some drummers feel they box in the sound a little.

Wooden hoop rims are the third alternative, although they are much less common. The Canadian company Ayotte has long made superb drums with wooden hoops, and in recent years wooden hoops have been offered on snare drums by Yamaha, Spaun and Premier among others. Wooden hoops make the sound of the drum a little softer and warmer, and again make for very pleasant rim shots and cross sticks.

Most 14″ diameter toms have eight tuning lugs per head while 14″ snare drums usually have

eight or ten. In the past there have even been snare drums with 12 or more lugs per head. What's going on here? Well, the idea is that snare drums are sensitive: the more lugs, the greater the tuning accuracy/flexibility. But there is also an argument that says the symmetry of eight lugs is preferable to ten. And what's more, using eight lugs means less hardware to stifle what is already a fairly small-shelled drum.

The matter is further complicated by the type of rim: are they die-cast or triple-flanged? The classic role models are Gretsch snare drums, which had eight lugs and die-cast rims, or the hugely popular Ludwig 400s, which had ten lugs and flanged rims.

Die-cast rims are extremely rigid and heavy, so an eight lug die-cast rim is very accurate. However, this very rigidity can lead to detuning because the shock of constant heavy rim shots is evenly transmitted, right round the rim. Flanged rims are less rigid, which makes tuning slightly more flexible. With the Ludwig's ten lug steel rim you're more likely to suffer from detuning of just the lugs closest to where you strike rim shots. Anyone who's ever owned one will have experienced this. If you play heavy, it's a good idea to use Lug Locks, particularly in the areas where you strike rim shots.

SNARE STRAINERS

The snares are held against the bottom snare head by the action of the 'snare strainer'. The strainer is operated by a thumb screw that pulls the snare up and stretches it flat as you turn it to tighten it.

Attached to the strainer is a 'throw-off' lever that is an integral part of the mechanism. When you push the lever into its 'off' position, it releases the tension on the snares and they drop away below the drum. On the opposite side of the drum, the snare wires are usually attached to a simple 'butt end' plate, although sometimes this also has a thumb screw strainer so that tension can be adjusted at both ends. This secondary strainer will not have a release lever, though.

A good throw-off should be sturdy, smooth, silent and positive, while the strainer should be easy to adjust – a large knurled thumb screw helps here. The snares themselves, which are attached by special snare cord or plastic tape, should be even and neatly soldered so they lie flat and don't prick the thin snare head. The commonest and most foolproof throw-off design has a side lever that simply takes the tension off the snares and lets them drop loosely beneath the drum. A less common version involves a die cast lever that pulls out and away from the drum.

One irritating problem with many throw-offs is that they don't throw the snares off far enough. When you put the lever into the 'off' position, the snares drop a little way but are still close enough to the bottom head to rattle against it, especially if you play hard or there's any serious vibration going on onstage. Designs which pull away from the shell, like those made by Gretsch or Noble and Cooley, work well because they drop right down, sometimes all the way through 180 degrees.

One reason why the independently made Nickell Drumworks Piston strainer is so popular with

Snare strainers/throw-offs. FAR LEFT: Nickel Drumworks' Piston Drive is a very popular, independently made strainer, which is fitted to drums by DW, Premier, Spaun and – here – a Fibes fibreglass snare drum. SECOND LEFT: some drums have strainers and thumb screws on the butt side of the snare as is the case with this Yamaha Manu Katche black-nickel-over-brass signature model. CENTRE AND RIGHT: the Ludwig Supraphonic 400 is the model of simplicity, with its modest side action lever and basic butt plate. Note also the use of cord/string to attach the snare wires. FAR RIGHT: Pearl snare drum with pull away throw-off and also a roller bar to accommodate extended length snare wires.

many drum companies is that it has a seriously good throw distance, despite using a side lever action. Another solution to snare clearance is the so-called parallel action strainer. With these the snare is carried in a frame below the drum, and the whole frame is dropped while the snare itself remains under tension. The problem with parallel actions is that they require precise adjustment and once disturbed can be difficult to set up again. They are not so popular as they once were, especially in the current climate, where it is unfashionable to burden your drums with bulky hardware.

Occasionally a drum will have two sets of snares. For example, Dave Weckl's Yamaha signature snare drums are fitted with dual, independent snare strainers. One has stainless steel snares and the other has hi-carbon snares. Dave claims, "The combination of tight tension on the hi-carbon snares with loose tension on the stainless steel snares provides both the precision necessary for sharp and clean strokes with an open airy sound."

> **"Snare wires are another area where people could experiment more. I quite often try plastic wires. I get sent strange things like very thin aircraft wire – which stretches from the front of the plane to the rudder. You have to be able to thread it but it sounds so bright and sharp."**
>
> *GEOFF DUGMORE (DIDO, ROD STEWART, ROBERT PALMER, TINA TURNER, ETC.)*

SNARE WIRES

Snare wires are commonly made from coiled steel wire, sometimes chrome plated and sometimes hardened with carbon or tungsten.

At other times snares are made from copper or bell brass. Snares are available in different lengths to fit different diameter drums, and with varying numbers of strands: 12, 16, 20, 24 or more. Good quality snares make quite a difference to your snare drum sound. Poor ones can rattle easily and choke the drum or give an indistinct sound. There have been times when the drum companies themselves have been guilty of fitting poor quality snares to otherwise very nice drums. Short-sighted or what?

The situation is better today, but if you're dissatisfied there are some specialist companies such as Puresound and Grover who make reliably high quality snares. Puresound's snares are made from hardened steel coils, soldered to copper end plates. It makes several different types, including the Equalizer snares, which have a gap running down the middle. The object of this is to cut down on sympathetic vibrations. Puresound also makes snares specifically for vintage snare drums, such as Slingerland Radio Kings and Rogers Dynasonics.

Grover Percussion concentrates on cable rather than coil snares. These are made from stainless steel cables and covered with nylon, nickel silver or phosphor bronze. They have brass end plates. Cable snares are much less liable to suffer from buzzing than coil snares, and for this reason are popular with classical percussionists who really don't need their snares buzzing through some delicate symphonic passage. But there are also many commercial and session drummers who appreciate the clean, dry sound made by a cable snare.

Snares come in various lengths and with varying numbers of individual wires made from steel or brass, etc. They are attached to the strainer by cord or plastic tape. The Ludwig Supersensitive snare (second left) has wires which can be tensioned individually.

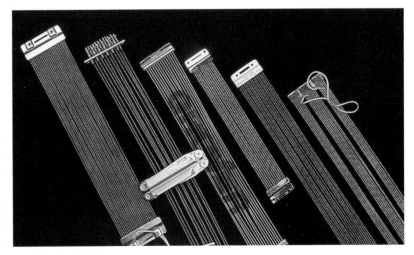

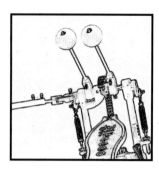

HARDWARE & ACCESSORIES

STANDS

Most major drum companies make three quality levels of stands and pedals. Spread across these levels there may be five models each of cymbal, snare and hi-hat stand: an enormous choice. The cheapest level will be the lightest and will have the fewest features. The most important distinguishing feature will usually be the single-braced tripod legs. This means that the fold-out tripod legs are made from single strips of chrome-plated steel as opposed to double strips.

All other ranges will have double braced legs. When it comes to cymbal stands each range will have a base section incorporating the legs, and two extra detachable telescopic extensions, so that you can attain the height you need. There will also be a boom arm extension in all but the most basic 'straight' model. It's usual now to be able to slot the boom into the upper tube to convert to a straight stand if necessary. This also helps with storage and transport.

The differences between the ranges will be in size and stability. On the top range kit, the base section may have wider diameter tubing and a tripod with a greater base area. The boom arm will reach further and will have a massive detachable counterweight. This is obviously intended for the drummer who has a mega kit, with heavy cymbals to support over the top of a dozen tom toms. For all other users, the second tier of stands will probably be sufficient. And for many drummers the basic entry level – even with single braced stands – will do nicely.

Obviously the drum companies will try to sell you top line hardware with a top line kit, if only because it costs more. This is fine if you've got roadies to haul them around for you. The stands will probably last longer and you (and your drum-tech) will be less likely to suffer the embarrassment of the cymbals toppling in front of a crowd of 50,000 adoring fans. But most players, especially those doing their own trucking, are better off with the middle ranges. These are strong enough for most purposes and far less of a nightmare when you have to unload at 4am in the pouring rain.

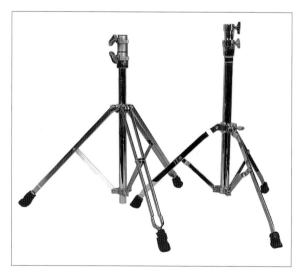

Tripod, fold out stand bases are said to be single or double braced. Stability is aided by large rubber feet.

Even the most basic ranges these days are terrific value and quite sturdy enough unless you're a pretty hard hitter. For the unbelievers out there, I suggest you check out old photos/videos of Buddy Rich and John Bonham. These dudes managed with measly single braced hardware and ride cymbals balanced on ancient bass drum mount bracket arms, precariously hinged straight onto the bass drum shell. Bonham even played a monstrous 24″ ride cymbal, which he gave some serious attitude. According to his roadie, Mick Hinton, it never toppled.

They did have to replace the wing nut on a regular basis, though. Overtightening of wing nuts, leading to stripped threads, was a major pain with the design of stands for decades. And this brings me to a really important part of modern hardware, introduced by Tama in the 1970s: the humble nylon bushing joint insert.

These are now routinely slotted into the telescopic housings at every section of every stand. Rarely has such an innocuous and simple solution done so much for the sanity of the drummer. No longer do you have to over-tighten any stand section, and no longer do stands sink slowly before your eyes like the setting sun.

As a final luxury, some stands have done away with wing nuts completely. Instead they have 'snap lock' one touch, quick release levers at each joint.

MOUNTING CYMBALS

The top of every cymbal stand has a spindle for mounting the cymbal itself. The spindle is invariably fitted with a tilting mechanism so that you can angle the cymbal as necessary. Tilters have traditionally had toothed gears, but gradually – starting with the top lines – they are being replaced by smooth, continuous tilter joints in brake-drum style. The way you mount the cymbal is very important. You want the cymbal to be free to resonate and you don't want there to be any metal-to-metal contact. The latter can cause unpleasant grating and rattling noises and worse, could possibly lead to the cymbal bell cracking. The cymbal must therefore be isolated from the central mounting spindle and from the base of the tilter on which it is sitting. This base often has a metal, plastic or fibre washer and then a couple of 'cymbal felts'. The cymbal is positioned between the felts. These can wear away quite quickly with normal use. Always make sure you have a spare supply, which you can buy in top-up packs.

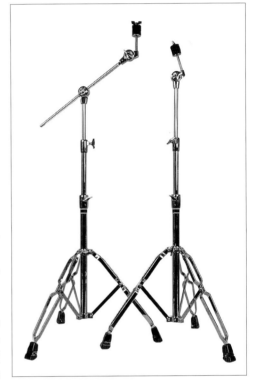

In order to reach over larger drum kits some cymbal stands have extendable boom arms. Others are simply referred to as straight stands. Both types have tilters for setting the desired cymbal angle.

Watch out also for the bottom washer, particularly if it is metal, because this is often in direct contact with the vertical mounting spindle, which can create very annoying rattles and squeaks when the cymbal is struck. If you have this design of stand, you might try inserting a narrow rubber or similar insulating washer beneath the metal washer to prevent metal-to-metal contact.

Next, the cymbal must be isolated from the vertical spindle on which it is mounted. The old solution for this was a short length of plastic tubing. These bits of tubing are easily mislaid: they spring off when you take the cymbal down at the end of the gig. So make sure you have spares handy. If you get caught short, improvise by wrapping strips of gaffer tape around the spindle until you have time to get to the drum store – or hardware store – to replace the tubing. Once more, modern designs aim to eliminate this problem. For example, there are cymbal sleeves that have the bottom washer moulded to the central tube, all in one.

The cymbal is actually secured in place by a wing nut, which should not be over tightened. Obviously you don't want it to come loose and fly off, but at the

same time you don't want to dampen the cymbal excessively. Tightening the cymbal down too much can lead to damaging, even cracking, the cymbal, because when struck it is unable to swing on the stand. Particularly with thin cymbals, you may wish to reduce the damping effect to a minimum by not having any felt in contact with the bell. Use a rubber central mount with no felts. Or you may be able to get a tilter that has felt below but none on top. Or simply make sure you use the smallest size top felt you can find. On the opposite tack – if a cymbal rings too much – rather than putting strips of tape on the underside, which I've seen many times, try using larger felt washers. They may just damp the response sufficiently. Or buy some small Zildjian stick-on foam dampers.

Cymbal tilters (left) are fitted with various protective sleeves, washers and felts to prevent the dreaded metal-to-metal contact.

SNARE DRUM STANDS

Snare drum stands require both the right height adjustment and a tilter mechanism to get the right angle. Because they only have the one height-adjustable section it is just possible to get lumbered with a stand that either won't extend high enough or won't go low enough for your needs. So, when choosing a stand, do be sure to try it out while you're sitting at your preferred height.

Tilter mechanisms generally have either a geared ratchet with interlocking teet, or a smooth,

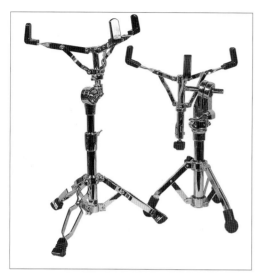

Snare drums are cradled in tri-armed baskets (above) which screw up from beneath gripping the drum's lower rim. Some stands are offset from the tripod base - which you may or may not find a help in positioning.

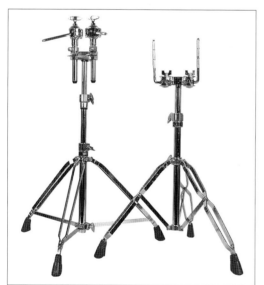

Two solutions to tom tom mounting. Yamaha's (left) hexagonal rod penetrates the tom shell or isolation mount horizontally, while Gibraltar's (right) vertical arms slot into isolation mounts or brackets bolted to the outside of each tom shell.

continuously adjustable tilter, which Tama calls a 'disc brake'. Occasionally you'll come across a ball-clamp infinite angle tilter: Sonor does one for example. Geared tilters are most common, and would seem to be more secure, but it's amazing how you can never get them to the exact angle you want. Or maybe that's just me?

Perhaps a bigger consideration is whether the triple-armed basket is mounted directly over the vertical stand base or is offset to one side. I always have trouble with the offset designs, but others swear by them. It really does depend on how you set up your drums. If you have a complicated set-up with double pedals crowding around your snare drum base, an offset design might be your saviour. Another solution to this sort of problem is the adjustable tripod base. Some stands allow you to change the angle of the tripod legs so that you literally push one leg out of the way. Sonor has this facility on all its top line stands, which enables you to move one leg up to 60 degrees to either side, where it is locked in position.

The triple-armed support basket itself is adjusted by screwing up a large wing bolt from beneath until the arms engage the bottom rim of the snare drum. The arms are optimised in reach to enclose a standard 14″ diameter drum. So, if you intend to mount a 12″ drum be sure the basket will grip it securely. Pearl sells adaptors especially to modify your stand for 12″ drums. Be sure not to over tighten the basket or the plastic/rubber grippers will stifle the life out of your drum. It's interesting that while tom toms are regularly fitted with resonance isolation mounts, we seem to worry less about our snare drums. Let the drum breathe, and you'll get quite a lot extra out of it. If the problem worries you, you might investigate Tama's Air Ride snare drum stand, which consists of a tripod base fitted with Tama's Star-Cast isolation mount bracket fixed to an 'Omniball' multi-directional arm. In other words, this is a snare drum stand fitted with a RIMS-style resonance mount to match up with your toms.

TOM MOUNTS

Until the advent of resonance isolation mounting systems, the small toms were mounted on the bass drum by a bass drum tom mount or tom holder. During the 1970s, these tom mounts were perfected by the new Japanese companies and tom slippage – a regular occurrence – was pretty well banished forever. The new mounts also provided increased reach and flexibility of positioning. My personal favourite is Yamaha's hexagonal rod and resin ball tom mount. I've had one for 20 years and it's as good as the day I first got it (and no, I'm not an official Yamaha endorsee). It's ridiculously fast and easy to set up and remains in place with a little elasticity to absorb the shock.

With this type of design the hexagonal rod passes through a receiving block mounted on each tom and actually penetrates the shell. A different solution is the type of holder used by Tama. This also has a resin ball clamp, but fixed to the ball is a vertical (rather than horizontal) knurled rod that hooks through the receiving block on the tom and in this case does not penetrate the tom. It does however sacrifice some lateral adjustment. A third type is used by Pearl. Pearl famously has two vertical mounting posts, one for each of the two mounted toms. Each of these has an elbow joint connecting the horizontal portion of the arm, which again penetrates the shell of the tom tom. The elbow joint has long had a geared ratchet but now, as we've seen on other stands, this is gradually being replaced by a non-geared 'Uni-Lock' brake-drum style tilter. The tilter allows the tom angle to be adjusted up and down, but Pearl has added yet more flexibility to the holder, by enabling the joint to swivel in a horizontal plane as well. Effectively this now gives the Pearl holder even more all-around positional flexibility than that achieved by ball clamp style holders.

MEMORY LOCKS

Talk of tom slippage brings us to another indispensible bit of modern mounting hardware – the memory lock. This started life as a small clamp that could be fixed immediately above each joint of a stand or mount. In the early days of rock, drummers and their roadies had used 'Jubilee'-style car hose clips to prevent their flimsy stands from collapsing. The memory lock put an end to this.

The way to use memory locks is to leave them loose when you first set up your kit and only when you have everything positioned exactly as you like it then go around and tighten all the memory locks in position using a drum key. Once set like this memory locks can be left on breakdown so that whenever you set up in future your positions are 'memorised'. Note, however, that memory locks come in several different sizes for use on the various diameters of stand tubing, etc. Each company has its own design of lock, which is usually a solid, die-cast ring with a small ridge that slots into a receiver 'notch' on all the mounting plates, stand joints, tom leg brackets, etc. It's a beautiful thing. It simply cannot move and has solved one particularly exasperating problem, which was the way knurled rods – found on tom mounts and floor tom legs, etc – would always slip in their receiver blocks.

There are some very clever designs of memory lock. I particularly like the Premier Series locks, which are sliced out of the bottom quarter of each oval mounting block and thus effectively hidden as part of the overall design. Neat.

Memory locks come in many shapes and sizes and are one of the most useful hardware inventions ever.

RESONANCE ISOLATION MOUNTING

For decades small tom toms were fixed on to the bass drum by a mounting bracket or tom holder. The toms had receiving blocks for the tom arms, which often protruded inside the shells. Then, in 1982, Gary Gauger came up with his idea of Resonance Isolation Mounting System, or RIMS. The RIMS concept recognised that if you hold a drum by its rim and strike it there is greater resonance than if you mount it on a traditional tom tom bracket and screw it down tight. With the obsessive pursuit of unimpeded shell resonance that characterized the 1990s, every major drum manufacturer was compelled to devise its own version of the RIMS concept. So we got Tama's Star Cast, Yamaha's Enhanced Suspension System (YESS), Mapex's Isolated Tom System (ITS) and so on.

The RIMS mount is a curved metal bracket, which attaches to the tension bolts of the drum beneath the top rim, is isolated by rubber grommets and has no other contact. RIMS is a universal design that can be fitted to any make of drum. This is not true of various manufacturers' in-house designs, so be careful if you try to mix and match. The original RIMS were made from steel, and one major drawback was that they added a massive amount to the weight of your toms. And then you needed over-sized cases to transport them. However, RIMS are now made using an aluminium design, which is just a third of the weight of the old steel brackets – a significant relief.

Another advantage of isolation mounting is that toms no longer have holes drilled into them to accept penetrating tom holder arms. However, there is a serious downside to this, which is that the lateral reach of the tom brackets is considerably reduced. I recently reviewed a drum kit that

The original RIMS (Resonance Isolation Mounts) adapts to most makes of drum, whereas some proprietary makes, like DW's (centre-right) fit only their own drums. Other examples shown are Sonor's Total Acoustic Resonance System (centre-left) and Pearl's Optimount (right) which grip both top and bottom.

had a typically modern 18″ deep bass drum with a central tom mount and a 10″ diameter tom fitted with a RIMS-style bracket. Try as I might, I couldn't get the 10″ tom anywhere near me. The answer to this is either to make sure the mount is fixed close to you on the bass drum shell, or to mount the toms from floor/cymbal stands and do away with the bass drum mount altogether. In fact it's increasingly common to have no mounting hardware on the bass drum, so that the shell is not penetrated and benefits from the same freedom accorded the toms. This way you also lose much of the sympathetic resonance between kick and mounted toms that was a feature of traditional mounts. Every time you thumped the bass drum, the toms would hum appreciatively. Studio engineers are happier, but some drummers rather miss it.

Isolation mounting is now incorporated wherever possible. For example, floor toms are routinely mounted from floor stands (see below) with isolation brackets. Where the floor toms still have legs the manufacturers do their best to incorporate an isolating feature, such as Pearl's Air Suspension legs or Mapex's Shock Mounted spring-loaded legs.

There is no doubt that isolating the drums leads to less damping of the natural sustain. It's easy enough to demonstrate. Just hang a tom from its rim between your finger and thumb and strike it. Then mount it tight on its old fashioned bracket: you should observe a lessening in sustain. My personal view though – and I stress this is a personal and rather unpopular view – is so what? How much sustain do you want anyway? Most decent drums sustain quite long enough, however they are mounted. I've lost count of the number of drummers I've seen with isolation mounts who routinely apply top head damping, particularly when they go in the studio or are miked up live. One dollop of Moongel is enough to cancel out a fortune spent on isolation mounts.

So I'm still not convinced they're worth all the extra bulk and hazardous mounting for the average player. I do, however, bow to the greater experience of the top drummers I know, many of whom swear by isolation mounting. So I'll leave it at that. What's for sure is that the classic tom bracket is an endangered species, as every company gradually turns over to isolation mounting on all its ranges, right down to the humblest.

> "I think isolation mounting does make a difference. If you have as much sustain as possible you can cut it down, but if the drum doesn't really resonate you can't go anywhere."
> DAVE MATTACKS

FLOOR STANDS

Floor stands are another invention of the 1980s, and today characterise what is often termed the 'fusion' kit. They were first introduced to mount floor toms with rather shallower depths than the classic standard 14x14 or 16x16. With a floor stand there is no need for the large toms to have legs. At first this meant they were fitted with the same mounting brackets as the small, bass drum

mounted toms. But today it's more usual to have no brackets and simply to use RIMS style isolation mounts. One floor stand can usually mount two toms plus a cymbal arm. However it's essential to get the tripod legs in exactly the right position for balance, as floor tom stands are notoriously easy to topple. Many kits today use floor stands to mount the smaller toms as well as the larger ones. This means you no longer need a traditional bass drum tom bracket.

RACK SYSTEMS

In 1983, Pearl, in conjunction with the late great studio drummer Jeff Porcaro, produced the first rack system, reminiscent of the console racks of the 1930s. Pearl's rack uses squared sections of lightweight aluminium. Subsequent rack systems have often used tubular sections of steel. Racks eliminate the sort of clutter that a half-dozen tripod stand bases create. Using clamps, brackets and stands you can mount any combination of cymbals, percussion, electronic pads, small snare drums and so on. Racks can also make microphone placement a lot easier, because again you don't need stand bases. Positions are easily marked and clamps can be left attached for transport, which speeds set-up and breakdown. However, racks are cumbersome in themselves and once positioned are difficult to move. If you're top of the bill they might be fine, but if you're supporting then they are not the easiest of contraptions to get off stage quickly. In fact they're a nightmare, and can easily get ripped apart in desperation by the headliner's road crew … I've seen it happen.

MULTI CLAMPS

The multi-clamp, another gem introduced by Tama and now used by everyone, is a most useful gizmo that can jazz up the set of any drummer. Multi-clamps come in many different sizes and designs and can be used to mount virtually anything you can think of: cowbells, closed hi-hats, woodblocks, boom arms for splash cymbals, small snare drums or electronic pads, stuffed bears, you name it.

THRONES OR STOOLS

In days all but forgotten, when bass drums were just 'feathered' with a light four to the bar pulse, the drummer was content to sit on the nearest chair or barstool. Nowadays, when ferocious stamping, jarring of knees, and spraining of back are just for starters, a first class throne or stool is paramount.

As we've seen, quality drum sets are not sold with stools. The drum companies reckon that you don't want to change your stool every time you upgrade your kit. So the motto is: buy the very best you can afford at the earliest opportunity. It will see you through a good many years and save a fortune on physiotherapy.

The major drum companies all market their own stools. Alternatively you can try the specialist hardware companies, like Gibraltar or Dixon. And there are good deals to be had from the same companies who import the generic Taiwanese/Chinese drum kits. You'll notice close similarities between stools offered by all these companies, so shop around for the best deal.

BASES AND HEIGHT ADJUSTMENT

Ideally, you want a stool that stands up to heavy use, but, like your other hardware, it must be relatively lightweight and fold away easily. Most stools use the same tripod bases found in snare drum stands – with single or, preferably, double braced legs. For even greater stability some top-end stools have four braced legs rather than three. Gibraltar also has a tripod base that you can tilt to compensate for uneven stage surfaces. Since drummers come in all shapes and sizes, it's important you check that your prospective stool will adjust to the height you want. You'd be surprised how often it doesn't. Some stools simply won't go low enough.

The simplest height adjustment is by 'pegging'. Height is determined by lining up holes drilled through the adjustable stem and base post, slotting a bolt though the two and securing with a wing nut. The problem with this type (apart from your own weight jamming the bolt so you have to take a hammer to get it out) is that since there's an inch or more between each hole you never get the exact height you want. This type of design is increasingly rare.

For continuous height adjustment the principle used on snare drum stands is adopted. The central stem slots into the base post and once adjusted to the right height is secured by a wing nut and beefy memory lock for strength. For the most secure design, though, the central post takes the form of a continuously spiraling threaded shaft. The seat is spun around until it's exactly the height you want and is then locked in position by a large clamping ring-nut of metal or nylon.

> **"I've been incredibly lucky, bearing in mind I still practise a lot. I bought a Roc'n'Soc throne (with a back rest) because I had a little bit of back trouble."**
>
> *STEVE WHITE (THE STYLE COUNCIL, PAUL WELLER)*

One further design uses the hydraulic principle found in office chairs. These have a side lever which you lift to glide to whatever height you like on a gas-filled pneumatic cushion. The problem is that if the mechanism breaks it can't be repaired: as a result these stools are not often seen. I think that's a pity. I've had one for 15 years and it's never let me down (pun intended) – and this despite the fact I don't seem to be getting any lighter with the advancing years.

Finally, DW has resurrected the old idea of the canister throne, which was a feature of the swing era. DW's 'Barrel Throne' is a height adjustable canister which doubles as a storage case for stands, etc, and has the circular seat mounted on the top.

SEATS

In order to mount the seat on the base stand, the underside of the seat has a large clamp, often made from die-cast aluminium. The more expensive the stool, the more massive this clamp, which is necessary as cheaper ones soon become wobbly. Obviously, the comfort of the seat is paramount. Round seats are the commonest, and the cheapest have the least depth and padding. Motorbike-style saddle seats are usual on more expensive thrones. The more you pay, the bigger, deeper and more sumptuously cushioned they get. Black vinyl is the usual covering material; more expensive seats are cloth covered, while others are real leather. Yamaha also offers a fabric mesh seat with increased ventilation designed to reduce the build up of moisture and heat. Hmm, nice.

For ultimate support, a backrest is the answer. Gibraltar's Roc-N-Soc range includes oversized seats and back rests. Roc-N-Soc also offers a retrofit System whereby you can add a backrest to your own stool. Whichever type you buy, make sure that the backrest will detach for transporting. Large seats always pose a carriage problem. Do you give them their own drum case? Or can you squeeze the seat into one of your tom cases? If you don't protect the seat the vinyl/fabric gets torn easily. The old solution of wrapping in a blanket and stuffing inside the bass drum is less used now that front heads are often kept on bass drums. Since most drummers sit on the front edge of the seat, assuming you've got a dainty derrière, a smaller seat might be more convenient.

Generally speaking, the more you pay for a stool, the sturdier and more comfortable it is. But even the cheapest stool is infinitely better than a household chair, and is fine for starters. If you're going to take drumming at all seriously, though, a quality stool is an essential purchase.

BASS DRUM PEDALS

Bass drum pedals, like drum sticks, are highly personal items of equipment that can make or break a drummer's performance. It's worth investing in a good pedal as soon as possible, since this will greatly ease your bass drum playing, which is not the easiest part of drumming at the best of

Bass drum pedals are highly personal items of equipment. The more you pay the more refinements you will get and the more adjustments you will be able to make.

times. The quality and action of bass drum pedals varies quite dramatically and it may take you quite some time and experimentation to find the pedal or pedal type that suits your playing the best. The reason for this is that pedals are mechanical devices that can have quite a wide range of adjustment and variations in set-up. They can be light and fast, or heavy and stiff.

ATTACHMENT

The bass pedal has a jaw clamp at the front of the base frame that attaches to the bottom hoop of the bass drum. The hoop should have a protective sleeve at this point to prevent it from being eaten away. The jaws attach via a thumb screw. Old designs have the screw located centrally underneath the front of the foot board, and this can be quite awkward to get to. More modern and expensive designs have the clamp screw jutting out to the side so that it is much easier to reach.

Basic design pedals have a steel wire frame, connected to the heel plate, which hooks into the main frame when the pedal is set up and ready to go. Unhooking from the frame allows the pedal to be folded up for carriage. But top line pedals now all have a full size base plate. This is fixed, and makes carriage more awkward, but means the pedal is more stable. The underside of the base plate is usually fitted with Velcro, which means the pedal won't slide. The pedal will also often have a pair of sharp, screw-down spurs in the outer edges of the main frame.

ADJUSTMENT

Perhaps the most crucial adjustment is the spring tension, which alters the weight and return of the stroke in combination with the variable length of the beater shaft. Adjusting the length of the beater shaft is easy but crucial. The longer the shaft, the greater the throw and power of the beater, and vice versa. Some pedals have small counterweights that can be positioned up and down the shaft to help balance the feel you like with the length of shaft and the type of beater head.

Many drummers like to have the spring tension fairly loose, although there have been some notable examples of famous drummers who like their spring tension really hard. The thinking here is that you have to work to make each stroke, and the spring then pulls the beater back off the head quickly and cleanly. However, I think it's safe to say most drummers prefer the spring medium to slack. In this position, when the foot is taken off the pedal board the beater will be facing back towards your shin. Once you place your foot back on the board, the weight of your foot at rest should take the beater up close to vertical. This creates a nice balance, helping to make sure that tension doesn't build up in the foot, shin or thigh.

> "I've gone through footboards – split one right down the middle. I learned a little trick, though: tape the underneath of the beater rod so that if the beater flies off, the rod doesn't go through the head on the next beat. I've seen that happen!"
>
> MATT SORUM (GUNS'N'ROSES, THE CULT)

Most pedals have a single spring to one side of the pedal. Tension is adjusted by slackening off the locking nut. This allows you to stretch the spring, taking up the slack on the large lower nut to increase tension, or to slacken it off. The action of playing the pedal causes the spring to stretch and then to return. The upper end of the spring is attached to a small rocker plate, which is directly connected to the drive and thus affects the stroke of the beater, pulling it forward or back a little way. The rocker may have several settings or be continuously adjustable. (Occasionally pedals work by compressing the spring rather than stretching it. The famous old Ludwig Speedking pedals worked this way, with twin compression springs enclosed in the side posts.)

Most pedals today are chain driven, although there is still usually the option of a strap drive. Chains drives tend to be more direct and inflexible, while strap drives have a little bit of play. Chains are single or double, while straps are made from extremely tough materials such as nylon, Kevlar or plastic embedded with steel cable. They are unlikely to snap so readily as they did in the bad old days of leather and fabric.

The chain drive fashion was fostered more than 20 years ago by Tama, which successfully re-introduced the original Camco chain-drive pedal (leading eventually to the ultra-flexible Iron Cobra), and Drum Workshop (which took up where George Way/Camco left off) with its 5000 series Turbo pedals.

The action of the pedal is determined by the chain/strap and the type of cam drive fitted. The original chain drive is similar to that in a bicycle, where the chain engages with the sprockets on a circular cam. This creates the very direct action found in, for example, DW's Turbo and Tama's Rolling Glide. For a more aggressive action the cam is offset – or 'eccentric' – and what this does is to increase the speed as the beater reaches the end of its stroke. This is the basis of DW's Accelerator and Tama's Power Glide. With strap drives, the cam is extended forward a little and seems to throw the beater at the batter head rather like a sling. Tama calls this the Flexi-Drive.

Some sophisticated pedals have further options. For example, the angle of your foot board can be changed without affecting your spring tension or stroke adjustment. And likewise, the angle of your beater can be changed without affecting the angle of your footboard. With Pearl's Powershifter design you can actually adjust the length of the footboard itself, by pulling it backwards or forwards, which will again influence the feel and action. Since bass pedals have to withstand so much punishment, the quality of the build is all-important, particularly in the moving parts. The use of quality bearings in crucial parts of the drive and in the heel hinge plate will ensure long life and a smooth, quiet and tight action.

BEATERS

The beater rod itself has to withstand intense sustained pressure, and if it snaps you can say goodbye to your bass drum's batter head: the jagged shaft will hit the drum so hard it will almost certainly tear through. The beater rod must therefore be made from hardened steel. Some are even made from titanium. The most popular type of beater has a hard felt head, which gives the warmest and fattest sound with the most pleasant, cushioned feel. However, you can get beaters made from wood, plastic or Plexiglas, amongst other materials, and many beaters are multi-faceted so that you can easily change between say felt and plastic for different tunes. Because bass drums are sometimes angled slightly upwards, and stages sometimes slope, it's possible the beater head won't make flat contact with the drumhead. Tama addressed this problem with its Iron Cobra beater, which has an independently adjustable head angle.

DOUBLE PEDALS

DW followed up its acclaimed 5000 Turbo pedal with the 5002 double pedal, back in the 1983, and that really started the double pedal fashion. Double pedals are now made by all the drum manufacturers and many specialist hardware companies too. The double pedal consists of a slave pedal, which is the same as the main pedal except it doesn't have a beater or spring. Instead it's linked to the main pedal, which has two beaters and springs. Needless to say, the quality of the linkage must be superb. There can be no play or looseness since the action is remote, and it's vital that the slave pedal feels the same as the main pedal.

DW's hugely popular 5002 double bass drum pedal, here fitted with Aquarian white 'golf ball' beaters.

An unusual way round this problem is to have a symmetrical arrangement, with the bass drum in between a double pedal unit. This idea was first tried by Sleishman in Australia many years ago and has recently been resurrected by Sonor with its Giant Step double pedal. It remains to be seen how popular it proves.

Because of the mechanical nature of the pedal there have been many attempts to revolutionise the action, to make it easier and more flexible. The Duallist, made in Scotland, is a double pedal in a single unit. It has two beaters that work in opposition and allow you to get two beats for one stroke. It's an ingenious system, but takes quite a bit of practice to master. So does the heel raising plate of the Vruk pedal, which, once you've conquered the rocking action, allows you to play at a terrific speed. Or at least it does if you're prepared to put in the hours of practice. If you do, though, you will be amply rewarded.

HI HATS

The hi-hat pedal is not quite so crucial as the bass drum pedal action-wise, but still there have been many improvements and variations over the years. Hi-hats have gradually become more sophisticated in the wake of the ever improving standard of bass drum pedals. The hi-hat works via a direct pull central chain or strap, and has a spring to alter the tension, in the same way as the bass pedal. The spring, though, is not usually external but is adjusted by turning a large knurled plastic/nylon ring just above the base frame.

The top hi-hat cymbal is held in place by the 'clutch'. As with your other cymbals, it's a good idea not to overtighten the clutch, as it will choke the sound of the top cymbal. Try clamping the top cymbals more loosely for a change and you may be surprized to hear the result. The two cymbals will also slosh together in a looser fashion – something the old swing drummers had down to a fine art, but which got lost with tight rock and funk hi-hat styles. The bottom cymbal sits in a moulded plastic cup, which is usually topped with a cymbal felt. Alternatively, the cup may be made from ribbed rubber or small rubber balls, which don't get squashed so easily and make the cymbal livelier again. The cup has a small screw underneath which tilts the bottom cymbal slightly. The angle of the bottom cymbal is crucial to getting a good 'chick' sound. It needs to be angled slightly, because if the two cymbals clash perfectly flat on you get an air lock and a flat response. Experiment with the angle to get the volume level and sound you like.

There is always a problem with the position of the hi-hat tripod when playing double bass pedals. There are a few solutions, which include stands with just two back legs (in place of the usual tripod) or tripods which swivel out of the way, allowing the slave bass pedal to snuggle in tight up

> "There was a time when I wasn't able to do double bass – not so fluently. I was sitting higher and I was getting backache. The legs have to be level with the seat – and your shin must come down at 45 degrees when your heel's on the pedal. The foot's straight on – no angle across the pedal, and no heel/toe. The movement comes from a balance: my whole leg doesn't move, just the ball of my foot."
>
> **DAVE LOMBARDO (SLAYER, GRIP INC.)**

The top hi hat cymbal is suspended between two felts in a clutch (right). The clutch is in two parts which screw together to grip the cymbal.

against the hi-hat foot pedal. If you use two bass drums, there's a third option, which is simply to fold up the hi-hat tripod base flat and then clamp the hi-hat stand tube to the hoop of the bass drum using a specially adapted multi-clamp.

Playing hi-hat at the same time as double bass drums also led to the development of the 'drop clutch', which keeps the hi-hat closed without the need for foot pressure. Some drummers have two hi-hats – the normal one and a 'remote hat' operated by cable and usually pedaled from the left, although it can be positioned anywhere convenient. If you don't want the inconvenience of cables the remote hat can simply be mounted on a special short stand and kept permanently closed. In that case it is called an 'X hat'.

I must finally mention the Mapex Janus pedal, which, so far as I know, is the only attempted marriage between a hi-hat and a double bass drum pedal.

The idea is that instead of having two left foot pedals snuggling against one another, you have a single pedal that can operate either the hi-hat or the left kick pedal. You switch between hi-hat and bass drum with a lateral sweep of your left foot. The pedal rests inside a guiding 'tray' with raised sides, which your foot pushes against to move back and forth between hi-hat and bass drum functions. Mapex describe this ingenious contraption as a 'shoe wing bicycle-type derailleur'. Well of course!

Hi hat stands (left) are simpler than bass drum pedals and usually have just a simple spring tension adjustment for the desired feel and foot pressure.

CYMBALS

A quick look at a recent cymbal catalogue by a major manufacturer reveals dozens of types and categories, with literally hundreds of sizes and weights. In fact there are more types of cymbal than there are types of drum. One reason for this is that the sound of a cymbal is fixed in manufacture, while the sound of a drum can be changed repeatedly by tuning and by the use of different types of head. So every time a cymbal manufacturer, or one of its endorsees, thinks of a new sound it would like to hear, off it goes to manufacture a new cymbal.

The layperson would be amazed and bewildered to discover this unbelievable variety, yet there seems to be no end to the variations cymbal companies can produce. Although cymbal making is an ancient craft, recent advances in metallurgy and manufacturing techniques have enabled them to design sounds with startling accuracy and finesse. As with drums, cymbals can be loosely categorised into the three levels: budget, middle and top lines. What makes a cymbal cost more and hopefully sound better is, first of all, down to the particular metal alloy that is used in its manufacture and thereafter to the complexity and expertise of the manufacturing process. Top cymbals go through many processes before they become the golden beauties that amaze you with their shimmering response.

The cymbals thrown in with the cheapest starter kits are not meant to be anything special. They do not resonate or sustain to any great extent and have poor tone and response. They can be unpleasantly thin and shrill, or more often plain dull. They easily dent and buckle. They serve a purpose, but once you've tried a 'proper' cymbal you will never go back. The point about a cymbal is that, like a drum, it needs to be of non-specific pitch with plenty of well-balanced overtones so that it will blend in with whatever music you're playing. But, unlike a drum, a cymbal cannot be tuned – what you buy is what you're stuck with.

Starter cymbals with very little resonance have a definite note that will soon drive you nuts. To make a cymbal that blends in with any musical key requires a whole different level of craftsmanship. To a large extent you get what you pay for. Medium priced cymbals are pretty good and expensive ones are even better. To put it another way, a medium priced drum kit can sound almost as good as a top line kit if you fit it with quality heads and tune it well. But a medium priced cymbal will always sound the way it does. You can't improve it.

CHOOSING AND BUYING CYMBALS

Choosing cymbals is quite daunting for the beginner. Luckily the task has been made much simpler now that all the major manufacturers offer boxed sets in many of their ranges. This is particularly useful in the budget and middle fields as this is where a drummer is likely to need a complete matched set to accompany a new drum kit. It's also a way to get three or four cymbals at a better price than buying them individually. And if you buy them with a kit the dealer will undoubtedly have a good offer for you.

> "The first live drummer I saw was Bob Turner with the Northern Dance Orchestra. It was such a thrilling thing because he had this fantastic old-time all-around cymbal. He'd get right underneath the brass, shimmering away with this big majestic cymbal sound and I was filled with awe – I thought every woman in the world must fall in love with a drummer who can make a sound like that."
>
> GARY HUSBAND (ALAN HOLDSWORTH, LEVEL 42)

Starter boxes may have just a pair of 13″ or 14″ hi-hats with a 16″ or 18″ dual purpose crash/ride cymbal. If you can afford it, a better choice would be the next pack with hi-hats and a separate 16″ crash and 20″ ride. Very often these packs will include a 'free' padded fabric cymbal bag. After this, you might want to add an effects pack including a splash and a Chinese cymbal. This would complete your basic standard cymbal set-up.

These packs are undoubtedly a great help both to new drummers and storeowners. As one dealer put it to me: "They come in colourful boxes and they basically sell themselves." Inevitably they will proliferate, and already you see boxed sets of more expensive high-end cymbals. For example, Sabian have Dave Weckl HHX Evolution Performance sets with hats, crash and ride, plus a free deluxe cymbal bag or hard-shell case. Or you may prefer their HHX Effects pack with 10″ splash and 18″ Chinese together with free video and towel.

> "My favourite cymbal? Wow, that's a hard one... probably my 20″ Zildjian 'K' Custom Ride. I've had it ten years and it sounds great."
>
> STEVE BARNEY (JEFF BECK, ANNIE LENNOX, THEA GILMORE)

Boxed sets are a way of getting matched cymbals and add-ons at favourable prices. However, over the years most drummers build up a collection of cymbals of different types and quality, often by saving up and making one-off purchases. While it's normal to trade in your old drums, if only for the sake of space, cymbals take up little room. Obviously, you sell off the ones you don't like in the hope of finding something better or to raise cash. It's a never-ending search, looking for that 'perfect' ride cymbal and hotter-than-hot hi-hat.

In the end, only you know what you're looking for and what turns you on. You're going to have to rely on your own ears and taste and not the marketing hype of the big companies. And one thing to consider in passing is that there is nothing wrong with collecting cymbals from different manufacturers and playing them next to one another.

Don't forget that your heroes plays one brand of cymbal because they have an endorsement deal which stipulates they will be seen in public playing those cymbals and no others. (Which is not to say they don't have cymbals by other manufacturers at home or for use in the studio if needs be.)

Let's get down to brass tacks – or rather, bronze discs. When you walk in the store looking for the elusive cymbal that is going to change your life, where do you begin? For in-store display, manufacturers supply 'trees' capable of mounting a couple of dozen cymbals on individual branches that can be pulled in and out for inspection. This is always a tempting spectacle. It doesn't mean the storeowner is going to be pleased if you start pulling them all out, getting your sticky paw prints all over the shiny surfaces and smashing them at random. Always ask for assistance, and show you have an idea of what you're looking for: you're not just there for a little Saturday morning sport.

Although the store will no doubt have a few pairs of sticks ready for cymbal testing, you will create a much better impression if you take along your own. The sound a cymbal makes is affected considerably by the size and type of stick. You should also consider taking along one or two of your own cymbals – cymbals whose sound you know well – for

> **"I have a 22″ 'K' Zildjian that I found in Istanbul that is the 'end all' jazz ride cymbal. This cymbal has the dark tones and not too much build up, a perfect combination."**
>
> *STEVE SMITH (VITAL INFORMATION)*

comparison. Ideally, you should ask to take the cymbal you're interested in, plus perhaps one or two alternative choices, into a demo room and mount them on a kit. Mounting your prospective buy next to your familiar cymbal(s) will give you a better sense of whether it's really what you're missing.

Make sure the cymbal is sloping towards you a little so that it's not crashed edge-on – a glancing shoulder slice is much kinder to cymbals, and to sticks. Play it the way you would normally use it, not to impress onlookers. Take it slowly and listen carefully to each individual beat. Make a single stroke and listen to the overtones as the sound dies away – is there a pleasant blend or a nasty aftertaste?

If it's a ride play the whole surface from edge to middle. Play a ride pattern, crash the edge and carry on riding. Can the cymbal take it and retain its clarity or does it 'wash' out? Check how much stick definition there is and how much 'spread' – is the balance between the two how you want it? If it's a crash cymbal strike it once and check for sustain, clarity and purity of tone. How is the pitch in relation to the ride and your other cymbals?

Next, go and stand at some distance away while the sales assistant plays the cymbals for you so you can hear how the new cymbal projects and blends. Try putting your fingers in your ears, cutting out the overtones and ring, for a better picture of how the cymbal will sound with the band playing, or when it's recorded.

SOUND CHARACTERISTICS

Like the acoustic drum, the cymbal needs to blend in with whatever is being played. The sound of a good cymbal is very complex. Although it will tend to sound predominantly high or low in pitch, there will be numerous overtones that mean that it can blend into the music, whatever the key. As mentioned above, good cymbals are made from bronze, the same alloy as is used in the manufacture of bells. Bells, of course, have a definite pitch – you can play tunes on a set of bells. The main reason for this is that bells are very much thicker, producing more of a ding than a ping when tapped. Cymbals are very thin by comparison and therefore much more washy.

So the first thing to realise is that if you have heavy cymbals they will have a more defined sound and a tendency towards producing a recognisable pitch. (The relatively thicker central bell dome of any cymbal has a much more defined pitch.) And this is a clue to why cymbals sound the way they do. If you slice a cymbal exactly down the middle you will see that it starts out thick at the bell and gets progressively thinner as it approaches the edges.

By striking the cymbal in different places on its surface you elicit tones from high (where the cymbal is thicker) to low (where the cymbal is thinner). But since the whole cymbal is a single resonating body – an idiophone – whichever part of the cymbal you strike, the whole of the cymbal is gradually set in motion, contributing to the overall sound. So you get a blend of many tones and timbres, and it is the way these blend that determines whether you like what you hear or not.

You can tell a lot about the sort of sound a cymbal will make by studying its shape and size. Everything in cymbals is a trade-off between one feature and several others. For example, the greater the diameter of the cymbal, the deeper its pitch. But the heavier (thicker) the cymbal, the higher its pitch.

So a large diameter, heavy cymbal may well be stronger, and probably louder than a medium weight (because of the extra mass), but it will be brighter to the point where you may find it too piercing. Larger diameter cymbals respond more slowly than smaller cymbals because of the time it takes to get the larger mass vibrating. But then they will go on vibrating for longer, like a large truck taking a lot of stopping. So the heavier the cymbal, the longer the sustain.

To take another example, a lighter, thinner cymbal will respond more quickly than a thicker cymbal of the same diameter and be shorter on sustain. This sometimes causes confusion because often a drummer might want a fast crash – so chooses a thinner cymbal than usual – and is then surprised to find that although it indeed responds more quickly, it is surprisingly low in pitch. This is sometimes described as a 'darker' sound. Cymbals that are described as dark are often thinner.

The opposite is also true: the same diameter cymbal, if thicker than normal, will have a higher pitch and will be described as 'brighter'. It will not respond quite so quickly (the greater mass taking longer to energise) but will be loud and penetrating – ideal for heavy rock. There was a period in the mid-1980s, when stadium rock was massive and drummers were playing at volume levels previously unheard of, when really heavy cymbals were all the rage. I have to say though that I sometimes questioned how loud they were.

> "I used to break cymbals all the time – I didn't hit 'em right. I think I'm more wrist oriented now. There's a right and wrong way to hit and it works for me."
>
> CHAD SMITH (RED HOT CHILI PEPPERS)

It seemed to me on occasion that they were so heavy they became 'muscle-bound' (excuse the technical term). I'm convinced that some medium weight cymbals were as loud or louder. My perception is that a cymbal can be so heavy that even the biggest stick has trouble extracting the full sound. Bear this in mind: if you go for the heaviest cymbals you will also need to play with extra thick sticks.

The medium weight cymbal is the best all-rounder. Although there's no obvious consensus between manufacturers about the diameter to weight ratio, they've all discovered a medium that works as the best all-rounder for them. So this is always a good starting point in your search. Check the medium crash and then think: would I like this darker and faster (check the lighter weight) or louder and brighter (check the heavier weight)?

There's another factor that may sway you and that is durability. Extremely fast and thin crashes are very attractive, but they are correspondingly easy to break.

It's as well to remember that your heroes, whose names are silk-screened on those lovely paper-thin signature crashes, are getting a steady supply of these babies for free. They probably use them mostly in the studio, and are miked up live so they don't have to wallop them with the force of a baseball champion to cut through the din of the guitarists' amp set at 11. Choose what's appropriate for your band and your style, not your heroes'.

Applying the same principles to ride cymbals, a 'dark' ride is usually thinner. The heavier the ride, the fewer overtones, the more pronounced the apparent pitch: while the thinner ride has a complex sound of many overtones. The sound is often said to have more spread, to be warmer and darker.

This is the reason certain cymbals of the 'K' Zildjian type are often preferred by the small-group jazz player. They are not so loud as a heavy cymbal like a 'Z' Zildjian but blend better. The warm spread is more suited to binding the music when the ride rhythm is the main rhythmic element in the sound. The extreme thinness of some (by no means all) of these cymbals however means they spread so much it is easy for them to wash out. The player has to play 'off' the cymbal with a light touch and a stick that is not too heavy.

As you can see, there are often three or more factors vying with one another. I know this can be confusing, so let me summarise what we have so far. The sound is a trade-off between various parameters. For example:

- **The heavier the cymbal the higher the pitch;**
- **But the greater the diameter the lower the pitch.**
- **A small crash will generally have a higher pitch;**
- **But a thin crash will have a lower pitch than a thick one of the same diameter.**
- **A big heavy ride cymbal will suit a loud rock player;**
- **A big thin cymbal will produce a darker sound more suitable for jazz.**

CYMBAL MAKERS

Since cymbal making really is an ancient and mysterious craft, it's as well to know a bit of background. The cymbals market is largely divided between the North Americans, the Europeans and the Chinese. The Japanese, who have dominated the drum market over the past couple of decades, have – so far at least – left the cymbal market alone. Don't ask me why.

The modern story of cymbals starts in America in 1929, where the Zildjian family brought its ancient cymbal-making craft. The Zildjians (Zildjian is Turkish for cymbal smith) had been making cymbals in Constantinople (Istanbul) on the eastern border of Europe since 1623. The secret Zildjian process was passed down the generations and the burden came to rest on Avedis Zildjian III, who was already settled in America and successfully making candy. His Uncle Aram asked Avedis to return to Istanbul to carry on the tradition. Instead, Avedis stayed put and wisely initiated cymbal making in the USA, in the Boston area of Massachusetts. Avedis Zildjian cymbals soon began their evolution into the modern 'A' Zildjians we know today, developing alongside jazz and, later, rock drumming.

The Sabian company, which launched its first cymbals in January 1982, started as a breakaway from Zildjian when, in typical Dynasty fashion, the two brothers and heirs to the Zildjian fortune (Armand and Robert) went their separate ways. The younger brother, Robert, took over Zildjian's erstwhile plant in Meductic, Canada. Sabian has done extraordinarily well to establish itself as Zildjian's principal competitor over the past 20 years.

It's interesting to note that both Sabian and Zildjian are built on the same ancient cymbal making philosophy, although they have obviously diverged over the intervening years. These two companies today dominate the market. They have massive ranges intended to suit every musical style and pocket. European competition has come largely from Paiste and Meinl, based in Switzerland and Germany. Paiste is comparable in quality and scope to Zildjian and Sabian. Meanwhile, Meinl is steadily gaining ground and stretching the boundaries of cymbal technology. Smaller, though significant, competition hails from Italy (Ufip) and Turkey. Turkish cymbals are made in the Istanbul area by a number of craftsmen who have links with the old Kerope 'K' Zildjian company (the forerunner of the modern American Zildjian company). These companies include Istanbul Agop, Istanbul Mehmet, Bosphorus, Masterworks and Turkish.

There is also the emerging Chinese market. Like the Turks, the Chinese have been making cymbals for centuries. The traditional Chinese style of cymbal differs from the Turkish, but cymbals made by Chinese companies in the Turkish/American style have recently started to appear in the West at very competitive prices.

MATERIALS

For years there was a divide between the American philosophy (meaning traditional Turkish-style, every cymbal hand made and therefore unique) and that practised in Europe (meaning hi-tech Swiss/German, every cymbal consistent and reliable). To understand this requires a short primer in cymbal science.

Nearly all good cymbals are made from bronze alloy. However, some budget lines are made from other alloys, including nickel-silver (88 per cent copper, 12 per cent nickel NS12) and brass (63 per cent copper, 37 per cent zinc MS63). Traditionally these alloys are not considered as good as bronze and the process of making them into cymbals is necessarily simpler. The resulting cymbals, though, can still produce a reasonable sound that can serve you for a while. Paiste has always been good at this low-end market. It produces brass 302-Plus and nickel-silver 402-Plus lines. Sabian currently has a line of brass cymbals called Solar, which is very popular with budget kits as well. Some of these starter cymbals are also occasionally supplied to other companies who stamp them with their own names.

If you're wondering what your unbranded starter cymbals are made from, you can probably guess from their appearance. Nickel-silver cymbals are indeed a silvery colour while brass cymbals have the gaudy yellow of brass door and window furniture. Bronze cymbals are rather darker with a more browny-gold appearance.

Once you are through this trial period you enter the proper world of bronze cymbals. Bronze is an alloy of copper with a smaller proportion of tin. Top quality cymbals are traditionally 80 per cent copper to 20 per cent tin, an alloy that is known as $CuSn20$, or simply 'B20'. B20 also includes tiny traces of silver that acts as a catalyst helping the copper and tin to bond. B20 is the material used for top line cymbals by Zildjian, Sabian, Ufip, Istanbul, Bosphorus and Turkish, etc. It's also employed by the Chinese to make their best cymbals. And, by the way, this is the bronze alloy that has been used for centuries in casting bells.

In 1963, Paiste started to make professional cymbals from a second bronze alloy, $CuSn8$ or 'B8', which is 92 per cent copper with 8 per cent tin. And from 1989 Paiste has used its own Paiste Sound Alloy for its top cymbals, the composition of which remains secret, although it's presumably not a million miles from B20 bronze.

MANUFACTURING PROCESSES

The manufacturing process for quality cymbals involves many stages. These include casting the alloy, multiple reheating and rolling, shaping the cup or bell, tempering, shaping the profile, hammering, lathing, truing (for perfect symmetry), smoothing the edges, maturing or ageing, polishing and applying a finish. All these processes affect the final sound. Whereas they were once all done by hand, today the cymbal smith generally uses machines to make the work lighter, quicker and more consistent. The exception to this are the cymbals still made in the traditional way in Istanbul and also, presumably, those made in China. But even in the modern Western factories there is still a fair amount of hands-on skilled craftsmanship. The exception is the Meinl factory, where the aim is to develop as much computer-controlled automation as is possible.

CAST VERSUS ROLLED

Paiste first launched its 'Giant Beat' B8 cymbals in the mid-1960s. These gave way to the 2002 series in 1971, which offered rock drummers a clean, cutting, warm and powerful sound designed to compete with increasingly loud amps. The success of relative newcomers Paiste sparked a

rivalry with Zildjian in which, inevitably, Zildjian played on its long and distinguished heritage – the mystique of their centuries old secret process – while Paiste retaliated with claims of consistency and the benefits of modern metallurgical science.

This was the start of the great 'cast versus rolled' debate. B8 cymbals are made from discs stamped out of large sheets of bronze, while B20 cymbals are usually worked up from individual blobs of molten alloy. The B8 is bought in from specialist suppliers, while the B20 is usually cast by the cymbal company itself. B20 cymbals are therefore referred to as 'cast' Turkish-American style cymbals as opposed to B8 European-style cymbals, which are often (with a derisory sniff) called 'rolled', 'pressed' or 'sheet' cymbals. In fact all cymbals are cast, since any alloy inevitably has to be cast in the first place. The distinction is a bit like cake making – using a cake cutter to slice circles out of an already rolled sheet, or taking a separate blob ('casting') and rolling it into an individual 'pancake' or 'muffin'. Actually, the closest to truly individually cast cymbals are those made by Ufip in Italy. Ufip use a unique method called roto-casting in which the alloy is poured into a rotating mould and the cymbal emerges almost fully pre-formed.

Both B20 and B8 cymbals are therefore cast – and they are also both rolled. However, the individually cast B20 cymbals are cross-rolled, while the B8 sheet is rolled in one direction: 'uni-rolled', as Sabian puts it. The B20 casting may be re-heated and cross-rolled as many as 15 times, each time in a different direction. The idea is to cause the crystals in the metal to become interwoven and thus make the cymbal stronger. This is necessary since the B20, with its high tin content, would otherwise be too fragile.

Whatever the process of manufacture, B20 is considered superior in tone by the traditionalists. B8 has a more compact sound while B20 has a wider possible frequency spectrum. So now we reach the crux: the B8 cymbal was pioneered by Paiste to produce a clean and consistent sound which worked very well in the newly emerging loud rock context, but perhaps was lacked a little complexity or 'mystery' for the more acoustic jazz player.

But over the years the backbiting has subsided. Paiste and Zildjian – and more importantly drummers – have all benefited hugely from the range of sounds that have been coaxed from both alloys. Zildjian and Sabian have now developed very successful B8 lines, which they market as their budget series. These include Zildjian's ZBT and ZXT and Sabian's B8, Pro and Pro Sonics. Paiste and latterly Meinl have continued to do wonders with B8 cymbals, and produce many lines that work well for budget or professional purposes. Paiste have their professional 2002s, mid-range Alphas and budget 802-Plus and 502-Plus. Meinl have many lines including Raker, Lightning, Amun, Classic and MCS.

All of the lines by the Turkish manufacturers in Istanbul, plus the pro lines from Zildjian and Sabian are B20, as are the very fine cymbals from the Italian cymbal co-operative Ufip. Cymbals from China are also B20. Meinl has its single B20 Byzance line. And from Paiste we have the Paiste Line, Signature and Sound Formula lines which use the Paiste secret formula. At the time of writing Sabian has just released its first budget B20 line, XS20. This means it can compete on price with the incredibly cheap and surprisingly good Chinese B20 cymbals currently marketed under the name Stagg. It remains to be seen if B20 budget cymbals become widespread.

To summarise: although B20 and Paiste alloy cymbals are most often chosen by the professionals, it's quite possible to prefer some B8 cymbals to some B20 cymbals: it just depends on the sound and effect you're after. B8 cymbals such as Paiste's 2002 series have long been favoured by certain top drummers, including Led Zeppelin's John Bonham. They have a pure and less complicated sound that suits many rock drummers. Also, Meinl in particular has developed cymbals made from combinations of B8, brass and a new alloy called FX9 geared towards a new generation of drummers whose aim is to mimic programmed drum tracks (see 'Specialist' below). FX9 is 69 per cent copper, 15 per cent manganese, 15 per cent tin and 1 per cent aluminium. It has a similar appearance to nickel-silver and is described as flexible, soft and durable.

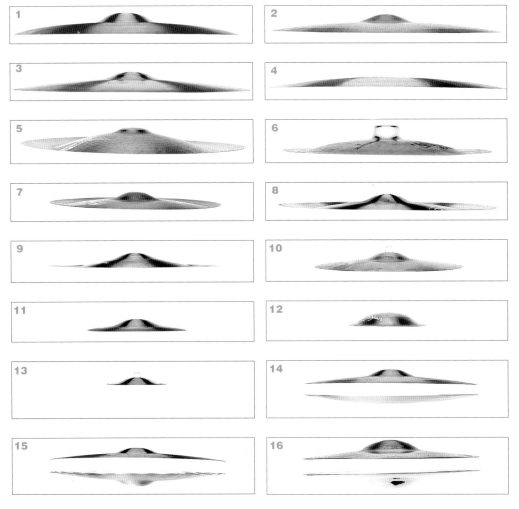

Variations in cymbal profile
1. 'A' Zildjian Crash/Ride 20" with large domed bell.
2. Sabian 20" ride with standard rounded bell.
3. Paiste 20" '2002' ride with smaller flat topped bell and six rivets.
4. Paiste Signature 20" Flat Ride with no bell.

CHINAS
5. 'K' Zildjian 19" China Boy with domed profile and small flattened bell.
6. Paiste Rude Boy 18" with high squared bell.
7. Sabian 'AA' 14" Chinese with rounded bell.
8. 'A' Zildjian 18" Swish with low profile, not domed.
9. 'K' Zildjian Mini Chinese 14" with high domed profile.

SPECIALIST
10. Sabian 'AA' 12" Splash with brilliant finish.
11. Zildjian 8" Splash.
12. 'A' Zildjian Zil-Bel
13. Paiste Cup Chime.

HI HATS
14. 'A' Zildjian 14" Quick Beats, with almost flat bottom cymbal.
15. Paiste 14" '2002' Sound Edge with wavy-edged bottom cymbal.
16. Zildjian 'A' Custom 14" with large domed bells top and bottom for extra projection.

SHAPING THE PROFILE

Bisecting a cymbal through its centre reveals its profile. In the middle is the bell or cup and arching away gradually from the bell to the edge there is the 'bow'. The bell has the thickest cross section and the cymbal gradually thins out as its profile tapers towards the edge. Every cymbal starts out as a flat disc of alloy, and the arch of the profile and the exaggerated arch of the bell are pressed and hammered into the disc during manufacture. A crash cymbal usually tapers quite noticeably so that its edges are quite thin. This makes for a faster response and shorter sustain. A ride cymbal tapers less, so that its rim is still quite thick. This gives a cleaner, more defined response, and elongates the decay.

The bell varies in size and in profile, as do cymbals generally. Some cymbals – usually rides – have no bell at all and are therefore described as 'flat'. These have a very defined stick sound, are rather low in volume and sound great for acoustic jazz and sometimes for recording. From this it can be inferred that the addition of a bell opens up the sound and increases volume and sustain. The larger the bell, the more overtones and body. For that reason, crash cymbals quite often have larger bells. Also, some very heavy rock rides have large bells to compensate for the overall thickness of the metal and to maximise the volume.

LATHING

Lathing is the process whereby the concentric 'tone grooves' are cut into the cymbal's surface. The cymbal is clamped to a machine that rotates it as the operator presses various types of cutter against the cymbal's surface. The resulting grooves can be broad or narrow, shallow or deep, regular, irregular and above, below or both. The lathing makes the cymbal shine and again drastically alters its sound, opening it up. By shaving away metal the process effectively makes the cymbal thinner and lowers its pitch. Unlathed cymbals will therefore have higher metallic tones with fewer harmonics. Lathing the top surface reduces the high-end stick ping while lathing the underside lowers the pitch without taking away the ping so much.

HAMMERING

Hammering is a crucial part of cymbal manufacturing, which is why today we have so many different hammering types and patterns. They are not there just for aesthetics. Hammering compresses the metal in particular spots, making it more robust and at the same time altering the pitch, the overtones and sustain. The more irregular the hammering pattern, the shorter the sustain and the darker the sound. Hammering causes indentations and compressions that affect the way vibrations travel through the body of the cymbal. The vibrations are disrupted making the sound more complex. Traditionally cymbals were hammered by hand, which inevitably made each cymbal slightly different. This still takes place today, although the description 'hand hammered' includes the use of mechanical hammers under direct human control, and even computer-controlled hammering. It no longer necessarily means a grizzled old Turk with a sharpened lump hammer banging a disc over a glorified shoe-last. Nowadays, with so many closely defined cymbal models in the catalogue, it's necessary for each manufacturer to achieve strict hammering consistency.

FINISH

Most cymbals have a satiny sheen that is the result of the lathing during manufacture. But other cymbals are polished to a bright reflective finish. Zildjian and Sabian call this their Brilliant finish as opposed to their Traditional or Natural finish and many of their lines are offered in both versions. Ufip also offers its Experience cymbals in a brilliant finish, which it says is a natural hand buffing process not involving any chemical polishes. It's natural when you see such bright looking cymbals

Cymbals: lathing, hammering and finish.
1. Sabian 'AA' 12" 'AA' Splash with Brilliant finish.
2. Zildjian 17" Re-Mix Ride with electro-style concentric square hammering.
3. Paiste Signature 20" Flat Ride with wavy broad lathing and hammering.
4. Paiste 18" Crash with regular deep and broad lathing.
5. 'K' Zildjian 20" Custom Dry.
6. Paiste 18" Rude China Type with Rude finish.

to think they must also sound brighter. However, this is not necessarily the case. Buffing a cymbal smooths the lathed grooves a little and removes a small amount of the metal: it's a bit like sandpapering wood to get a smooth and shiny appearance. The buffing process also hardens the cymbal a little and the overall effect, if anything, is to make the sound a little mellower and warmer.

MELLOWING AND AGEING

Newly made cymbals are stored for a period in the cymbal factories to allow them to settle down before finally being distributed.

Although the cymbal may appear to be an inert object, it is in fact a highly tempered and in some senses fragile instrument. Because of the violent nature of the heating and cooling and hammering processes the molecular structure of a new cymbal is disturbed. Eventually this molecular structure settles down and the molecules, which start off disjointed, gradually clump together.

What this means is that over time, especially with consistent playing, the sound of the cymbal does change slightly. Like fine wine – and indeed like drums made from fine timber – the cymbal should mellow and mature nicely with age. Mind you, they also get fractionally duller because they get dirty: and there are many drummers who say you should never clean them.

Perhaps this is a good time to recount a cautionary story that a friend – a respected jazz drummer – once told me. He and I have long discussed and compared our hearing problems and one day he phoned me and said, "You know what? I've just had my ears syringed and I had to completely change my cymbal set-up. I was playing these incredibly bright cymbals and never realised". I'm afraid it's a fact that all of us – and particularly drummers – lose the high end of our hearing as we get older. Lord knows what we are inflicting on the public and the rest of our band mates.

> "I do think cymbals wear in. And I've had this conversation with people high up in the cymbal business who say they don't: but I think they do, especially rides and hi hats. My tech cleans them for live – he hates dirty cymbals. But the older cymbals I use for the studio don't get cleaned."
>
> *STEVE WHITE (THE STYLE COUNCIL, PAUL WELLER)*

CYMBAL TYPES

Time was when a cymbal was defined simply by its size and weight, eg, Heavy 20″. Today, there are hundreds of types, each with a specific designation, such as Custom Dry Light Ride, Paper Thin Crash or Fusion Hats. Whereas the old jazz drummer would get a dozen different tones out of his single ride, the modern drummer wants a dozen cymbals. It's great for the cymbal business.

THE BASIC TYPES

The cymbal explosion really began during the 1980s. Before that there was a much more limited selection. And if we go back to the time when rock first came along, there was only a handful of cymbals beyond the basic categories of ride, crash and hi-hat. In fact these categories are still the cornerstones of cymbal selection.

The ride cymbal is usually a relatively heavy/thick cymbal with a diameter between 18″ and 24″ (20″ being the standard). It's called a ride cymbal because it's used to play continuous 'ride' patterns, whether the straight eighth-notes of rock, the 'ding-dinga-ding' of jazz, or perhaps the more syncopated patterns of Latin. The crash cymbal is usually thinner and often smaller – commonly between 13″ and 20″ – and is used to make explosive accents in the music. While the

> "Another concession to arena gigs is large cymbals, 18″ to 22″ crashes, because in a big live stadium you need that decay, especially out in the house over the PA. In the studio I still use smaller ones."
>
> *MATT SORUM (GUNS'N'ROSES, THE CULT)*

ride cymbal is played predominantly with the tip of the stick for a clear, concise sound, the crash is struck with a glancing blow using the shoulder of the stick.

Finally, the hi-hats are paired cymbals, generally between 12″ and 15″ in diameter, with 14″ being the standard. The bottom hi-hat cymbal is normally slightly heavier than the top, and this gives the brightness and solidity to the 'chick' sound when the two cymbals are clashed together by depressing the hi-hat pedal foot plate. The bottom cymbal is often designed to release the air trapped between the two cymbals when they're closed together. That's why you'll see bottom hats with wavy edges (Paiste's Sound Edge) or holes drilled through them (Zildjian's Quick Beat).

These four cymbals – ride, crash and paired hi-hats – are considered the essentials of virtually every drummer's set up, whatever the style of music. When it comes to extending cymbal choice, many drummers add a second crash, smaller or larger than the first. This gives you a crash cymbal on both sides of the kit, which makes life easier and more fun. After that you may decide to add a splash cymbal – which is basically a mini crash cymbal (from around 6″ to 12″). Splash cymbals obviously make a shorter, faster and softer accent. Next you might want to try a China, or Chinese type cymbal.

CHINA TYPE CYMBALS

A brief detour here. Most modern cymbals are descended from the Turkish type, but cymbals have also been made in China for centuries. Chinese or China type cymbals have a squared rather than a rounded bell profile, and the rim of the cymbal is upturned slightly. The effect of this is to give the China cymbal a more gong-like, clouded timbre, often referred to as 'trashy' or simply oriental. There has been a place for the Chinese type of cymbal in jazz and rock over the last 100 years, but the China cymbal has usually been relegated to a single, exotic addition to the standard Turkish-American style set up. Today, all the main companies make their own versions of the Chinese style of cymbal. Indeed they have developed many variations in just the same way they have extended the Turkish-style cymbal. Genuine Chinese-made cymbals are available from the Wuhan company. And recently Chinese-made B20 cymbals in the traditional Turkish style have appeared, with names such as Stagg. Although it's evident the quality control is not up to the standard of the Western companies, some of these are surprisingly good and are offered at truly bargain prices.

> "I love Chinas especially for doing shuffley things."
>
> *KENNEY JONES (THE FACES, THE WHO)*

RIVETED CYMBALS

Riveted or sizzle cymbals have always been popular in jazz, though less common elsewhere. They were familiar in the 1960s rock boom, when drummers used the washing sound of their riveted rides to sustain a wall of noise, which was useful in the days before amplification of drums. Apparently, many years ago, drummers would actually bang nails through their cymbals, though you would think this must surely have led to cracking.

The idea of riveting may have arisen from the desire to reflect the earlier practice of 'riding' on the snare drum with pressed rolls. That was how the original jazz beat was expressed. The effect of just a single rivet on the sound of the cymbal is quite amazing. Since a good cymbal reverberates and resonates for ages, the rivet will go on dancing for minutes, creating a tingly, jangly sound – a sizzle, in fact – like bacon in a frying pan. The sound is softer and more pleasant than the trashy, abrasive effect of riding on a China cymbal. The gentlest touch from a brush also calls forth a prolonged sizzling, which is great for ballads.

Many drummers start off with a cymbal with a half dozen rivets and gradually remove two or three. Nickel alloy rivets are sold in packs of 25 by Sabian. It's rare to need more than three or four rivets: after that the weight of the rivets can have a damping effect. Riveting works best also on a cymbal which has a good long resonant response in the first place, as the effect of rivets on a short sounding cymbal will again most likely be to dampen it rather than extend its sizzle. Rivets may also be placed in the perimeter of China-type cymbals, producing what are known as 'pang' or 'swish' cymbals. Zildjian's delightfully named Swish Knocker is a perennial favourite. There you get the best of both worlds. When a large number of rivets are placed around the edge, the weight of the rivets can actually have a damping effect. This gives an amazing crash response.

Zildjian will supply any of its cymbals with rivets to order. It suggests the best use is in a dry ride cymbal and offers two popular layouts: six evenly placed rivets around the perimeter, or three rivets placed in a cluster one inch apart and one-and-a-half inches from the edge. This latter configuration produces a more subtle effect.

There is, of course, nothing to stop you drilling a cymbal yourself if you're adept at this sort of thing and have a good sharp 3/16″ metal bit and preferably a press drill for stability. But be warned, you could easily crack the cymbal, or you might simply overheat the area around the drill hole, affecting the tempering and weakening the cymbal.

The holes should be quite close to the edge, maybe an inch or two in at most. The cymbal is most sensitive and reverberates the most near the edge and so the rivets will have the most effect here. I've heard it suggested that the holes should not be symmetrically positioned. That is, it's not a good idea to have all the holes at the same distance from the cymbal's edge as this could cause latitudinal weakening. Similarly, it's probably not a good idea to drill on directly opposite sides of the cymbal where a 'longitudinal' line joining the two holes would pass through the centre hole. Better to be safe than sorry.

> **"The sizzle cymbal on the ballads album [*Warm And Tender* by the Charlie Watts Quintet] album is a 22″ Avedis. Actually it might be a 'K' – it's quite thick. It's got an awful lot of rivets. I've had it years. I never use sizzles with the Stones – they tend to wash over (sustain) too much."**
>
> *CHARLIE WATTS (THE ROLLING STONES)*

You don't know exactly what effect the holes and rivets will have on the sound, so it's best to do one hole at a time until you get the amount of sizzle you're looking for. If you don't like the result, you can always take out the rivets and hope your original cymbal sound won't have been noticeably affected. But if you want to sell the cymbal, it won't be easy.

An easier way of getting a sizzle sound is to hang a light chain around the cymbal. I've seen everything from large paper clips through delicate neck chains to heavier lavatory chains. You can also buy the commercially made Pro-Mark chain Sizzler. This has the great advantage of being adjustable and removable.

TECHNO CYMBALS

Today a huge amount of popular music is programmed with highly processed and compressed rhythm tracks. This is particularly the case in the fields of dance, hip-hop and drum'n'bass, etc. Drummers have responded to the programmed beats and taken up the challenge of playing in a manner that reflects them. You might have thought the easiest way to achieve this would be to use electronic kits with the appropriate sounds, and yet, perversely, many drummers are using the acoustic kit. The ingenuity involved is staggering and I'd like to take this opportunity to name-check a few pioneers. They include Jo Jo Mayer, Andy Gangadeen, Marque Gilmore, Zach Danziger, ?uestlove (Ahmir-Khalib Thompson), Thomas Lang, Marco Minneman, Johnny Rabb, Zoro, and Tony Verderosa. We've seen 'jungle' drum kits and mini-snare drums with treble pitches, and the cymbal companies have risen to the challenge by developing lines that also clearly do not follow the golden rules of past generations. These cymbals include Sabian's V-FX, designed in collaboration with Tony Verderosa, Zildjian's Re-Mix and Paiste's Noise Works.

But of all the companies, Meinl seems to be leading the trend. This new area suits Meinl's technology-led image. The Generation X cymbals use the new FX9 alloy, which is described as flexible, soft and durable. They include a set designed by Thomas Lang with crashes that "resemble artificially engineered cymbal samples" and are said to be "db compressed" – which roughly means they're quieter. Meinl also has Johnny Rabb's 'Rabb Pack' Generation X cymbals designed for house, techno and drum'n'bass styles again made from FX9. Rabb's Safari 16″ crash, 18″ ride and 12″ hi-hats are topped by 8″ wavy-edged brass cymbals which can be 'tuned' by the amount of pressure applied to the mounting wing nut. As Rabb says, the effect is to "transform an acoustic drumset into an acoustic drum machine". Finally, Meinl has 8″ and 10″ Drumbals, made from brass with wavy edges again. Placing a Drumbal on the snare batter head enables the drummer to simulate electronic snare sounds, white noise or handclaps.

The interesting point about all these techno cymbals is that they cannot be evaluated in the same way as traditional Turkish style cymbals. They are more akin to the 'trashy' sounds of Chinese or Latin cymbals, or to earlier ideas like Terry Bozzio's Spoxe hi-hats, which were made from the die-cast frames of Roto-toms. This is a fascinating and fast developing area of modern drumming and we can look forward to many more strange inventions in the near future.

LIVING WITH CYMBALS
SWEET SPOT AND ORIENTATION

You may hear drummers talking about a cymbal's 'sweet spot'. This simply means that the drummer has found an area on the cymbal that seems to his ears to sound the best for playing ride patterns. It also necessarily implies the cymbal is not uniform all around. This is quite possible, particularly with cymbals that have been genuinely hand hammered with more random patterns. You'll know if the cymbal is fractionally unbalanced by the way it shifts on its stand, ie, revolves round to the same position (observe the way the manufacturer's logo always ends up in the same place). This may or may not be a problem, but if it bugs you and it's an expensive new cymbal you might want to consider taking it back for a replacement.

Alternatively, by sweet spot the drummer may simply mean that if he plays the cymbal three quarters of the way towards the bell, say, that's the best spot for cutting through. That is, the cymbal may be uniform, but a certain concentric band is the preferred playing region.

HANDLING

Cymbals always require careful handling. Just because you attack them with sticks, never forget they are thin brittle discs that can easily get damaged. Never stand them on end except on a very soft carpeted floor, and then only with extreme care. Get a cymbal bag that has cushioning in the bottom, and if it doesn't, stick an inch of tough foam or similar in the inner bottom. Some drummers use a section of old bicycle tyre. Sooner or later someone is going to drop the bag: probably you. Try to pick up cymbals by their edges, using both hands so that you don't get fingerprints all over them.

When you crash a cymbal, use a glancing, slightly off-centre blow from the shoulder of the stick. If you smash at the cymbal square-on, you create a shock wave through the cymbal (and your hand), which will eventually lead to cracking (cymbal and hand). In the meantime you will chew sticks faster than a panda in a bamboo forest. If, in fact, you notice your sticks are always chipped then you probably need to evaluate how you're striking your cymbals. Some drummers like to have their cymbals mounted horizontally rather than angled slightly towards them. Admittedly this can look very cool. And there's an argument that they sound better, since they are freer to resonate symmetrically. However, drummers who do this usually develop a glancing attack or manage to get over the cymbals. Check out the many videos of Buddy Rich to see how he played his horizontal crash cymbals from all angles.

The opposite approach is to mount your cymbals at an extreme angle, closer to vertical. This is not common, but there are some drummers who swear by it. If you play ride patterns with your thumb up – a lot of players do – this more upright angle can be quite comfortable. It's not so good for crash cymbals, though, as you have to contort your wrists to get a shoulder crash. Obviously if you mount your cymbals in this fashion the central mounting hole through the cymbal will come under a lot of pressure. You will need to be extra vigilant with the plastic mounting sleeves on your cymbal stand tilters, which will get sliced through much more quickly. The chances of metal-to-metal contact are considerably increased: and that is something you really don't want.

CRACKS

Metal-to-metal contact can lead to cracks around the bell hole, not to mention nasty grating sounds every time you strike the cymbal. Hairline cracks can appear in the perimeter or inside the bell of any cymbal that has been abused.

Cymbals are highly tempered and obviously vulnerable. Aside from being mounted badly on their stands they can be damaged simply by playing them too roughly. Or, of course, from being dropped. Hairline cracks are something you should always look out for, particularly when buying second hand. Go round the edge and the bell, with a magnifying glass if necessary. Really. If there's a crack don't waste any more time.

If you have a cymbal that breaks inside the usual one-year warranty, you must take it back to the store where you bought it. Be ready to answer some tough questions. The store may ask you to play the cymbal so it can see what you're doing wrong. It's a good idea to ask the store before you buy what the return policy is.

Different cymbal companies have different attitudes. Some will replace cymbals with virtually no questions asked, just to promote good relations. Others may only replace the cymbal if they are satisfied it's not the drummer's fault. It's your responsibility to buy appropriate cymbals and the store has a certain responsibility to advise you – or warn you if they think you're eyeing up a cymbal that is inappropriate.

The obvious problem is young guys who don't know their own strength walloping too thin crashes and splashes edge-on. Today's rock drummers play unbelievably hard and they do break cymbals. Cymbal companies are only too aware of that, but they make cymbals for every type of drummer, not just the heavy guys. This includes thin cymbals catering for much lighter players. Thin crashes nearly always sound good when you're toying with them in the drum store. But It's no good if once you're on your gig you play twice as hard and trash it first time out. It's up to you to buy heavier models if you're a heavy player.

A cracked cymbal cannot be restored, but it can be salvaged. Edge cracks can be sawn out into a gradual arc using a fine hacksaw and filed smooth. Even splits in the middle of a cymbal can be arrested by drilling a small circular hole at each end of the crack and sawing and/or filing the crack in between.

Cracks in the bell are tricky. They're hard to access, the metal's thicker and you don't want to enlarge the mounting hole. Any vigorous sawing or filing of a cymbal will raise the temperature of the metal and can upset the tempering. But then once a lump has been cut away the cymbal is obviously going to sound different anyway. The cymbal will lose some of its resonance and sustain but will still produce a fair amount of sound. The fix is only temporary, though: the cymbal will most likely eventually crack again.

Once a section of the perimeter has been cut away the cymbal will be lopsided and will always turn on the stand in a particular way. This may cause you to strike it in the damaged area, which will again lead to an early failure. So a lot more care will have to be taken with a broken cymbal. But I should point out that many drummers have found a place for a cracked cymbal in their set-ups, just because it will produce a unique sound, usually shorter and maybe crunchily trashy.

SIGNATURE CYMBALS

Ever since Avedis Zildjian III started to make cymbals, in Boston in 1929, the opinions and suggestions of great drummers have been sought in the evolution of the modern instrument. But while there have always been 'signature' drum kits, snare drums and sticks, signature cymbals have been a rarity.

Now that so much is understood about the process of working with cymbal alloys and so much is under the controlled environment of the modern factory, it is quite possible to design unusual cymbals according to the specific whims of the endorsers. Still, Zildjian has so far resisted the temptation to market artist signature models. Sabian, however, has numerous artist models aiming to fulfil particular musical dreams. They include Terry Bozzio's Radia and Cup Chimes, Will Calhoun's Alien Disc, Jack DeJohnette's Encore Flat Ride and Richie Garcia's Salsero Ride.

It seems to me that signature cymbals, like signature snare drums, are a reasonable idea. They offer unique sounds, which might otherwise never be realised. The idea, though, doesn't yet seem to be widespread. Bosphorus has a small range of Jeff Hamilton signature cymbals, called Hammer, while Ufip has Experience cymbals, which are said to be custom made prototypes suggested by Ufip artists. Meinl has an interesting variation with its 'One Of A Kind' custom service, which anyone can take advantage of, rather than just endorsers. Customers are invited to specify their ideal cymbal and Meinl's craftsmen will hand make it in B8 alloy. Thereafter, the cymbal can be copied exactly by computer, if requested, and becomes what Meinl calls a Custom Shop model. There is one area, though, where Meinl has developed artist signature lines and this is at the cutting edge of dance and programmed beats.

SOME RECOMMENDATIONS

There is no law that says you have to use a particular type of cymbal to play a particular type of music, although obviously ranges are designed with certain stylistic applications in mind. Certain types of cymbal might sound brash in jazz, whereas others may be too thin to last long in a punk metal band. Otherwise, you're at liberty to play what you want in any fashion you desire. As a starting point, I've attempted to categorise some current cymbal lines into broad areas of music.

All-round:	A Zildjian, Sabian AA, Paiste Signature and Sound Formula, Ufip Class.
Rock and heavy rock:	Zildjian Z Custom, Sabian AA Metal X, Paiste Classic Rude, 2002 and Dimensions, Meinl Raker, Istanbul Turk, Ufip Bionic, Bosphorus Gold (polished) Traditionals.
Traditional Jazz (swing, be bop, etc):	Zildjian K, K Constantinople and Zildjian & Cie, Sabian HH and Manhattan, Paiste Traditional, Meinl Byzance, Istanbul Sultan and Nostalgia, Bosphorus Masters, Ufip Vintage.
Contemporary	Zildjian K Custom, Sabian HHX, Paiste Traditional, Istanbul Traditional, Ufip Natural, Bosphorus Ferit Antique.
Studio/Fusion:	Zildjian A Custom, Sabian AAX, Paiste Signature and Sound Formula, Meinl Amun, Istanbul Vezir, Bosphorus Ferit Turk.
Dance/Techno/Cutting Edge:	Meinl Generation X, Zildjian Re-Mix, Sabian HHX Evolution, Paiste Noise Works and Innovations.
World/Exotic:	Zildjian Oriental, Azuka, Earth Plates, EFX and Zil-Bels, Sabian El Sabor and Roctagon, Meinl Candela, Paiste Exotic Percussion.

STICKS

When someone asks a drummer "Hey man, what sticks do you use?" they're usually trying to be funny. But to tell the truth, drummers probably spend less time examining sticks than they should. And as drumming gets more precise and physically exacting, choice of stick is all the more important. When your technique sucks and you hit a dead-end, it could partly, at least, be due to your sticks.

Here's a little experiment: tap your ride cymbal with your favourite stick. Now tap it with your mother's knitting needle or a chopstick. (Don't laugh; top jazz drummer Joey Baron uses chopsticks for real). Amazing change in sound, right? Obviously. But the point is that the sort of stick you use affects your sound more than you might realise. Drummers are so concerned with the feel of their sticks, the size, weight, length and balance, that they don't stop to think just how different each stick sounds: not only on your ride cymbal and hi-hat, but also when it comes to whether your toms and backbeats come over as fat or thin.

The problem is that finding a stick you're totally comfortable with can be almost as hard as finding that perfect ride cymbal. So it's not surprising that once you find a stick that seems pretty comfortable you stay with it. Thereafter it's easy to forget how important it is. But that humble looking stick is the interface between you and your instrument, and there are a surprising number of factors to consider.

The strength and feel of the stick is partly determined by the way the 'lumber' is treated: in particular, how much it's kiln-dried. This is crucial to maximising the eventual strength of the stick and its resistance to warping. Dry it too little and the stick is sluggish and warps; dry it too much and it becomes light and brittle. Each company chooses the optimum moisture content that it thinks is the best – maybe around six percent. So far as I'm aware, the only company that offers a choice in this is Johnny Rabb. They offer three different weights of each stick type according to the moisture content.

The method of production is similar for all the manufacturers, although quality control procedures vary. The selection of the wood is critical: no one wants knots or discoloured wood. Pale, straight-grained woods are preferred, although in truth darker woods may be just as sound. Logs are ripped into boards, then (usually) kiln dried. Then they are cut into billets with a square cross section before rounding into dowels. The dowels are lathed or ground into the required profile for each model. The sticks are usually finished with a sealant to stop them drying further or absorbing further moisture.

The finish is also chosen for its effect on the feel of the stick in the hand. Gripping the stick can be a problem, particularly playing under hot stage lights when your hands start to sweat. Sticks are usually sealed with a light varnish/lacquer and/or a light wax. Non-slip coatings and high gloss lacquers are less popular than they used to be. For example, the French company Pro Orca uses a non-slip varnish in its Soft Touch Process. Some companies like Pro-Mark make natural finish sticks – 'The Natural' – with no coating at all. Danish B-Sticks are uniquely treated with genuine beeswax. You can even apply Drum Science's H3 drumstick wax directly to your sticks yourself to improve grip. The alternative solution to the sweaty grip problem is to try one of the several available stick wrap

> **"When I started playing major arenas with The Cult, it was in Canada in mid-winter. It was really cold and I got terrible blisters, and then the blisters peeled off and the skin cracked beneath. For two months, every time I hit the backbeat it was excruciating. So I got some really thin gloves from Pro-Mark. Now I've got calluses, but no blisters."**
>
> *MATT SORUM*

tapes, eg, Pro-Mark's Stick-Rapp, which is non-sticky, reusable and offered in ten colours. Or you could try some of the drummers' gloves made by Zildjian and Easton among others. Always remember, though, that a drummer can take off his vest or he can wear gloves… but never both.

Other efforts to improve grip have included sticks with narrowed waist areas. Trueline sticks do the opposite: they are specially contoured so that there is a bulge just behind the grip area. Trueline also do a newer, Natural Diamond Grip stick, which has fine diamond patterned knurling in the handle. Some drummers achieve a similar result by simply sanding the grip area to remove varnish and rough it up a little. Yet another solution is Aquarian's Power-Sleeve sticks, which are hickory sticks with a nylon sleeve moulded around the middle.

A typical stick profile

TIP   TAPER   SHOULDER

NECK   GRIP AREA   BUTT END

Before examining sticks in detail, let's just take a moment to run through the basic checklist for when you drop by the drum store. Assuming you've already found a model of stick that suits you, check each pair by rolling them on the flat store counter. If they are at all warped you will know straight away. Expensive sticks are guaranteed to be straight but you need to be sure. They may well have been straight when they left the factory, but they've probably travelled half way across the world. And how long have they been lying around in the shop? Wood is organic: it responds to changes in temperature and humidity. In fact, just about every stick will warp eventually. So if you hang on to them forever a good pair may eventually turn out to be bananas by the time you use them.

Assuming they're true, now look for a relatively straight grain, particularly running through the neck – the weakest part of the stick – and on through the tip, which can easily chip and flake. Don't worry so much about colour variations, but do check for balance and evenness of weight. Tap them together like a pair of claves, or singly on a hard wooden surface. They should have the same pitch. High-pitched sticks are generally good – the higher the pitch the denser the wood.

Manufacturers rely on various quality control and pairing strategies, encompassing colour, grain, density, pitch and weight. Exact matching is frankly impossible when dealing with an organic material like wood. You assume a good pair of sticks weighs the same but they may only be guaranteed to within four grams. That could be five per cent or more of the overall weight and it's amazing how sensitive you can be to fractional differences in each hand. Synthetic stick manufacturers generally claim a one per cent tolerance (see below).

Expensive sticks are guaranteed against warping, are closely matched and should be made from quality wood, which will last longer than cheap sticks made from poorer, softer timber. However, all sticks chip and shred if you play with rim shots and loud crashes. If you're just sitting there bashing out backbeats all night you may not need the perfect stick. Some manufacturers allow seconds – their reject sticks – to come on to the market. Often these sticks are unbranded and you just take pot luck.

Many drum stores have a bargain bin where you'll find cheap unbranded sticks and rejects of full price sticks with have a slight perceived warp or grain inconsistency. Occasionally, a well known stick company may offer sticks made from 'second best quality' hickory, say – wood which has not quite made the grade for their top notch lines. I'm all for this. It's an eco-friendly way of using up timber that otherwise might go to waste.

Don't be a total meany though. I've seen drummers hang on grimly to sticks that are ragged and literally half the thickness they started out at. Worse, I've even seen sticks still in use with their tips broken off – I mean, come on – the sound is non existent and you'll ruin your heads, which is really stupid and altogether more expensive. You know who you are…

Incidentally, if you regularly chop a lot of sticks, one solution might be HQ Percussion's Stick Saver. This is a vinyl coated aluminium ridge that clips over your snare drum's top rim in the area where you make rim shots.

NAMES AND NUMBERS

Now let's get down to detail. There are, as with cymbals, literally dozens of models offered by each company. But you'll soon discover what appear to be common standard designations with puzzling code names like 5A or 2B. Ignoring the numbers for a moment, the letters came about in the USA decades ago when they loosely referred to the field of music the drummer inhabited. Thus 'A' was for orchestral players, 'B' for concert band players and 'S' for street players, which in those days meant marching bands. Roughly speaking that meant A would be light, B medium and S would be heavy.

The lengths of the various sticks didn't vary that much – maybe between 15.5" (39.5cm) and 17" (43cm) hovering roughly around 16" (41cm). As and Bs might have similar lengths, but the As would be slightly slimmer and lighter than the Bs. The marching S sticks would generally be heavier and fatter than the other two and probably slightly longer.

Over the years these classification bands have survived but the A designation has come to serve jazz, lighter pop players and young beginners as well as orchestral players, while the Bs have become all-round sticks for commercial rock/R&B, etc. The S group are still mainly for marching and parade drummers and occasionally for HM sloggers. The significance of the numbers has long since disappeared, but don't worry: only a few numbers seem to be in common use, and the most popular designations today are 7A (light, jazzy), 5A and 5B (all-round) and 2B (medium heavy). However, this does not mean every manufacturer's 7A or 2B is the same. Each manufacturer has its own interpretation. To give an extreme example, Zildjian's hickory 5A weighs in at 48 grams while Regal Tip's hickory 5A is around 58 grams – quite a difference.

Beyond these and a few other less common code numbers, manufacturers have generally resorted to descriptive names like 'jazz', 'studio', 'techno', 'rock' and so on. There are also a huge number of star signature lines available. As with everything else, star players get to have their own model sticks. In practice, what happens is that they start from the nearest standard or previously available model they prefer and ask the stick company to make adjustments, adding a bit here and shaving a bit off there, until they arrive at their perfect profile stick.

Now, a word about buying signature sticks. Almost every name drummer has a signature model so it's obviously a successful marketing ploy for the manufacturers. And this is worrying

The four commonest stick designations, in order of weight from heaviest to lightest: 2B, 5B, 5A and 7A.

because it implies that many drummers choose their sticks simply because someone they admire plays them. Signature snare drums and cymbals I can understand – they may make a sound you like. But as we've seen, stick choice has a lot to do with your own personal anatomy, or at least your hand size and shape. Your hero's hands might be dainty and yours like a heavyweight boxer's. Your hero might be in a stadium metal band while you play wedding gigs. What certainly makes sense is to look at the brand of stick the player uses and then find a model in the range that suits your specific needs and physique. The endorsement of a particular manufacturer may be more relevant than a particular stick design.

> "On the first Living Colour European tour – 29 shows in 31 days – I was using a 3A. But it was too short and too thin and you spend all your energy squeezing before you even play. There were a couple of nights where my tendons locked and the sticks got locked in my hands: Cory [Glover, the band's lead singer] said to me, put your sticks down man, the show's over – and I couldn't take them out of my hands!"
>
> *WILL CALHOUN (LIVING COLOUR)*

WOODS

Next, what about the wood the sticks are made from? This also affects the feel, sound and weight. Nine out of ten drumsticks are made from hickory or oak and the rest are made from rock maple, along with rarities that include almost any wood you can name. I've come across ash, rosewood, bamboo, birch, bubinga, hornbeam, ebony, walnut, poplar and rosewood.

The hickory usually comes from North America (Alabama, Tennessee, the Carolinas and Florida), while the Asian White Oak often comes from Japan. Hickory is a tough wood but it flexes a bit because of its long, open gain. This absorbs some impact, which is kinder to your hands – and to the sticks. For this reason hickory is also used to make handles for hammers and picks, etc. Hickory is stringy and more susceptible to warping. While oak and maple are likely to chip and snap, hickory shreds: it sometimes tears in great long strips. Oak is harder than both hickory and maple. It's denser with a shorter grain and therefore it feels less flexible and absorbs shock less well. It's the least supple, so it appeals to those who like a direct, hard response with a sharp cymbal bite.

Maple is less commonly used and is the lightest of the trio. It has a very fine, tight grain and a velvety smooth feel. It's not so dense as oak or hickory, so you can have a bigger stick without it being too heavy. It has elasticity, although I've personally found it to feel rather brittle. Maple sticks are light and fast, great for jazz and symphony players, but heavy-handed rockers may break them too easily.

As for more exotic wood sticks, they tend to be a lot more expensive because they are made in extremely small quantities. They all feel slightly different with varying qualities of sound and durability. If you're interested I can only commend you to the specialist makers such as Johnny Rabb.

STICK SHAPE

Your sticks are as crucial to your performance as golf clubs are to Tiger Woods. But he's got a dozen different clubs to choose from, while you most likely approach your whole performance with a single model stick. Obviously there's going to be a trade-off between various parameters. So hang onto your hat and I'll see you at the end of the next paragraph. Here goes …

The thickness, taper and length of the stick, the position and profile of the shoulder, they all affect your stroke, control and sound. Longer sticks have greater reach and leverage but can slow you down. The length of stick you find comfortable also has to do with the size of your hands and the place where you grip and make a fulcrum. If the stick is too short you'll end up holding it too far back and losing the bounce. Ideally you want the stick to work for you, to maximise the rebound. If the stick also has a thick and heavy shoulder, the further back you hold it the less chance there is of getting any rebound: the stick will just drop.

A stick with a long thin taper or neck, by contrast, will seem light and fast. But this is a trade-off against durability: a long, thin neck is easy to break. So, to put it another way, the stick's shoulder is the counter-balance to your grip/fulcrum and dictates the way the stick rebounds. If the shoulder is too near to your hand the tip appears to have less weight; if it's too close to the tip the stick feels heavy. The latter will give you volume and the stick itself will be stronger. But it will also reduce the rebound and make you work harder. This may be okay for slamming, but it will hamper your attempts at speedy fills. Nevertheless, if you're a heavy player you obviously don't want the neck to be too thin or it will definitely snap.

Simple enough, really. Whatever the stick's profile, each drummer will find a balance point that suits. But if you're breaking a lot of sticks it could be you're putting too much pressure on the stick in the wrong place. Try changing your stick – or your fulcrum position – and you might find you get more rebound and fewer broken sticks. And you might even get more volume and tone.

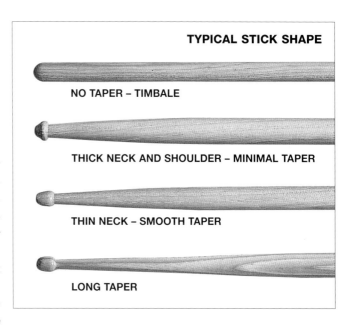

TYPICAL STICK SHAPE

NO TAPER – TIMBALE

THICK NECK AND SHOULDER – MINIMAL TAPER

THIN NECK – SMOOTH TAPER

LONG TAPER

Four different stick tapers. From the top: a timbale stick which has no taper, neck or defined tip; a heavy stick with thick neck and shoulder and minimal taper; a light stick with thin neck and smooth taper; and a medium stick with an extended neck area.

STICK WEIGHT

So we've established there may be some advantage to a heavy stick with a thicker girth, in that it gives you more volume so you don't have to put in quite so much effort. You'll also get a fatter tone out of the toms, which can be attractive: but the downside is that the heavy stick might obliterate your cymbals, particularly your ride definition. Conversely, if you use too thin a stick and still try to play loud you can have other problems. You find yourself gripping too tightly and end up with cramp. Will Calhoun of Living Colour told me how he came off stage one night and couldn't put his sticks down. His hands had cramped around them because they were too thin. He changed to a thicker shaft.

Here's an old chestnut. Should you use a heavier stick for practising? The jury on this one is split. The idea is you use a heavy stick – even a steel stick – to build up stamina and muscle in the hands and wrists. Many people over the last century have sworn that by using heftier sticks you can increase your power and then when you get back to your real sticks on the kit you just float. Some great drummers have advocated this so there's no way I'm going to rule it out. But personally I find it worrying. Do golfers and tennis players use heavy steel oversized clubs and rackets to practise with? I doubt it.

An overweight stick might make sense just for building hand strength, as does using those Chinese squeeze balls or some other gym workout. But for serious practice surely you should use the correct tool – the stick you actually play with?

There's a similar controversy about another old favourite, which is practising on a pillow. The idea again is to make your hands and wrists work harder and improve your endurance. That sounds like a safer idea, but because you're not getting any rebound it's the complete opposite of current thinking on technique. Everyone today talks about getting the stick to do the work – to control the rebound – to master that graceful, ergonomically sound technique which bears the name of Sanford Moeller. Drummers who've mastered the Moeller method hold their sticks very lightly, just guiding them and keeping them bouncing. Well you can't do that with steel sticks on a pillow. Can you?

Examples of various tip shapes and types.

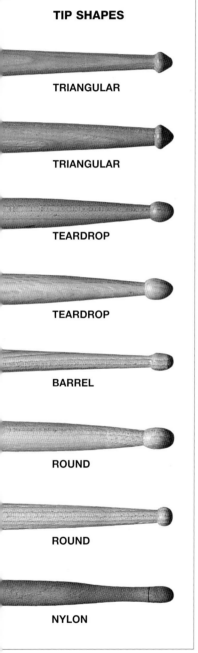

TIP SHAPES

TRIANGULAR

TRIANGULAR

TEARDROP

TEARDROP

BARREL

ROUND

ROUND

NYLON

Still, to reiterate: I know there are great drummers out there who say they've benefited from one or both of these techniques, so I'll say no more.

TIP SHAPE

The shape of the tip or bead greatly affects your feel and sound, particularly on cymbals. Tips come in all varieties, but there are may be four main types. These are teardrop (or acorn), barrel (oval or olive), round (or ball), and triangular (arrow-tip or mushroom) shaped. There are also some sticks – like timbale sticks for example – which have no sculpted bead at all. If you've never thought much about tips, now's the time to try a selection on a ride cymbal and be amazed. (Rather than changing your ride cymbal you might end up changing your stick.)

At its simplest, a round tipped stick only touches the cymbal or drum in a single spot and therefore produces a sharp sound with plenty of highs. A flatter, barrel-shaped tip makes contact over a bigger area and produces a broader and deeper sound. So you might say small round tips are great for jazzy ride cymbal playing with pinpoint definition, while barrel tips are good for getting that fat studio back-beat on your snare drum. Tear-shaped tips are an effective compromise while triangular-shaped tips can offer the best of both worlds – pinpoint or flat – depending on how you angle the stroke. Generally speaking, a smaller tip elicits higher tones. On the ride cymbal a smaller tip doesn't cause so much build up of complex overtones and so gives a sharper, clearer 'ping'. A broader tip meanwhile covers more surface area and extracts more overtones, including the deeper ones.

Another advantage of a perfectly round tip is that it will always give you the same response no matter what angle you play at. This can be useful if for example you have a large, extended set-up where some items are at a distance and awkward angles. The advantage of elongated oval and acorn shapes is that it means you can play your ride cymbal and hi-hat with a thin tip sound if you wish, while you can lay the stick closer to flat to get a fatter snare sound or tom sound. On the other hand, some acorn shaped tips have quite a defined point to them and if you have your toms set at extreme angles towards you then you will not only get a very thin contact but you can soon find you're pitting the heads.

You can learn a lot by checking out the signature models of top drummers and comparing them with their musical styles. This is one way in which signature sticks can be helpful. For example, Peter Erskine uses a small round tip, which suits clean jazzy ride cymbal work, while Steve Gadd uses a medium barrel tip, which suits his fat, warm studio sound. And Terry Bozzio uses a special enlarged 'helmet' shaped tip that gives him a big tom tom sound for his melodic solo pieces.

Wooden tips have a tendency to chip or break off, often way before the rest of the stick is worn out. For this reason, the Regal Tip nylon-tipped stick was invented by Joe Calato back in the 1950s. Most manufacturers now offer nylon tip alternatives to their wood tip models, and they've all devised ways of fusing the tip onto the stick so that it doesn't fly off.

Nylon tips last longer so long as they don't snap off completely, which can happen, particularly if the stick's neck is narrowed for clasping into the nylon. Nylon tips tend to have less variety in shape and they produce a hard and bright sound. This works well on drums but not all drummers like the harsh effect it has on their ride cymbal sound.

UNUSUAL AND SPECIALIST STICKS

Over the years manufacturers have regularly tried to tempt drummers with unusual sticks. Louie Bellson had jingles on his sticks way back in the 1940s. An intriguing modern invention is Johnny Rabb's serrated RhythmSaw stick. Take a look at Johnny Rabb's video (see Education chapter) and you'll be amazed at what he does with his RhythmSaws, recreating DJ style scratch effects, for example. In fact the advent of machine-inspired/drum'n'bass style drumming with its exacting beats has given manufacturers a new category of stick. 'Techno' sticks have long thin tapers for those frighteningly fast, yet light and sensitive beats.

Besides these variations on standard sticks there are of course the two staples: beaters and brushes. Felt beaters or mallets are made in all sorts of grades for timpanists. It's a whole world in itself with dozens of designs available. Just about every kit drummer will find a use for at least one pair somewhere in their music.

Brushes were traditionally made from wires set into a wooden handle in the shape of a fan and used for many styles of music. Nowadays brushes are just as often made from nylon and these tend to vary more in size.

The nylon brushes are very versatile, but wire brushes are probably better for tackling the sweeping motions of traditional jazz ballads. This type of playing is an art in itself. Brushes are sometimes telescopic with rubber handles, the idea being that by retracting them the strands are protected from breaking and bending. Also, the arc of the spread of the fan can be adjusted from narrow to wide depending on the effect you are looking for.

Somewhere between brushes and sticks we have Regal Tip Calato Blasticks and Pro-Mark Hot Rods. Both these products bridge the gap between brushes and sticks. Blasticks have brush-like strands of thermo-plastic, but they are tightly packed, not spread out like a brush. Hot Rods consist of tightly bound dowels of birch in four different thicknesses from fine Cool Rods to thick Thunder Rods. Once more, each stick company now makes its own version of these two original products. Both these 'brushes-sticks' can be used in normal playing situations to create varying effects and dynamics. I also find Hot Rods in particular are great for practising quietly and for rehearsing: working out material quietly to save everyone's ears. You can talk over them and give the singer a break. Then when the arrangement is sorted you can go back to sticks and let rip.

SIGNATURE MODELS

Four signature model sticks from different manufacturers.

Some unusual stick designs including Johnny Rabb's rubber-tipped practice model and Aquarian's answer to rim shot damage - the protective Power-Sleeve.

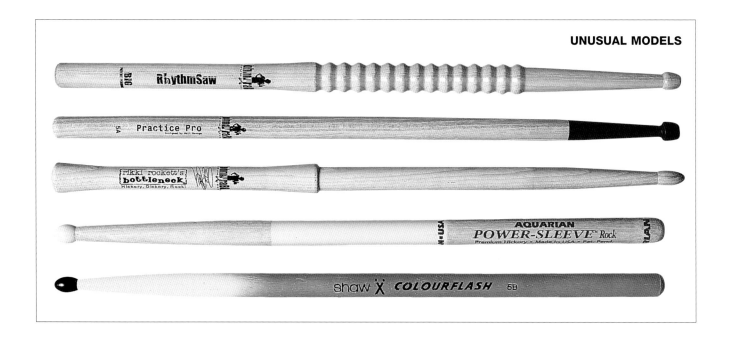

UNUSUAL MODELS

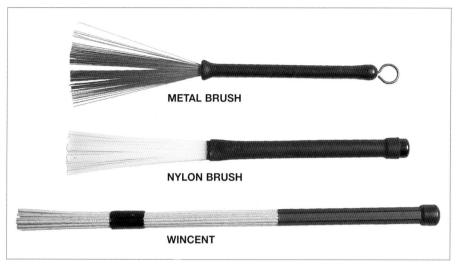

METAL BRUSH

NYLON BRUSH

WINCENT

Metal and nylon brushes, both retractable to protect the easily bent strands. Plus Wincent's version of the original Pro-Mark Hot Rod.

Some synthetic sticks by Carbostick, Mainline, Aquarian and Easton. The Easton Ahead stick has an aluminium handle with a replaceable polyurethane sheath.

SYNTHETIC STICKS

Making sticks is a very wasteful process. Wood being a natural product that is extremely variable, the manufacturers get through a lot of lumber by the time they arrive at the end product. All the knotted, unevenly grained, flawed, outer and heartwood or dark wood is rejected. All that trashed prime hickory and oak.

Do you feel guilty? We are assured that American, European and Japanese sticks generally come from sustainable supplies. Herb Brochstein, the founder and owner of Pro-Mark says American hickory is growing faster than it is harvested, while the Japanese white oak is strictly conserved to assure sustainability, with only limited amounts cut each year. And the eco-friendly Vic Firth meanwhile use 'matchbox' recycled card wrappers (100 per cent recycled paperboard printed with soy bean ink) rather than the ubiquitous plastic. Vic Firth also uses sawdust from the wood mills to heat its drying kilns, with the rest going for animal bedding.

This is all good news and yet it still seems horribly wasteful, apart from it being very expensive, with drummers worldwide shredding sticks by the box load. Attempts to prolong stick usage have had limited success. Nylon tips have been around for a long while but the harsh, pingy ride sound stops them from being overly popular. The answer is surely synthetic sticks, but these have also been slow to catch on. The problem is feel. Wood has great shock absorbing properties while synthetics and metals generally do not.

Some synthetic stick manufacturers turn the tables, claiming it's a good thing their sticks don't perform like wood. Why would you want them to when wood is imperfect? Synthetic sticks offer greater durability with greater consistency. They are more expensive but can repay you by

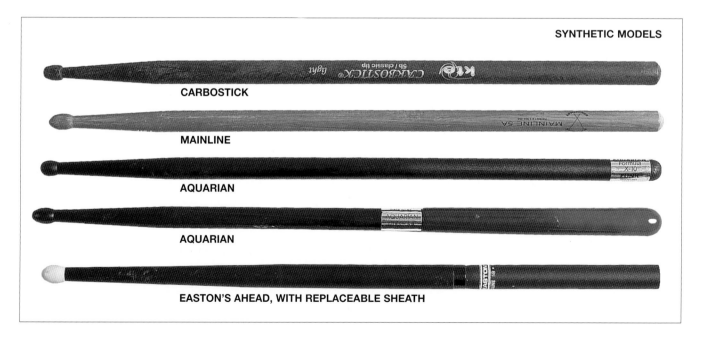

SYNTHETIC MODELS

CARBOSTICK

MAINLINE

AQUARIAN

AQUARIAN

EASTON'S AHEAD, WITH REPLACEABLE SHEATH

outlasting wood many times, typically five to eight times and more with careful use. (Of course, if they last you five times longer and they are five times as expensive – which some are – then you may want to rethink.) Synthetic sticks will not warp like wooden sticks and they will probably remain functional right up to the moment when they finally break up. Also, because they are uniform, if one in a pair breaks the other will still be useful – it will match up perfectly with your next pair.

In fact, synthetic sticks could be made to last virtually forever. But then the manufacturers would like to sell you more than one pair. And, ironically, if the sticks are too strong they will destroy your heads and cymbals. Also, the more durable the stick the harder it is likely to be. Which means it will be inflexible and will convey greater shock through your hands. Wood may be relatively soft, but its very vulnerability offers you protection. So the synthetic stick manufacturers have to compromise by constructing their sticks in such a manner that they will last several times longer than a wooden stick, but are not hard as iron. All synthetic sticks must have a degree of wear – the inner core may be very tough indeed but the outer sleeve must give a little.

One drawback – or advantage – is that a synthetic stick with the same dimensions as a wooden stick will usually be heavier. Aquarian's nylon/graphite sticks are hollow or you'd never pick them up. But with synthetic sticks there is greater control over adjusting the distribution of mass along the length of the stick. They are often weighted towards the front to give more power. This is something you'll either like or find uncomfortable.

The materials used in making synthetic sticks include graphite, aluminium, nylon and Kevlar. There have been quite a few different designs, several of which have come and gone. Aluminium is a lightweight material and is used in sticks by Verisonic and Easton. Verisonic claims it was the first to make a non-wood stick back in the 1960s, using aircraft grade recyclable aluminium. Today it has Classic sticks in six bright colours and Rock sticks in eight colours. Verisonic reckon they give you an extra 3dB in volume.

Easton makes Ahead sticks, favoured by many heavy rock players. The handle is aircraft alloy so you have to be very careful not to strike your cymbals with it. But the shoulder and neck is a replaceable polyurethane sleeve. When this wears out you can change it simply and cheaply. The beads are nylon and screw onto the shaft tip. Easton also makes Crossroads Ahead sticks, aimed at the country market. These have hardened wood-coloured urethane sleeves to give you a good cross-stick sound.

> **"I've been using the Easton Ahead stick which has an aluminium inner shaft with replaceable carbon fibre tip – no wood at all. They have the same weight and give as a wooden stick. I do stretches and sometimes use a deep heat rub because sometimes my wrists will cramp up, but since using these sticks I've had fewer problems – there's less of a shock."**
>
> *MATT SORUM (GUNS'N'ROSES, THE CULT)*

Graphite has formerly been used to replace wood in other comparable instruments such as tennis rackets and golf clubs. It made sense therefore to give it a whirl with drumsticks. But graphite is heavy and so Riff Rite's original graphite sticks were partially hollow. They also had cork handles to reduce the shock. German made Carbosticks are said to give a 'realistic wood feel' but are three to eight times longer lasting. Carbostick claims they don't bruise, split, crack or splinter and have good shock absorbing properties.

Aquarian offers all the popular stick sizes in its X-10 series and its cheaper Lite series, which has a little less graphite. Both series have red Shock-Grip handles for protection against excessive vibration and fatigue. Finally, Mainline makes synthetic composite sticks that aim to look and feel similar to wood but last eight times longer. They are also available in standard sizes and even have wood or nylon tips.

DELIBERATE IMBALANCE

To play a fast but light samba or bossa nova, some drummers use a brush in one hand and a stick in the other. So there are times when you don't necessarily want perfect balance between the two hands. The sound you need will change, depending on what you're playing. You might want a sharply defined ride sound and so you need a good stick tip. But you might at the same time want a fat backbeat, in which case you may well turn your left stick around and play with the butt end. The same technique of reversing the stick is also useful for playing fatter cross stick sounds. You might also go for a Latin pattern on the bell of your ride cymbal and use the shoulder of your stick for a fuller tone.

The most interesting example of this purposeful imbalance between the hands I've encountered is from the great reggae drummer Sly Dunbar. He would play with completely different sticks in each hand and the right hand (hi-hat) stick was wrapped in tape around the shoulder to give it extra oomph.

This may seem to go against all the standard rudimental balance, but it is a perfectly legitimate way to play the drum kit if that's the sound you're looking for. Orchestral percussionists often use different sticks and beaters in each hand to play on different surfaces. But many kit drummers have one type of stick and that's it – in accordance with rock dynamics: "Whaddya mean, dynamics? I'm playing as loud as I can." Perhaps we should routinely carry several weights and types of stick and change them for different tunes and gigs?

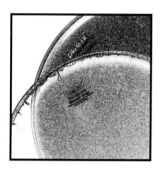

DRUMHEADS

I once heard the story of a drummer with a good quality kit who went into a drum store to get his toms fitted with RIMS-style resonance mounts because he wanted them to ring more. Before taking his money the store very responsibly asked him what heads he was using. "The heads that came with the kit," was the reply. And how long had he had the kit? "About five years."

While it's understandable to spend so much time drooling over the latest kits we should never forget it's the drumheads that actually generate the sound. The shells are merely projection chambers that alter the timbre. This is why a budget kit with good heads can sound almost indistinguishable from an expensive kit.

That is a very hard fact to assimilate when you're confronted with the beautiful shells that are the main selling point of most drum kits. Nevertheless it's true, and good heads and careful tuning are the main key to getting a great sound. But heads wear out, become distorted and lose their elasticity. They need care and attention, and, particularly if you're a fairly heavy player, they need replacing from time to time.

MATERIALS AND MAKERS

Today 99 per cent of heads are synthetic, although there is a small lingering market for real animal skins. Most synthetic heads are made from a tough, weatherproof and heat polyester, or plastic, called Mylar. This was invented during World War II as a heat resistant film used by night reconnaissance aircraft. The idea was it wouldn't melt during the intense heat of bombing raids.

There are really only four major companies producing professional standard heads and they are all based in the USA. They are Remo, Evans, Aquarian and Attack. Evans, Remo and Ludwig in the USA, and Premier in Britain pioneered the synthetic drumhead market, from around 1957. Aquarian started in 1980 and now boasts a massive range, while relative newcomer Attack has a more concise and clearly labelled range. Remo has always had the lion's share of the market, while

Evans, Aquarian and Attack offer excellent alternative choices. Ludwig's famous Weather Master heads are mostly found on Ludwig drums.

The unbranded heads on starter kits are made in the Far East. As we've seen, they serve a purpose, but they are thin, dent easily and lack tone. They soon wear out and should be replaced with quality heads straight away. All the branded heads can be considered professional; which brand you choose is down to personal preference and the type of sound/music you're into.

In the past some of the major drum companies – notably Premier, Sonor and Ludwig – also made their own heads. Ludwig still does, but today Premier and Sonor, like just about everyone else, fit Remos on their drums as standard. Premier made their own Everplay heads from 1957 until very recently; but although they have resurrected the Everplay name for their latest drums the heads are actually Remos. This is not unusual. You will often see a drum company's name and head description, such as Gretsch Permatone, stamped on the heads, but the small print usually tells you the heads are made by Remo or, occasionally, by Evans.

An exception is Pearl's ProTone. Until a few years ago, Mylar was exclusively produced by the chemical giant Dupont. But since Dupont surrendered its world licence, Pearl has started to make its own ProTone Mylar heads. These heads are made by Pearl and fitted to its budget and mid priced drums, although even Pearl fits Remos to its professional lines.

It may be that other big drum companies will again make their own heads, but the experiences of companies like Premier and Sonor seem to point the other way. It's simpler for them to be supplied by Remo, Evans or the other dedicated manufacturers. Drummers who bought Premier and Sonor kits would often change to Remos (or Evans or Aquarian, etc,) as soon as the first heads wore out. It was uneconomical for Premier and Sonor to continue head production.

Many budget and mid-price kits, for instance those made by Yamaha, now use Remo's U2 heads, manufactured in Taiwan using Mylar film imported from the US. It's a way for the top manufacturers to fit good quality heads to their lower ranges without breaking the bank.

Today each drumhead company claims its Mylar supply is special, and, along with the various ways it treats the material, this accounts for any differences between makes. Aquarian, for example, says its X-R (extra resonance) Mylar film is exclusive and specifically developed for its own drumheads. Attack is different because most of its heads are made in Taiwan from a polyester nylon film it calls Dynaflex. However, Attack's Terry Bozzio Signature range is made from Mylar. Because of the extreme tensions employed by marching bands, a different type of head material is used, called Kevlar. Kevlar is a woven fabric, famously used in bulletproof vests. Other materials, such as fibreglass, have been tried at various times, though not at present.

Finally, just like the cymbal companies, the head companies produce boxed sets of heads so you can revamp your kit at a better price. Your local store will have Evans PrePaks, Attack Samplers and Remo Pro Packs, etc, hopefully of every description for every type and style of drummer. You may not be able to afford to change all your heads in one go, so boxes will contain a set of batter heads for your toms, say a 10″, 12″ and 14″, with a 14″ snare batter. The bottom resonant heads you can leave longer, assuming they're not damaged. Other packs contain paired bass drumheads such as the Evans EQ system series. Alternatively, stores sometimes offer deals whereby the more heads you buy the greater the percentage discount you're offered, ranging from 5 per cent up to maybe 20 per cent.

MANUFACTURING TECHNIQUES

Most manufacturers attach their Mylar to an aluminium hoop. Each company has its own way of clinching or crimping the plastic into the hoop. Remo, Evans and Aquarian use an epoxy resin to 'glue' the head into the aluminium channel. There are detail differences in each company's hoop – so, for example, Aquarian has its Safe-T-Loc hoop with its Triple Locking System, which prevents any chance of the plastic slipping. Attack heads are different again because they are secured via a pressing process – rather then by glue – into a rolled steel rim. But Attack is not the only company to do this. Premier and Sonor used a similar method when they made heads, as does Ludwig with its 'Headlock' clinching system today. And high-tension marching heads follow a similar principle, and are guaranteed not to pull out. Then there are Remo's budget U2 heads, which are made in Taiwan. Remo calls them 'crimped' rather than 'poured' heads since there is no epoxy poured into the hoop channel.

Glue or no glue, heads rarely pull out these days – you're more likely to put your stick through the centre first. Though even that requires you to be a beast of a player. The cracking sound made by the glued heads when you first tension them is nothing to worry about. All heads have a collar at their edge where they curve into the hoop. When you tighten the head, the collar of the plastic moulds to the bearing edge. This is called 'seating' the head. Collar profiles vary slightly from one manufacturer to the next. Some collars are curved and some have a squared ridge.

Attack and Aquarian claim their initially rounded collars help with tuning since there is no pre-formed ridge. Whether this makes a difference once the head is tightened fully I couldn't say. It affords some ammunition for the advertising copy, though, with Aquarian claiming its heads are musical because if you hold one of its heads by its hoop and tap it in the centre you get a musical tone. Attack, on the other hand, suggests the opposite is true: that the slack head should be toneless like a guitar string. Only when it's tensioned do you hear the note. Take your pick.

HEAD TYPES

Broadly speaking, synthetic heads come in two types: single or double ply. Single ply heads are brighter and ring more than double ply heads, which are harder wearing with more attack, but have less resonance. Heads are usually transparent or white coated. The coating is often slightly rough, the idea being to mimic the nap of real animal skin and to provide some friction for brush playing. Many drummers therefore have a coated head on their snare drum, even if they prefer transparent heads on their toms and bass drum.

Aquarians's Jack DeJohnette signature heads have a thicker, black coating creating a warmer, more calf-like tone. The coating on a head dampens some of the overtones and makes the head a little deeper in pitch. Both single and double ply heads can be modified by the addition of extra circles of Mylar or various perimeter damping rings, which accounts for the various laminated heads you will come across. Other heads, such as Remo's FiberSkyn-3, are also laminated, while Remo's Renaissance heads have a textured coating.

SINGLE PLY HEADS

The most common batter heads are single ply, around 10 mil (ten thousandths of an inch or 0.01", sometimes referred to as 1000 gauge) thick. The most popular single ply head is Remo's Weatherking Ambassador. This versatile head is played by every type of drummer imaginable.

The coated head is the most popular snare batter, while the clears are the most popular tom batters. Alternatives to the Ambassador coated are the Evans Genera G1, Aquarian Texture-Coated Satin Finish and Attack Coated. For more sensitive playing, Remo make a thinner single ply head called the Diplomat, which is 7.5 mil thick (750 gauge). Diplomats are popular with orchestral and small jazz group players. Equivalents include Aquarian's Hi-Frequency tom tom heads, Evans' Resonant heads and Attack's Thin Skin.

It's quite usual for your batter head to be thicker and more durable than your resonant head. For this reason it's good (and cheaper) to fit single ply heads to the bottom of your drums, whatever type of head you have on top. This will give you more projection and increase your tuning range. Thus an Ambassador tom batter might have a Diplomat bottom head. Other lightweight resonant tom heads include Evans G1 Resonants and Aquarian Classic Clears.

The resonant head of your snare drum is fitted with an even thinner, special 'snare-side' head.

Remo's Diplomat Snare is just 2 mil thick and feels almost as flimsy as kitchen cling-film. The Ambassador snare is 3 mil and the Emperor 5 mil. Snare heads are extra thin because you don't need to strike them (don't even think about it) and a thinner head gives a speedy and sensitive snare response. Aquarian's Hi-Performance snare head has two short patches laminated beneath the head at each side to prevent the snare wire ends from puncturing the thin head.

DOUBLE PLY HEADS

Heavier players benefit from the many double ply heads that are available. Two-ply heads have more attack, fewer overtones and a darker sound than single ply heads.

Remo's Emperors are a double thickness of 7 mil film, making 14mil. The combined strength of the two layers is actually greater than a single ply of 1400 gauge film. This is because much of the durability of the film is in the doubled surface area rather than simply the extra bulk. Two-ply heads are therefore more flexible and durable than a single ply of 1400.

Other double ply heads include the Evans G2, Attack-2 and Aquarian Response-2. Aquarian also makes a double ply tom head using thinner film, appropriately called the Double Thin, which is still durable but a little brighter. Attack's Blast Beat heads meanwhile have one medium and one heavy ply with an extra thick Duracoat coating for attack and power. Following the lighter bottom head principle, an Emperor batter works well with an Ambassador on the bottom.

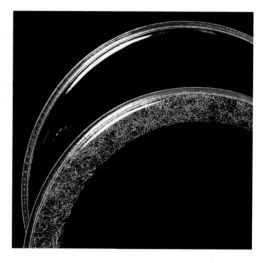

SPECIALISED HEADS

RIGHT: Remo's Clear Emperor and Clear Pinstripe are both popular double ply heads for the heavier player.
BELOW: centre reinforcing dots strengthen the head with a minimum degree of damping.

Back in the 1970s, when drummers really started playing loud and using close miking, Evans shook the drum world with its Hydraulic, a two ply head enclosing a drop of oil, giving a deep, fat and wet sound. In combination with the single headed concert toms of the day the sound was so clipped and dark it became known as the cardboard box sound.

Remo replied with the rather more rounded Pinstripe, which became the most popular head of the 1980s and is still a firm favourite with many. In fact many drum stores still advise less experienced players with budget and middle range kits to fit Pinstripes – or other double ply heads such as Evans' G2s – once their initial cheap heads wear out. The idea is that the double thickness heads are easier to tune and harder wearing. They also cut down on some of the nastier overtones associated with cheaper drums.

The Pinstripe, like the Emperor, has two plies of 7 mil film, but this time bonded around the perimeter inch or so with a thin black line. There is no oil inside the two layers of the Pinstripe, although sometimes it may look as though there is. This is just refraction of light, which results in a rainbow effect: a phenomenon called Newton's Rings, for the physicists among you.

Aquarian now produces a roughly equivalent design in the Performance-II. This does not have the rainbow, though, because Aquarian uses a vacuum system to seal the two layers of film before bonding the hoop.

Following the Pinstripe, Remo came up with the Controlled Sound (CS) Black Dot head. This is simply an Ambassador head with an extra circle of black Mylar stuck beneath

FAR LEFT: Remo's Fiberskyn-3FA (front) is a heavyweight head with a retro, calf-like texture and dark sound. Evans' Genera Dry (back) has a perimeter damping strip and pinhole vents for increased focus. LEFT: although these two heads may look similar, the Remo Ambassador Coated (back) is a single ply head while the Evans Genera G2 Coated (front) is a double ply head.

the centre. The black dot reinforces the head but only dampens it a little, so it's ideal for harder playing without loss of resonance. The design actually came about to help out jazz great Buddy Rich, who was kicking his way through a lot of bass drumheads. The reason the damping effect is minimal is because the centre of any head is already a relatively dead spot. The head's most resonant areas are nearer to the edges, which is why the Pinstripe has a more damped sound than the CS.

Again, the CS Dot idea has been echoed by most other manufacturers: eg, Aquarian's Power Dot, Ludwig's Silver Dot and Evans' Power Centre. Remo also now has the Emperor X, which is a double layer of Ambassador weight film: two 10 mil layers, making up 20 mil, with a black centre Mylar dot for extra durability. The head is also coated, which adds some warmth while increasing the crack.

Aquarian's equivalent is the Hi-Energy, which is essentially a single ply head but with a thin Power Dot layer bonded to the entire playing surface and a normal size Power Dot reinforcing the centre. As you've probably guessed, these two heads have been developed to cater for the extreme heavy hitters around today.

RETRO HEADS
Until the mid 1950s, drumheads were made from real animal hides. The advent of the Mylar head meant drummers could get consistent, weather resistant heads more cheaply and in unlimited

FAR LEFT: the snare drum is usually fitted with a rough white coated batter (back) and a rather thinner transparent bottom or snare head (front). LEFT: tom tom batters come in many guises, such as this Remo Ebony (back) and DW Clear with white damping band (front).

quantities. And they were much stronger. It's doubtful the real skin trade could ever have kept up with the demands of the rock generation.

However, the warm, deep sound of calfskin heads is something special and the synthetic head companies have tried to cater for that sound with retro-feel heads, like Remo's FiberSkyn-3. This is made by "fusing a single ply of Mylar with poly-spun fibres in a proprietary high temperature bonding process".

The heads are produced in four weights – FT (Diplomat), FD (Ambassador), FA (equivalent to two ply though, it's a single ply) and heavyweight F1. The other companies' corresponding series include Attack's admirably named 'Calf-like' heads and Aquarian's Modern Vintage and American-Vintage. The latter have a slightly larger hoop diameter that allows them to fit better on many vintage drum shells.

Although Remo say the FiberSkyn-3 was originally created in an attempt to copy the classic sound of bebop jazz, all of these retro-heads find fans in many styles of music, particularly those with more traditional, earthy grooves, from jazz and world/folk to Latin, African and Caribbean.

Since the advent of the FiberSkyn-3, Remo have developed the Renaissance head, which it says claim combines modern and retro properties in the best of all worlds. The heads have a permanently bonded coating to the top and bottom of the Mylar film, which will not degrade under the hardest of playing. Remo hit on this process of sanding and coating while looking to improve its timpani heads. Inevitably the process was applied to standard drum kit heads and found to be equally impressive.

The coating is like a fine grade of glass paper, great for brush playing. And the harder, abrasive surface gives your sticking an extra snap too. Remo say the heads "combine the warmth and depth of laminated heads, the clarity and response of coated heads, with the resonance and projection of clear heads". Despite that promise, Renaissance heads have not really dented the universal popularity of Ambassadors: possibly because they are more expensive.

A typical Premier big band kit from the 1930s, fitted with calfskin heads

ANIMAL SKINS

Real calfskin heads are rare these days, although some drummers do still use them. You might come across a vintage drum that won't accommodate the standard plastic sizes and requires a calfskin head. Also, tough animal heads are still commonly fitted to congas and other ethnic percussion instruments (although Remo has developed synthetic 'Mondo' heads for this purpose).

The problem with calfskin vellums is that they have to be individually selected and mounted – 'shrunk' – onto hoops known as flesh hoops before they can be fitted to the drum. This is an expensive business and requires a certain amount of skill and know-how. There are specialists who will undertake the work – check your local store for leads.

A viable alternative is offered by Earthtone, a specialist company which markets calf skin heads already pre-mounted and stretched onto aluminium hoops ready to fit straight onto your drums. They're more expensive than plastic heads, obviously, but if you're after vintage authenticity, then Earthtone provides a great service.

SILENT HEADS

Silent heads are a great idea, whether fitted to electronic kits or when used for quiet practice sessions on both electronic and acoustic kits. They are often black, and you'll find them on electronic kits by Roland, Pintech and Koby, amongst others.

Roland's V-drum system uses what is basically the Remo Legero shallow-shelled kit, fitted with special heads, also made by Remo, which are tensioned as normal but made from a fine twin ply nylon mesh. You tension the heads to the feel you like, but they make hardly any sound of their own, just a soft ping. Pintech's range of electronic trigger pads is also fitted with a silent head, this time made from a woven fabric. The Pintech heads can be tuned up high and have a rather firmer feel, closer to a real head than the soft mesh of the Roland heads. But both types feel good.

Pearl also makes fabric 'Muffle' heads, which it first introduced on its shallow-shelled Rhythm Traveler acoustic kit, a cut-down version of its Forum budget kit. These heads do not have such a fine weave as the Pintech heads, but then – as you expect from Pearl – they are reasonably priced. The great thing is that you can use this type of head for silent practice sessions on your acoustic drums.

Silent heads are available now in all sizes and have conventional metal hoops, which means they can be fitted to any acoustic kit. They all feel slightly different and if you can find a dealer who has them mounted on different kits it's worth comparing them. Then you could perhaps get hold of a really cheap second hand snare drum, fit a silent head on it and use it as an ultra-realistic practise pad. Just a thought.

One final use of the fabric head has been identified by Evans with its Retro Screen Resonant bass drumhead. This is a fabric head that you fit to the front of your bass drum. It gives you the contemporary black look of a full front head, but sounds as if the front head is absent – a real 1970s thud.

BASS DRUM HEADS

Bass drums can be fitted with the same heads as the other drums but they usually require special treatment as regards damping. This is because bass drums are by far the biggest drum in the kit and also because they are struck with a felt beater rather than a thin stick. One way of reducing the boom of the drum is to cut a 'port' hole in the front head. From the mid 1970s to the mid 1990s this was standard practice.

The bigger the hole the more boom is reduced and the more attack you hear. The smaller the hole the more resonance is retained and the rounder the attack. Today you will often see quite a small hole, maybe 4″ to 6″ in diameter, usually off-centre towards the bottom and to one side. This serves also as a miking hole. Many drummers also use it to stuff damping material – towels, pillows or whatever, inside the drum. Heads can still be bought with a pre-cut hole, but since the mid-1990s there has been a gradual move towards keeping the front head intact. In fact almost all kits today are sold with the front bass drumhead intact.

This move back towards fuller bass drum sounds was given a big boost with the introduction of the Evans' Genera EQ system in 1990. The idea here was to incorporate sufficient damping into the head system (front and batter) along with a small offset miking hole in the front head, so that no other damping would be required. The EQ heads have a removable perimeter muffling ring of Mylar on the inside.

Later, Evans came up with its EMAD (externally mounted adjustable damping) heads, which have the adjustable damping on the outside, making life even easier. Evans offers different types of EQ heads for different types of music. The EQ1 is for lighter jazz and bop fusion, the EQ3 is the popular all-rounder, the EQ2 more focused and punchy, the EQ4 more durable with extra low end. The other companies have, of course, devised their own counterparts, like Remo's single ply Powerstroke-3 and twin ply, Emperor-style, Powerstroke-4; Aquarian's Full Force and Force II; and Attack's No Overtone. Aquarian also makes several other bass drumheads, like the Impact and Super-Kick, which have 'floating' muffling rings. These rings are mounted a little way in from the perimeter edge of the head so that they do not obstruct the collar. The Super-Kick muffling ring is made from felt rather than Mylar.

Finally, you'll have noticed that standard front heads on bass drums are very often black, like Remo's Ebony. As well as looking cool, the black pigment actually gives the head a slightly darker sound.The internal perimeter damping ring idea worked so well on bass drums it was soon applied to other heads. So now, for example, we have Attack's Tone Ridge snare and tom heads. Evans has taken the idea further with its Genera Dry heads, which are also 'vented', with pin-sized holes around the perimeter. The holes allow free movement of air and thereby control decay and focus the sound a bit more.

MARCHING DRUM HEADS

The marching band sound is quite different from the normal drum-set snare drum sound. It is much higher, so that you are virtually playing on a solid surface. Marching band heads are mostly made from Kevlar, which will withstand the fantastically high tensions without pulling out or breaking. Examples include the Remo Falam, Attack Force and Aquarian Chieftain. Evans has its Aramid Fiber marching heads (Kevlar is an Aramid fibre, so we're talking the same sort of chemistry here).

All these heads will outlast even the toughest Mylar head and so they sometimes find an alternative home – tuned rather lower – on the snare drums of heavier kit drummers. In fact Evans now has the Rock AF Aramid head, which has been specially developed for heavy rock players. The sound is warm with plenty of initial crack. And Bear Percussion produces three styles of Kevlar head – the Studio, which is virtually overtone free, the Concert, with medium overtones, and the Stadium, which is the brightest.

SECTION 3 | PRACTICAL TIPS FROM THE PROS

SETTING UP

In this chapter we will first take a brief look at assembling a new drum kit out of the cardboard boxes in which it has been shipped. That will lead to a more detailed examination of setting up for performing. Then we come to gigging, and a list of things you should never leave home without.

ASSEMBLING A NEW KIT

Drum kits are bulky and incur large shipping costs. Starter, budget and middle priced kits have all probably come from the Far East, and will inevitably arrive partly disassembled. The drum store will sometimes help you put the kit together. It may charge you a small amount, but if you're new to drumming this is money well spent, as it will show you how to tune the drums at the same time.

The cheaper the kit, the fewer cardboard boxes it will come packed in. There will usually be at least two boxes. One will contain the bass drum and the toms packed inside one another concertina-fashion. The other holds the snare drum, thankfully fully assembled, plus the hardware and stands. You will need quite a large space to work in and you should allow at least an hour if it's the first time you've assembled a kit.

Take all the parts out of the boxes and lay them to one side. You should find a parts inventory and basic written instructions – or, if you're lucky, a getting-started video. Constructing a drum kit is easier than assembling a flat-pack wardrobe. It just involves fitting the heads and rims to the toms and bass drum, followed by slotting the stands and mounts together. The only tricky part is tuning the drums, and that is dealt with in a separate chapter. You will be able to construct the kit using just the supplied keys: a drum key and maybe an Allen key.

Take the largest shell – the bass drum – and lay it down on its front. Make sure you have the drum the right way around – the spurs will be nearest the front of the shell, so place it down with the spurs

Stages in assembling a brand new Pearl Export ELX drum kit. With a mid range kit, like this one, the snare and small toms are shipped already assembled.

nearest the floor. Fit the batter head first, ie, the one you play. This will most likely be a transparent head, while the front head will be black.

Place the batter head over the bearing edge and fit the hoop (either hoop will do) over the head. Take out half the claws and tuning rods (usually eight of each) and place them on top of the head. Be careful you don't lose the washers that come with each rod. Lay the claws over the hoop, then slot one rod through each claw eye and locate the tension bracket housings.

You can now take up each rod to finger tightness and proceed to seat the head as explained in the chapter on tuning.Once the batter head is in place, turn the drum over and fit the front head. Make sure any logos are centred and the right way up (assuming you're not bolshie and want them upside down). Fold out the spurs and set the drum upright facing away from you. Then fix the protective rubber sleeve on to the bottom of the batter hoop and now you're ready to attach the bass drum pedal.

The one item of hardware that is sometimes perplexing to assemble is the bass drum pedal, since the way it's packed means it appears to be turned inside out. This is simply because the tension spring is not attached, but it can take a minute or two to figure out how to turn it the right way around.

The best thing is to look at a picture of an assembled pedal and you'll soon see what's happened. Because the pedal is packed with the tension spring unhooked, the rotating cam which has the drive chain (or strap) attached to it will have pulled itself round 'backwards'.

Place the pedal base on the floor and pull the cam and chain around until the footplate lifts off the ground into its playing position, an angle of about 20-30 degrees. You will feel the tension that the spring is there to counteract. Now if you hook up the spring the pedal will right itself and all you have to do is to fit the beater.

You now have to assemble your toms. It's best to fit the bottom heads first. With cheap kits, the top and bottom heads will probably be the same. On budget kits and above, the batter heads will most likely be labelled as such. Fitting the heads is simple enough. You just slip the head over the

bearing edge and secure the metal rim using the tension bolts, again taking care not to lose the washers. For tuning details refer again to the tuning chapter.

The rest of the hardware and stands should be easy to erect. With stands, it's just a matter of folding out tripod legs and slotting in the tubular, height adjustable extensions as necessary. Each extension tube has a nylon insert, which provides enough friction to prevent slipping without the need for over-tightening the wing nuts. So go easy on your wing nuts and your stands will last longer. Most joints are also fitted with drum key tightened clamps, called memory locks. You can leave these loose until you're happy with the height and angle of everything in the set.

Then go round and tighten them all in place: your kit shouldn't budge under the wildest of assaults. Floor toms will either have three legs, or, in 'fusion' kits, a floor stand. Floor stands you'll either love or hate. They can easily topple over if you don't get the tripod base legs in just the right position. The floor stand may also have a socket for a cymbal arm, which will further complicate the balancing act. The larger and heavier the tripod base, the safer the floor stand. The actual tom mount bracket fitted to the floor stand can usually be positioned pointing upwards or downwards. Which way you decide to use it will depend on how high or low you prefer to set your tom(s). The bass drum mounted tom bracket by contrast only works one way up, but this will be self-evident.

When it comes to mounting your cymbals on their stands remove the wing nut and one felt from each stand tilter and place the cymbals onto the bottom felts. Make sure the small tubular plastic sleeve is shielding the cymbal hole from the threaded metal spindle mount and then replace the top felt and screw down the wing nut. It's best not to tighten the wing nut too much as you don't want to muffle the cymbal's sound. Also, over-tightening the wing nut can put harmful pressure on the cymbal – particularly a small and thin one. Cymbals need to be free to sway on their stands when they are struck.

SETTING UP FOR GIGGING
POSITIONING AND MARKING

Let's now move on to examine in closer detail the ritual of setting up your drum kit for serious practising, band rehearsals and gigging. To stop your kit creeping forward as you play, it's usually only necessary to place it on a carpet. For gigging you'll need a square or oblong of carpet, maybe around six foot square. You can buy a dedicated 'gig rug' from companies like Promark, who make a five foot square black mat that folds up to store in your drum case. Alternatively, you can just look out for a suitably coloured off-cut from the local discount carpet store. Rubber-backed carpet is good as it will not slip on a shiny stage, although the quality of the carpet itself may not be as good as woven.

When you set up your kit at home, be aware that the various spurs can easily do damage and that there may be some soiling from, say, the bases of the kick pedal and hi-hat, especially if you grease or oil them. You may want to lay your gigging carpet over the room carpet to protect against this. I find bass drums are easy to anchor, but some snare drum and hi-hat stands are more likely to start moving as you play harder.

Sometimes a strip of gaffer tape applied round the feet of the snare stand is all it takes to prevent movement, though it's not the prettiest solution. It depends largely on how hard you play. If you find your snare drum stand is jumping around mid-gig then you need to fold the tripod legs as flat as they will go, and failing that you will probably have to get a heavier modern stand with massive rubber feet. Hi-hats usually have their own spurs and better still, up-market hi-hats and bass drum pedals often have Velcro grip bases.

Your own gigging carpet is essential gear because many stages are polished hardwood. The drums and stands will slide all over the place and if you hammer spurs or nails into the stage you'll be very unpopular (though not the first, by any means, to do it). However, you may prefer the livelier sound of placing the kit on a wooden base, avoiding the damping effect of a carpet. In this case you might want to consider constructing a hinged, fold-in-half square of plywood or chipboard/MDF, etc, possibly painted with matt black stage paint. In such a case you will need to screw wooden blocks in various positions as buffers for the bass drum and stands to butt against. How far you go with this is up to you. Some drummers have intricate and foolproof bases with small u-shaped wooden battens surrounding the feet of each stand. Others like to have some freedom to move things around night by night.

With a carpet, it's easier to move and reposition stands. Roadies and drum-techs tend to mark out the position of stands on the carpet using strips of tape or felt tip pens. The latter is less noticeable. If you do your own roadying you'll probably not need to do this, as you know your own set-up instinctively. If you use a rack system then the situation is even simpler, because everything is fixed in position. Racks, though, are too cumbersome for the majority of average players who find stands easier to deal with.

MOUNTING THE SMALL TOMS

The order in which you set up your kit is largely down to what works for you. However, it is usual to place your bass drum down first and build around that. It's a good idea to extend your bass drum spurs until the front of your bass drum rises off the floor by an inch or so. This gives you a bit more forward projection and prevents the loss of resonance by having the drum's shell in contact with the floor. Be careful not to raise the bass drum too much or it will affect the stroke of your pedal and may even result in the bass drum pedal's own die-cast frame touching the batter head. There are special cradles available, such as that made by D'Amico, which lift the bass drum clean off the floor – a sort of resonance-enhancing mount for bass drums. It's a great idea, though at present most drummers don't feel the need to go that far.

Once the bass drum is positioned you can attach the bass pedal. In order not to damage the wooden hoop of your bass drum you should fit a rubber sleeve over the hoop in the area of the pedal clamp. These sleeves are usually included with the pedal or the drum. You can easily make something suitable yourself if you mislay one. If you have a double bass drum pedal you need to make sure it comfortably spans the snare stand base and that there's room for the hi-hat pedal to snuggle up to the slave pedal.

Next you can mount the small tom toms on the bass drum. The bass drum has a central mount with adjustable arms to support and position the two small toms. The small toms may have the traditional receiving blocks for the support arms or they may be fitted with so-called 'resonance enhancing' mounts, based on the original Gauger RIMS™ concept. Finally, erect the cymbal stands, mount the cymbals, slot in your snare drum and position your stool. Fine height adjustments and cymbal angles can only be assessed once you're sitting behind the kit.

The Fibes Sta-Way bumper prevents the snare drum rim damaging the small tom shell.

Many drummers position their snare drum on the stand with the snare wires crossing from left to right rather than from front to back. The reason for this is so that you can easily reach the throw-off/strainer with your left hand and also so that the throw-off or opposing butt plate is not knocking against the bass drum hoop or small tom. If you can find one, a Fibes Stay-Way bumper is a great attachment that stops your snare drum's metal rim digging holes in the small tom shell. I don't believe they are manufactured any more. If someone wants to produce one I'm sure they would sell like hot cakes. A common problem with the normal triple-arm snare basket is that once you get the snare strainer throw-off positioned on your left, in between two of the three arms, the far butt-side always seems to be obstructed by the third arm. You can only do your best to find a compromise position. Yamaha has produced a stand with a *four arm* basket to overcome this problem if it really bugs you. Whatever stand you use, be careful not to tighten the basket arms too securely around the snare drum. If you do, the rubber grippers will stifle the drum and you can lose quite a lot of resonance.

Most hardware today is equipped with memory locks, whether for simple up-and-down stands or for more complicated set-ups with boom arms and clamps, etc. Memory locks not only help to speed your set-up, they also make the kit much more stable. They come in all shapes and sizes, cleverly designed to fit into the hardware of each particular company. It's worth taking the trouble to make sure they are slotted in properly at every opportunity. Multi-clamps are very useful for floor tom stands and for mounting extra items, from cowbells to remote hi-hats.

Always try to leave the clamp attached, undisturbed, to at least one section of stand when you come to break the kit down. This means it's in the right position ready for the next time you set up. In fact, the less you have to break down hardware items, the easier and faster your set-up becomes. You probably know your own gear inside out, but with bigger set-ups it can sometimes be helpful to use drum-tech tricks like colour coding stands, maybe with small stick-on dots. Or you can use a permanent marker with a simple numbering system. Markers can also be used to indicate things like the angles of boom stand arms.

MIKING UP

If you play a gig where you are miked up, try to arrive in plenty of time otherwise the minute you place your bass drum down an engineer will be fussing around trying to position his mikes. The problem with this is that once you start to make fine adjustments the mikes will have to be re-positioned. It's best if you can politely ask the engineer to back off until you're happy with your set-up.

Don't let engineers position mikes so that it's impossible for you to play. This is particularly likely when miking the snare drum. The engineer has to get in between your hi-hat and snare and will try to get the mike over the drum and aiming down towards the centre for a full, fat sound. There's going to be some compromise here, but you don't want to spend all night worrying about hitting the mike. At the end of the gig, make sure the mikes are removed before you start breaking down or they can easily get damaged.

> **"The drums dictate my posture, and with the toms on either side I centralise my power by staying very stable and centred."**
>
> **BILLY COBHAM (JAZZ-ROCK PIONEER)**

GETTING COMFORTABLE

Most drummers soon manage to find ergonomically sensible positions for their drums and cymbals. The more comfortable you are, the more relaxed you will be and the better you will play. However, now and then you'll meet a drummer with the most amazing – well, crazy – set-up. One young guy I met recently set up his kit with his floor tom so low that the tom legs were protruding above the top rim. I never did find out why. The incredible thing was this guy could get round his kit, and thought nothing of stooping right down when the roll came around to the floor tom. Another drummer I met had his ride cymbal on exactly the same level as his floor tom batter head. The cymbal was to the right of his bass drum and so he was forced to move the floor tom way out to the right beyond the cymbal.

I'm not going to suggest these set-ups were 'wrong', but there's no doubt they contributed to problems the drummers were having with their technique and execution. And as for their posture … The latter drummer played his snare backbeats with his left wrist resting on his left thigh. He certainly liked the low down, laid back approach.

There are no hard and fast rules about how you set up. In fact developing your own unique layout is one of the best things about drumming, and a major factor in stamping your personality on your playing. However, there are a few common pitfalls (rather more common than the above extreme examples) that many drummers fall into and which you might want to consider.

It's generally considered correct to adjust the height of your stool so that when you play the bass drum your thighs are horizontal, or just slightly sloping down towards the bass drum. To achieve this you should sit on the front edge of the stool so that the padded seat is not supporting your thighs, just your butt. You should then try to maintain an erect, but relaxed, posture and avoid slouching. In this position you will find the best place to position your snare drum and from there your toms and cymbals. The easier they are to reach, the better, though obviously if you have a large set-up you will have to stretch to reach some items.

It's a great idea if you can set up in front of a mirror or get someone to video you as you play. You can see straight away if your posture and playing are ungainly or lopsided. The fashion for sitting high (like Buddy Rich) or sitting low (like Vinnie Colaiuta) seems to go in cycles. Be careful when copying your heroes. They may be much taller or much shorter than you and their angles might be impossible for you to emulate. At the time of writing we seem to have come out of the low sitting fashion and are returning to a higher position. But the important thing is to be comfortable.

Once you're happy with your seating position you can angle your snare drum. If you play matched grip it's normal to have the snare drum close to level, but if you play traditional grip then most drummers slope the snare drum down and slightly away to the right. This obviously suits the angle of the left hand traditional grip better and it also explains why it feels good to play jazz that way. You'll see many jazz drummers, when they are comping lightly on the snare, hold the left stick close to vertical. This purposely creates a thin contact between the stick tip and the head and yields the light feathery touch they're looking for. This is very difficult to do using matched grip.

With your snare in place you can now turn your attention to your toms and cymbals. Because your mounted small toms are usually above the bass drum it's normal to have them sloped towards you. This is fine so long as the angle is not too steep. If it is, then your sticks will dig into the heads with their tips. This will give you a thin sound, make you play harder, and will also soon dent your heads. In fact, if your heads are full of dimples, this is probably your problem. Try levelling off the toms a little and you'll get a fatter tone. However, if you have a large bass drum (over 22″ diameter) and use deep mounted toms this might be impossible. Your own height will be a factor here also. If you're tall and your tom brackets have good vertical reach you can overcome the problem. If not, you're in trouble.

Tall drummers can have problems as well, though. Playing an 18″ kick jazz set is always going to be awkward. You will undoubtedly stoop. You might need to sit further back, increase the height of your snare stand, mount your small tom higher, etc. I've seen tall drummers who insist on sitting low and then have a problem with their snare position and foot technique as their knees graze their chin like Easy Rider.

One solution to the – quite common – problem of mounted toms is to take them off the bass drum altogether. Have just a single mounted tom and put it on a snare drum stand (or an isolation bracket mounted on a cymbal stand) to the side of the bass drum. There are some great drummers, like Abe Laboriel Jnr, currently with Paul McCartney, who do this. It creates a larger gap between your mounted tom and your floor tom, but it has the advantage that you can now get your ride cymbal in closer. This is not to be underestimated, especially if you use the ride a lot. The strain of holding up your right arm is immense, particularly if you have to reach over a row of mounted toms. Using a single tom means you hardly have to lift your ride arm and your playing will be much more relaxed and steady.

> **"You need to fine tune your set up – you don't want a ride cymbal that's sitting three feet above your stick level so that all the blood's in the bottom of your arm. You want the ride at the extension of where your arm comes out, and your toms at a reasonable angle."**
>
> *J R ROBINSON (MICHAEL JACKSON)*

Not wanting to be a spoilsport, I repeat that sometimes it's cool to use unorthodox positioning if it suits your style and you're trying to achieve a particular effect. For example, some drummers have their crash cymbals ridiculously high which forces them to really stretch. But the idea is to create visual impact. The world loves acrobatic and energetic drummers, even the occasional show-offs. Just be aware that you can damage yourself by overdoing it.

A note for the left-handed: in your case it's normal to set up in exactly the same way, but in a mirror image of the pictures shown here. Alternatively, you could try playing in an 'open-handed' style. That is, you play a right-sided kit, but lead with your left hand on the hi-hat and play your backbeats on the snare drum with your right hand. Then, when you go to the ride cymbal, lead with your right and play backbeats with your left. The advantage of this approach is that you don't have to cross your hands over to the hi-hat. This style was pioneered by the great jazz-fusion drummer Billy Cobham. It is eminently logical and although it's still not widespread, more and more drummers are tempted to try it occasionally.

I've always believed that being a 'lefty' is actually an advantage for a drummer. Most of us who are right handed have pretty poor left hands and face a constant struggle, willing our left hands to catch up. But drummers who are left-handed always have pretty good right hands too. The right biased environment we all grow up in has forced them to use their right hands constantly against their natural inclination. This means that lefties are much closer to being ambidextrous than righties, and when it comes to playing the drums this is a massive plus.

There was a time when left-handed players were regularly persuaded by teachers to play right-handed. Personally, I think that was shortsighted, and I imagine in today's climate it's a rare occurrence. If you are a lefty, be grateful – you'll make a great kit drummer. And for any right handed drummer who's in the doldrums I'd suggest setting up your kit the 'wrong' way round and practising left-handed daily for a couple of weeks. When you go back to your normal set-up you will surely see a big improvement.

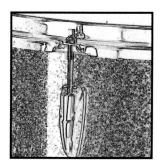

TUNING

I've spoken to dozens of top drummers and read hundreds of pages on drum tuning. And you know what: I don't believe there's a great deal of agreement on the subject. It is incredibly subjective. It's one of the things that make drums and drumming so fascinating, and – unfortunately – it's also the thing that causes drummers the biggest headache. There are no real rules. There are those who are really good at it and those who swear they can't tune to save their lives. And sometimes those who profess to be hopeless at it are drummers who are heroes to thousands and have a great sound. Figure that out. Perhaps they're just being modest?

What's for sure is that drummers get a lot of stick for not being able to tune their drums. So let's be clear that tuning drums is not a simple task like tuning a guitar. With a guitar there are defined pitches you have to attain, using a reference: an electronic tuner, or maybe a piano or keyboard. You apply tension until the string reaches the correct pitch. Then you move on to the next string. There is skill involved, but at least there's a strict target: you know precisely what you're aiming for.

But the drums are an instrument of non-specific pitch, with no absolute reference. You 'tune' them until they sound 'right'. Great. What the heck is that? A standard five-piece drum kit has maybe 80 tension rods. Half of them are on the underside of the drums and murder to reach: in fact you probably only ever alter the ones you can reach while sitting behind the kit. And – Sod's Law – those underneath are probably more crucial to your sound than the top ones. Each rod has to be tweaked 'just so'.

So tuning a kit is a laborious, complicated process. It's more akin to tuning a piano – and you get a specialist in to do that. And then you can leave it for months – years even – and the piano will still sound fine. It will stay pretty much in tune. Most pianists wouldn't have the foggiest idea how to tune their instrument. In fact many famous drummers in mega bands also have specialists who come in to tune their drums for them when they make records. It's not because they can't get a reasonable sound themselves, but, precisely because the sound of a drum kit is such a variable concept, a breed of drum-techs has grown up who make it their business to know how a load of different drums will perform in different studio and live environments. That way they can get the particular sound the producer or drummer is looking for. Oh yes, the room is another major factor. You tune the drums to suit the room, and the 'room' may vary from a heavily damped recording studio booth to a 60,000-seater open-air stadium.

Although tuning the drum kit can be almost as long-winded as tuning a piano, there is far more leeway with tuning drums, because they don't conform to exact pitches. But if there's no standard reference, how do you know if it's right? How do you know whether it's a good sound or a bad one? In truth, you can often get away with murder. So long as top and bottom heads are sufficiently taut that they don't flap or buzz, then you just play and few listeners will notice much difference. But go in the studio, with mics an inch away from each batter head, and your whole world can fall apart. Drummers are replaced on early recording dates by session players almost as much for unsuitable sound as for uneven playing ability.

> "I tune the bass low but not flapping, slightly muffled with a packing blanket and an old sand-bag sitting in the middle so it just touches each side of the head. The toms are tuned minor thirds away but not exactly – sometimes it goes down a full octave between one and four. The toms are definitely low. I like to build a track from a 'building a house' perspective: from the foundation up."
>
> *J R ROBINSON (MICHAEL JACKSON)*

Now I really have depressed you. Sorry about that, but by recognising the problem it's possible to get to grips with it. And the first thing to realise is that tuning your drums is a significant part of learning how to play the instrument. One reason drummers have so many problems is because they don't practise tuning regularly. Guitarists have to 'practise' tuning every time they play. They get very good at it. But drummers can easily leave their drums for weeks without going near a drum key. Top session players need a good sound at all times and so, not surprisingly, they get good at tuning. It's (almost) that simple. Make a point of regularly taking time to practise your tuning and experiment with it.

TUNING TOM TOMS

It's best to start with your tom toms, which are less complicated than the snare drum and bass drum. Don't try to tune while the drum is still attached to its mount. Take the drum(s) off the kit. Most toms today are double-headed. That is, they have a top (batter) head and a bottom (resonant) head. If you have single headed toms then the tuning process is much easier. You have half the number of heads to deal with and you don't have the complicating effects of the top and bottom heads conflicting with one another. However, most drums are double-headed, so we'll look at those.

We'll assume you are going to put new heads on the drums. If not, be aware that old heads may well be stretched to distortion or pitted and you'll never get them to sound good anyway. It's easy to tell if a head is worn out. Just slacken it off. If uneven dents or craters of various sizes appear, that means it's lost its elasticity. If it has a coated head and the coating is beginning to wear off, that is another sure sign. Even a bottom head will lose some of its elasticity and sparkle over time, although it's obviously subject to less wear than the top one. You can actually get away without changing the bottom heads for months – years even – but at some stage it's worth putting new ones on and seeing if they give you a bit more brightness and ease of tuning.

If you have two or three toms you can start with the smallest or largest first. It's probably easier to start with the smallest. First take both top and bottom heads off the drum. If you've not had the drums apart for a while, this is the perfect opportunity to clean everything up: the metal rims, the shells and lugs, etc. Most importantly, you must check the shell bearing edges to make sure they are free of any flakes of wood, fluff and dust, etc. You might want to check how good the bearing edges actually are, if you've not done so before. If a bearing edge is faulty then you will never be able to tune the drum perfectly.

Luckily, even cheap drums these days are well made and the edges are pretty level. If the edge is drastically wrong you will see with the naked eye. Just line up the shell at eye level so that you can look directly across from one side to the other. Any dips will reveal themselves. Also, if the peak of the bearing edge 'wanders' as it goes around the circumference, so that it's a bit nearer the outside edge at one point and then nearer to the inside edge at another, you've got problems. To check the edge is perfectly flat you need to have a perfectly flat surface.

Drum craftsmen use a marble, granite, slate or glass slab that is known to be perfectly flat. For rough checking you can use a hard kitchen work surface, glass table top or similar. Put down a sheet of thin black card and then lay the drum edge on to it. Shine a light around the inside edge, or pass a thin plastic playing card or similar underneath and see if there is the slightest inconsistency. If it looks suspicious to you, then unless you're a real woodworking whizz you should find a trusted drum craftsperson who can undertake the job of re-sanding or routing on your behalf with confidence.

A lot is made these days of the importance of bearing edges. Many top drummers will tell you this is the most important aspect of a drum's construction. The point is that if there is any inconsistency in the edge there will be a spot where the head has to be over-tightened or under-tightened in order to compensate. This will distort the head plastic slightly and create undesirable overtones so that the head will never speak clearly. This is the theory, but one thing's for sure – when you get a drum with a perfect bearing edge and you get a head that is itself consistent (not all heads are perfect, I'm afraid) then getting a nice clean note is a whole lot easier.

SEATING THE NEW HEAD

Assuming your shell edges are ready, it's a good idea to rub a smear of wax all around which will help to achieve a good, airtight and smooth contact with the head. Now take the bottom, resonant head and place it over the bearing edge. Replace the metal rim and tension bolts and screw the bolts with your fingers up to 'finger' tightness. Go round a couple of times to make sure the bolts are all as tight as you can get them with your fingers.

With some modern drums you may have to use a drum key because the lugs are designed to prevent slippage and so are deliberately tight after the first few turns. In this case, get the bolts up to the point where the washers and bolt heads are just firm against the rim. Now take your drum key and apply a full turn to each rod. Always work in zig-zags across the drum – from 12 o'clock to 6 o'clock, then from 9 o'clock to 3 o'clock, and so on, in order to take the tension up as evenly as possible.

You will need to feel your way here, as heads rarely take up tension perfectly evenly. After one turn press on the centre of the head firmly for a moment and then apply another half or full turn. With a smallish tom you may now find that the head is already starting to smooth out. Apply pressure to the centre again and check to see that the wrinkles are disappearing evenly all around the edges. Sometimes the wrinkling will be to one side, and you may need to apply a judicious extra quarter turn or so at this point. Be aware that you are trying to get the head to tension evenly. If the head gets pulled to one side too much at this stage, it may become distorted and then will never tune perfectly.

If you continue this even tensioning process, you will now start to hear cracking noises in the rims as the head pulls away from the glue channel. Don't be alarmed, this is perfectly natural: heads are constructed to withstand enormous pressure, and indeed they are often guaranteed not to pull out. You can carry on this process until the head has stopped cracking and is board hard.

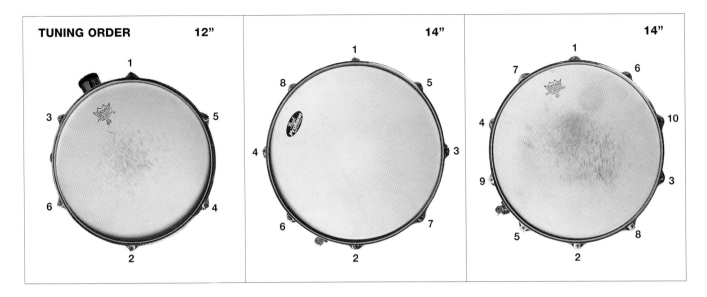

When you tap it in the middle it will make a high-pitched pinging sound. This process is called 'seating' the head, which means giving it a good over-stretching so that it settles in.

Next, take a couple of turns back off each rod – still criss-crossing the head – until the head is just above the wrinkling stage. Some drummers like to leave the head at this stage – when it is at its fattest sounding and deepest. This is particularly true of bass drum batters. Otherwise, from here you can fine-tune the head back up to the tension you like. Always try to tune up to a pitch rather than back down. This is done by tapping the head an inch or two in from the edge at each tension bolt and checking that you hear the same pitch all around.

Now it's time to come clean and state that this is much easier said than done. Since the head produces many overtones, it is often not at all obvious what you're listening for. It can take a lot of getting used to, so don't feel a dummy because you find it difficult. There are so many overtones it's sometimes difficult to recognise the predominant pitch. I'm sure I'm not the only drummer who's done this a million times and still occasionally gives up in despair.

The trick is not to linger at one place on the head, agonising. Use the 'guitar string' method where you tap next to one bolt, immediately and quickly de-tune and then turn it back up again so you can hear a definite pitch change. As you twist the bolt back up towards the target note it's much easier to hear when you reach the desired pitch. With practice you will get quicker at doing this, and the quicker you do it the easier it is. It's easier to keep the target pitch in your head and to blank out all the conflicting overtones.

And what might the target pitch be, you ask? Well, I think you will find it relatively easy to identify the pitch area where the whole drum sounds fullest with the most attractive timbre for you. Some drummers prefer a higher pitch, some lower. But whatever, this is the central area around which you should experiment. DW is very clever because it stamps all its drums with the fundamental pitch of the shell. This undoubtedly gives you something to aim at and is a great starting point. You can try to find the fundamental note for each of your own drums – whatever their make – and use this as a reference for when you tune.

The only way to do this properly is to take off every piece of hardware from the drum until you have the completely bare wooden shell, suspend it perhaps from a piece of thread and then tap it in the centre and listen for the shell's predominant fundamental note. If you were to do this for your whole kit it is to be hoped that the shells would reveal a nice descending set of pitches as the drums get larger. DW suggests that unfortunately this is not always the case and that it's one possible reason why many drummers feel they have problem drums in their set. Having identified

Suggested tensioning order for six, eight and ten lug drums.

this problem, DW stamps each of its shells inside with its fundamental pitch and guarantees that all its sets have been what it terms 'timbre matched'. I dare say this service has been a factor in DW's remarkable success story – it's such a blessed relief for a drummer to be given this information. You could say it gives them a head start.

THE TOP HEAD

Once you've got the bottom head sorted you can turn the drum over, place it on the floor and do the same with the batter head. You will want to dampen the bottom head somewhat so that you can concentrate on the top head, in which case you can sit the drum on a drum stool or on a cushion or settee or whatever. This will, however, impede the flow of air up and down the drum and so the response from the top head will be very pingy. Which just goes to show how much the bottom head is involved in the overall sound. But for now don't worry, just concentrate on getting the top head properly seated and evenly tensioned. Once you've achieved this you will be aware that there are three possibilities for tuning the whole drum. These are that the two heads can have the same pitch, that the top can be higher than the bottom, and vice versa. The only way you can decide which of these you prefer is to experiment.

It's often said that you tune the top head for feel and the bottom for tone. If you're playing fast music with fills that require fast sticking, it's normal to tune high, for rebound and clear articulation. So small group jazz drummers often prefer small drums with higher tuning. The opposite extreme would be a band that plays big, slow, open Elton John style ballads. Here you would probably prefer large toms with relatively deeper tuning for simple, broad, melodic fills. The trick therefore is to get the batter head how you like it to play on and adjust the resonant head for a decent overall sound and good projection.

Start by trying to get top and bottom heads to the same pitch. This should give a clear and full sound. Then try slackening the bottom head off a little and see how this affects things. You may get a slight drop in pitch after the initial beat, which can be quite an attractive, funky effect. Then try taking the bottom head up above the top head. This will give you a brighter, attacking sound with a shorter decay.

The permutations are immense. Depending on your starting pitch you can move the heads up and down relative to one another by exactly a tone, a second or a third, say. With, for example, a major third there's a clear difference between the two heads and a good chance the effect will be pleasantly harmonious. You can try to see just how far apart you can tune the two heads before the sound becomes truly appalling.

Then you can experiment tuning the heads closer and closer. The closer the two get together the greater the possibility of dissonant clashes. Worse, when the heads are really close you can start to get headache-inducing 'beats' – conflicting waves of harmonics that cause your drum to sound distorted. Large floor toms can begin humming uncontrollably as though they've got electronic feedback.

This, in a nutshell, is why drum tuning can be so fraught. There are simply thousands of permutations for each drum. There is no easy answer. You simply have to spend time in a room with your drums and experiment. Don't be disheartened when you seem to be going round in circles – we've all been there. If you get your kit sounding perfect one day try to make a note of all the pitches for future reference.

Before moving on, there are a couple of other points to consider. First, you may sometimes have to compromise a little with your batter head feel in order to get the best sound, particularly as you go from one room/gig to another. Second, the type of head you use obviously has a great effect on your sound and the way you play. And don't forget, it's quite common to use a resonant head that is thinner than the batter head, so the two will require different degrees of tension to achieve the same pitch.

TUNING BASS DRUMS

Bass drums and snare drums require somewhat different treatment from tom toms. Let's look at bass drums first. For most drummers, the aim of the bass drum is to provide a thud more than a note. The exception might be the small group modern jazz drummer with an 18″ or 20″ bass drum tuned quite high. Here the bass drum is an integral voice in the on-going improvisation and often sounds quite like another tom with a pronounced note. It is played with the same conversational freedom as the snare drum.

For virtually all other drummers, though, the bass drum is used to provide a much more regular thudding pulse. Many drummers therefore simply tune the batter head until it has the wrinkles out. To do this it's essential to seat the head and then stretch it as described previously by pressing firmly in the centre of the head while the drum is lying face down on the floor. Then slacken off the head and take it back up evenly until the wrinkles are just smoothed out. This will give the drum its lowest note and will also provide a good edgy crack. You can then experiment with the front head, perhaps tuning it a little higher for tone in the same way that you treat your toms.

Because over the past 20 years bass drums have had holes in their front heads, I've personally got used to the idea of putting the batter head on first. That is, the opposite way around to the other drums. I still have a small hole in my front head but many drummers today have completely intact front heads. In this case, you may want to put the front head on first and tune in the same way as for the toms.

The bass drum is generally more cavernous than the other drums and it's played with a felt or hard beater rather than a stick. It will inevitably have a greater resonance and boom than your other drums. Back in the 1970s and 1980s, it was common to either remove the front head completely or to cut a substantially large hole in the front head. This had the effect of making the drum virtually indistinguishable from a single headed drum. In fact you only have to cut a central hole of around 8″ or more in diameter for the drum to start sounding suspiciously like a single headed drum. For this reason, to get the best of both worlds, so called 'port' holes are now commonly seen. These are smaller holes – maybe around 4″ or 5″ in diameter – and positioned off to one side rather than centrally. Such a vent hole will reduce the booming a little without sacrificing the fat sound of the drum. It will increase low-end response and add some edge to the beat. The hole will also prove useful for miking up the drum and for arranging any internal damping material you might want to use.

CUTTING A PORT HOLE

If you decide to cut a port hole yourself you need to take great care because it's easy to tear slits in the edge of the hole and ruin your expensive head. The obvious method is to use a razor-sharp hobby knife and slice round a circular former. This is not as easy as it seems, though, and is a surefire way to get the aforementioned tears. A better approach is to adapt a circular 'cake cutting' technique. To do this you could use a metal vegetable or soup can of the appropriate diameter. You will need to cut the can with a tin opener of the type that leaves a sharp edge. You then heat up the edge of the can and use it to melt through the head. (Extreme care and a pair of thick oven gloves would be sensible precautions here.)

To further guard against tearing try the following. Get two cans, one 4″ (100mm) in diameter and the other 5″ (100mm). Use the 5″ can to cut a 5″ circle out of an old discarded head. Stick this over the inside of your bass drumhead in the position where you want your port hole. Now take the 4″ can and, preferably working from the front of the head, cut your 4″ port hole smack in the centre of your 5″ circle. Now you have a 4″ hole bordered by a 1″ (25mm) double thickness internal reinforcement.

If all this sounds like too much work then simply buy a head with an appropriately cut and reinforced hole such as those made by Aquarian and Attack.

BASS DRUM IMPACT

Although most drummers like to get good definition – and certainly in the commercial area, where drums are miked up, it's essential to get a good thwack – a large proportion of drummers still prefer to use felt beaters. This is a bit strange really, as the same player would never use a felt beater on a tom or snare in normal playing.

I think the reason has to do with the feel of a felt beater on a bass drum. It's easier on the foot, often responds faster and produces a warmer sound. Loud players often 'bury' the beater, and with a felt beater the impact is softer, with less of a 'boing' after-shock effect. However, those same players often stick an impact pad on the bass drum at the point of contact to get more 'click'. Impact pads such as Remo's Falam Slam pad, or Aquarian's Kick Pads (for single or double pedal beaters) protect the head while increasing definition. If you use a hard wood, plastic or Plexiglas beater an impact pad will also help extend the life of the head. Hard beaters are undeniably louder but the sound is drier, and sometimes the heavier type of beater can feel slower to respond.

Aquarian's Kick Pads are made from the same material as Aquarian's Power Dot head reinforcement dots, but are thicker and stronger. Of course, you can make your own impact pad from all sorts of source materials. A circle of old head material, or, for really hard hitters, a flat section of plastic milk carton, can be taped or stuck in place. In times gone by drummers used 'moleskin' pads or leather shoe soles: today you could use rubber ones. Some have even resorted to taping a coin at the exact point of impact to get a really bright click. Whatever you decide to stick on your batter head, though, be warned. You can use gaffer tape around the area of impact – but not over it. If you do, the beater will soon work its way through the fabric and then get stuck on the amazingly gooey adhesive beneath. Let one who's made this dumb mistake tell you, it can really slow you down.

BASS DRUM SIZE

While most drummers have a selection of tom toms, they have only one bass drum. The commonest diameter is 22″, which makes for a good all-round drum. As for depth, because modern music is obsessed with bass frequencies, the fashion is creeping towards deeper shells. While 16″ has been standard for years we're now seeing more and more 18″ deep bass drums. This also coincides with the ability of sound systems to cope better with deeper bass frequencies. In the studio it's long been a common practice to increase bass response by constructing a sort of tent over the bass drum and extending it forward like a sound tunnel chamber. Sometimes a second bass drum is positioned in front of the first to get twice the depth and a similar result. DW makes special shallow shelled extension 'Woofers'.

With regard to diameter, one important consideration is the position at which the bass drum beater strikes the head. As with the other drums, it can make a big difference to the sound, with the fattest tone coming from striking dead centre. The problem is that once the bass drum gets larger than 22″ – say 24″ or 26″ – your beater, even when fully extended, will strike below the centre point. This will give a thinner, higher pitched response. And vice-versa: with a 20″ or 18″ drum, you will find your beater strikes above the centre point (unless you reduce the length of stroke to a feeble few inches) with the same result. And while we're on this subject, many drummers suffer a similar frustration with their double bass pedal because the main beater hits dead centre while the slave beater inevitably hits slightly off to one side, producing a thinner tone.

However, despite the restrictions of pedal beater reach, it does seem it's possible to get a good sound with either a small or large drum. Bernard Purdie, who is one of the greatest recording drummers of all time (Aretha Franklin, Steely Dan and many more), has long favoured an 18″ Sonor bass drum. Yet he always gets a full and fat sound. And John Bonham of Led Zeppelin was famous for his monster sound using a 26″ Ludwig. Indeed, Bonzo's bass drum sound is pursued like a sort of Holy Grail for rock drummers. The drum was also a shallow 14″, which was normal for the

1970s. The shallow depth helped Bonham to get a fast response, even though the drum had a large diameter. Bonham also tuned his bass drum much higher than people realise. This stopped the drum sounding muddy and gave it an enormous crack like a heavy door slamming. So it is possible to use a big diameter drum, get a thunderous sound and nimble beats. I'm not quite so sure about the current fashion for considerably deeper – 18″ or even 20″ – drums, though. They certainly deliver lots of low-end oomph, but watch out for a slower response and, particularly when miked up, a cloudier tone.

TUNING SNARE DRUMS

The snare drum is the trickiest drum to tune because of the added complication of the snare wires. To replace the snare side resonant head it's necessary to take the snare wires off the drum. However, you can check the tuning of the bottom head without removing the snares. What you do is turn the drum over, release the snare mechanism and put a stick across the shell under the snares so that they are lifted off the bottom head. Now you can tap around the head and adjust the tuning with the snares safely out of the way. Be very careful with the bottom head – you should only tap it very gently or it will dent. It's best to tap it with a very light stick rather than your playing stick, or better still with just your index finger. And since the bottom snare head is so thin, it doesn't take a lot of tensioning to get it to ping. Get the wrinkles out and take it up a little and that may be enough. The same tuning methods apply as with tom toms. However, if the bottom is too slack it can cause the snare wires to snag and choke and make the drum dull. Too tight and you can start to lose the effect of the snares altogether, as they 'float' over the head making insufficient frictional contact.

The respected drum designer Bob Gatzen, in his extremely informative video, *Drum Tuning, Sound and Design*, is prepared to go right out on a limb. What he says is so specific I'd like to repeat it here. He says that he's found the bottom head often sounds good tuned somewhere around a G. He then tunes the top head a third, fourth or fifth above that (ie, to B, C or D). Intervals of a third produce a more woody sound, while intervals of a fourth or fifth produce a more metallic sound. Anyone who's prepared to be that explicit deserves respect. Check out the video.

> **"You've got to turn the snares off and go to each lug and go 1.5″ off each lug and tap. If one's down try to make it equal. Check your bottom head tuning is not too tight – and same with the toms."**
>
> *J R ROBINSON (MICHAEL JACKSON)*

And while I'm quoting, I have in front of me a fascinating article in *Modern Drummer* magazine from November 1999. In this, some of the world's leading drummers reveal their tuning preferences. I note that some tune their bottom snare head higher than their batter, and vice versa. That is the perfect illustration that there are no rights or wrongs when it comes to drum tuning. You just have to find what works best for you.

SNARE BUZZ

Sometimes the snares on the bottom of your drum will start buzzing for no apparent reason. This is a universal problem and is basically a 'design fault' of the instrument that is too late to fix now.

What you should know though is that your snare drum should have what's known as a 'snare bed'. This takes the form of two shallow dips on either side of the bottom bearing edge where the snares are attached. What the snare bed does is to cause the centre of the snare head to bow downwards a little, ie, to be slightly convex. As a result, the snares make good contact with the centre of the head when they're under tension. Without a bed the snares can droop slightly in the centre as they're stretched/pulled up from either side, and this increases the likelihood of buzzing. So before anything else, check the underside of your drum and what you should see is a gradual, shallow dip on either side. If there is no bed and you suffer persistent snare buzzing then you may want to take your drum to a specialist drum craftsman who can cut a proper bed.

> "So long as the snare bed's cut properly and the snares are in contact with the head, then you don't need to have them too tight, which will choke the drum. With a really good snare bed you can tune the bottom head unevenly, so it's like a big curve. The tension rods by the snare bed are quite tight and in the middle of the drum they're fairly loose."
>
> SIMON PHILIPS (THE WHO, TOTO)

Alternatively, you could check out Rhythm Tech's Active Snare System. With this the snares are pre-tensioned in a slight bow, thus increasing the pressure of the snares on the centre of the snare head and equalising the pressure overall. Some drummers also try to counteract drooping snare syndrome with their tuning. What they do is add an extra tweak to the two tension bolts on either side of the beds. It's worth a try.

Even with perfect snare beds, everyone suffers from snare buzz sometimes. Often it's set off when you strike one of your tom toms, the result of sympathetic resonance. Your small tom or middle tom may resonate at a similar frequency to your snare drum and if it's close enough it will cause the snare to respond. It's an annoying phenomenon, a bit like your drum kit's very own 'feedback' howl. All you can do is to try to minimise the nuisance. Start by checking that your snares are in good condition. For this you need to take the snares off the drum to examine them.

Since the snares will consist of, perhaps, 20 separate strands of tightly coiled steel wire, it's not unusual to find that some or all of the snares have become distorted. Some coils may be longer or shorter than others causing the whole contraption to twist. The wires have obviously responded to tensioning in different ways over time and some have sprung back and others have lost some of their elasticity. You may well find that when they are on the drum and tensioned they all appear to be even, but the truth is that some will still be slacker than others and this will increase the incidence of snare buzz. You can get some tin snips and remove the most disfigured coils, but this will probably upset the balance of the whole unit and cause further unequal strain. Your best bet is to get a new set of the best quality snares you can find. Just like getting the best heads, it's always a wise investment and will save you many a headache.

While you're changing your snare wires have a think about the type you're using. The average snare is 20 strands of coiled steel. But maybe a twelve strand snare will give you the snare response you want. Many drummers find that just half a dozen strands still gives them a good snare response. Other drummers like lots of coils – Gretsch has long made a 42-strand snare, which surely gives a very snarey response, but can be difficult to control. At the opposite end of the spectrum, some top drummers use gut snares, which produce a very dry sound but almost no buzz whatsoever. Simon Phillips once told me he was using snares specially made from shark fishing cable. No one says you can't experiment. Maybe you'll invent a unique snare drum sound.

Assuming your snares, whatever they may be, are in good shape and they are set up properly so that they are mounted square with the edges of the shell, there are various things you can do to minimise the chances of snare buzz spoiling your fun. However, just when you get things sorted the bass player will plug in and the snare will start resonating in sympathy with the bass. In fact anything can set the snares off, so it's an intractable problem. For this reason it's always advisable to turn your snares off when you're not on stage, and always at the start of a quiet song where the drums aren't playing.

The good news is that because most bands today play loud you simply won't notice snare buzz 99 per cent of the time. But in the studio, when the drums are isolated, it can be a problem.

Happily, the problem can usually be traced to one offending drum, often the small 12″ or 13″ tom next to the snare. You can try various counter-measures in whichever order is least objectionable.

You can fractionally loosen or tighten the snare wires themselves. Or you can loosen or tighten the two tension bolts on either side of the snare at each end. If this doesn't work you can adjust the tuning of the offending tom tom or the snare drum itself. Tune one slightly up and the other slightly down, in order to create a tonal gap. And don't forget that the bottom head of the tom might be causing the problem rather than the top.

If you just have a couple of toms then it shouldn't be hard to tune them both out of the register of your snare drum. If you have a lot of toms, it's more difficult, since they're going to be closer together pitch-wise. However, if all else fails, particularly if you're in the studio, you can always do away with the tom that's causing the trouble. How often are you going to play it anyway? Maybe not at all in the song you're recording. This may sound flippant, but even if you' ve got ten toms, the problem is no more complicated, since only one of them is actually causing you grief. Dump it. No one will ever know.

> "Snare buzz is basically sympathetic vibration created by one particular drum, and you have to get that drum pitch-wise away from where the snare is. It's that, plus the four tension rods on each side of the snare bed. It can upset everything, especially if you have good intervals on the toms. The snare drum is the highest pitch for me and then it goes down – the 10″ tom is below it. But if I'm doing something with a low pitched snare drum I make sure the nearest tom physically is above or below the pitch of the snare drum when you turn the snares off."
>
> *DAVE MATTACKS (PAUL McCARTNEY, XTC, MARY CHAPIN CARPENTER, ETC.)*

CORD OR TAPE?

Snares used to be strung on to their strainer using strong cord or wire. Nowadays, plastic tape is more common. There are pros and cons to each method. Tapes are easier to set up and tend to lie flat without distortion. If you string your snare you will have to adjust it more carefully to get it square, and then make sure you tie a good knot that isn't going to slip. But still some drummers prefer the stringing method, since they maintain that the four-point fixing allows you to fine adjust the snare position more accurately. Whichever method you choose, make sure you always carry spare tape or cord with you. There are plenty of alternatives to the commercially available cords if you find yourself short. Various garden wires or insulated electrical cables work well, while flat parcel tape or any super-strong plastic material can be cut into strips. An old Mylar drumhead is a great source of almost unbreakable snare tape. If the tape is too narrow, though, you run the risk of the snares twisting easily. The broader the tape, the better. And whether you use cord or tape, keep a regular check on them: if they break during the gig it's a nightmare.

CHANGING SNARES

Fitting new snare wires back onto the drum can be quite tricky. I find it's best to take off the old snare and then loosen the tension knob on the strainer right back, with the lever in the 'off' position. If there is a strainer knob on the butt end as well, then set this one at a medium tension. Attach the snare to the butt end and make sure the flat metal plates on each end of the snare are exactly square but slightly nearer to the drum's rim on the butt side. Now attach the snare to the strainer end and pull it up till the slack has been taken out of the tape or string and the snare lies perfectly flat. This is your slackest setting. If you turn the drum the right way up and leave the strainer lever in the 'off' position, the drum should play with no snare response, ie, like a tom tom.

Now apply some tension to the strainer knob and put the lever in the 'on' position. If you play the drum you should now get the snare sound. Hopefully by now the snare has been pulled almost into a central position on the snare head, equidistant from either rim, so that the snares should respond cleanly.

You will probably want to give the tension knob a couple more turns to get a snappy response and the snares should remain pretty central on the bottom head. If at this point you find the snares are still too far towards the butt end (or vice versa, too near the strainer end) then go back, start again and adjust the first position of the snare accordingly. The aim of course is to have the snares lying flat, square and centrally positioned when they are under tension and the drum is sounding the way you want it to. You have to go backwards and forwards a few times to find the optimum method of achieving this, but you'll soon be expert with your own drum.

FULL-LENGTH SNARES

The positioning of the snare can be tricky if the snare is too long. You want to get a response right up to the edges, of course, but a 13″ long snare on a 14″ diameter drum is plenty enough and gives you the leeway to square things up. The desire to maximise snare response has led to so-called full length snares. In these the snare goes right over the edge of the drum and is supported by outrider roller bars of metal or plastic. They would seem like a good idea, but they can sometimes make it harder to get the snares to lie flat. The roller bars have to be exactly level with the snare head or there is no way the snares can be adjusted to lie flat.

INDIVIDUALLY ADJUSTED SNARES

There are some snares that have individual screw adjustment for each coil. These were devised for orchestral players, where the ability to play whisper rolls on the edges of the snare drums with superlatively subtle dynamic control is paramount. Adjusting each individual coil is, as you can imagine, extraordinarily fiddly, and I wish you luck. As with other, earlier, often unnecessarily complicated strainer designs, they are rare these days and I think few drummers miss them.

A Rogers dynasonic snare drum (top) with parallel action snare mechanism. For comparison, a typical standard snare is shown below.

BALANCING THE WHOLE KIT

Let's now look at the kit as a single composite instrument, because as well as tuning each drum individually you also have to get the whole kit, of however many drums, to sound good as an entity. Many drummers start with the bass drum or the lowest tom and tune up from there, making sure that each drum has a recognisably higher pitch than the one before it. To state the obvious, the fewer drums, and the bigger the difference in their sizes, the easier it is to get good, clear pitch intervals. It's a good idea to hum a simple tune or riff as a guide to a nice melodic set of pitches. Try something like the US anthem, 'The Star-Spangled Banner'. Or try the Rod Stewart singalong 'Sailing', which would work nicely with a row of six toms.

Depending on how many toms you have, you can again go for intervals of thirds, fourths or fifths. If you have a large set up with four or more toms it's a good idea to work to a system. Here's one: starting with your largest floor tom, tune the bottom head to its lowest and the batter head a third above that. Now tune the bottom head of the next tom the same as the batter of the largest tom, and so on rising in thirds right through to the batter head of the smallest tom. I believe this is a system used by the brilliant and meticulous British drummer Jon Hiseman.

Although the idea with drums is that they are of non-specific pitch so that they will blend in with any key signature, it is still possible to single out the predominant pitches you're aiming for and tune your drums to a specific key to fit a particular tune. Some drummers like to do this, especially when recording. The great jazz-rock drummer Billy Cobham is one of them.

RECORDED AND PROCESSED SOUNDS

A drum kit in the flesh sounds quite different from anything we are used to hearing on records. Perhaps this is why so many new players cover their drumheads in tape to produce a sort of 'eq'-ed, 'cardboard box' sound. This is what they think a drum kit is meant to sound like, since this is how it appears on the recorded product.

> "I tune to the American roll call – 'Sergeant Bilko'. My bass drum is 22"x18" with no hole because I really like the boom, though I've had a hole in the front for touring – for the engineers."
>
> **FRANK TONTOH (CRAIG DAVID)**

The first thing that any new drummer should realise is that a drum should ring. Yes. It should have a nice long decay – everything in its manufacture is aimed towards producing a resonant, lively sound that will project a mile. Also, realise that most top drummers today try to tune their drums to achieve maximum resonance. The reason the drums don't seem to have a huge long decay on records is because most of that ringing after-sound and overtones are obscured by the sounds and noises made by the other instruments on the recording. If you went into the studio and isolated just the drum track you would find that it had a massive ambience. If you took that away the recording would sound lifeless and dull, mechanical and dry. Which is, of course, how many early machine tracks sounded. It is also the reason why, after the initial fascination with machines in the 1980s, popular music soon started to recruit real drummers on acoustic kits overdubbing the machines. Or started to use sampled break beats, liberated from 1960s funk records and the like.

The difficulty for all drummers is judging just how much of the ring from a good drum is acceptable in any given situation. For most live acoustic purposes, you want as much ring as you can get. That is, you need to tune the drums as open as possible and use as little damping as possible: probably none at all, particularly on the toms. If you're going to be close-miked, then you may need to apply a little bit of top-head damping. But probably not as much as your first inclination. The thing to remember is that there is good ring and bad ring. When the ringing is discordant and your tuning rods are all over the place, sticking a

> "The way I approach tuning is I'm always looking for as much sustain as possible. For me, one drum ringing more is not a problem – the problem is making the others ring that much. And not just ring – 'cos there's good and bad ring – but sustain."
>
> **DAVE MATTACKS**

mike next to the head is going to amplify that and embarrass the hell out of you. Which is why it's so easy just to dampen the heads. Make sure your ring is a good ring. It's very easy to use damping to cover up poor tuning.

Don't be frightened to spend a few minutes re-tuning. Don't be bullied by the other musicians or PA crew telling you to shut up. Be careful not to 'noodle' on the drums while they are tuning, but ask them to respect you also and allow you time to tune your instrument for the room or stage.

DAMPING TECHNIQUES

I believe the whole business of heavy damping came about because of the advent of close miking of drums during the 1970s. Before that drummers rarely damped their drums much – other than the bass drum – and once the initial miking-up 'panic' phase was over (a period of a decade or so) we went back to using as little damping as possible. If you think about it, it's obvious. What is the point of finely crafting a wooden resonating instrument, only to muffle out the resonance when you come to play it? And yet I'm constantly amazed when I go round schools or colleges to find how many young drummers (and inexperienced engineers, teachers and other musicians) stick all sorts of disgusting bits of tape and cloth on the heads and make a right mess of the drums. Usually the problem is compounded by the fact that there's no one around who can tune the kit properly, and the heads have been bashed senseless and shapeless.

Some light batter head damping: a loop of sticky tape and a strip of Moon Gel.

The important thing is to get the drums tuned and balanced well first. Only then, if it's necessary, apply a little damping – and as little as possible. If you position the damping in the right place you can get away with the minimum. To understand this, it helps to know a little bit about how the head actually resonates. A good head, well tuned, will be responsive right up to the edge of the drum. This is important if you want to play very soft press rolls, for instance, the sort of thing a jazz or an orchestral percussionist might regularly do.

However, the head is generally at its most responsive a few inches away from the edge. This is because heads have a complicated pattern of what acousticians call nodal vibrations, and the most responsive areas (or anti-nodes) are here. Around two or three inches in from the edge of a standard 14″ snare, say, you'll find it's at its liveliest with its longest decay. This is the area where most drummers play a press roll, since the head here has its greatest sustain and is at its most responsive. So if you want to dampen a drum this is the place to do it most effectively.

For most drummers, however, this is a bit too far in from the edge to be practical. And in any case, you don't want to deaden the drum completely, just take out a few overtones. Top head damping is therefore usually placed nearer the edge, or even right at the edge.

You may have noticed that the centre of the head has a very satisfying, quite dead, but loud and attacking spot. This is due to a combination of nodes and anti-nodes criss-crossing the centre. So striking the centre gives a strong, loud fundamental tone, but few higher overtones. In other words it's fat and slightly damped with good attack. So whacking dead centre is a great place for fat-back back-beats. If you want a more funky, high-pitched crack, then you make sure your stick tip strikes three or four inches in from the edge.

Combine that with a rim shot for maximum effect. Heads like Remo's CS black dot batters have an extra circle of Mylar glued below their centre point. This strengthens the head where it's at its weakest but only dampens out a small part of the overtones, particularly the fundamental, the lowest pitch. This is why these heads are strong and just a little damped, and yet remain quite high pitched and bright.

Until the 1970s, drums routinely came fitted with internal, mechanical screw-up felt damper pads. The problem was that the pad would cause a hump in the head, distorting the tuning at that spot and impeding the downward movement of the head when struck. They also had a tendency to work loose and rattle. Having said that, the venerable Ian Paice (Deep Purple) specified an old fashioned internal muffler on his Pearl Signature snare drum just a couple of years back. So screw-up dampers still have at least one fan.

Screw-down damper pads that attach to the outside of the drum are perhaps a better idea. With these the pad clips on to the rim, is screwed down towards the head and can be adjusted to make the lightest of contacts. Large circular dampers of this type were commonly employed on bass drums, from the 1920s through to the 1950s when felt strips became widespread.

A variation on the internal damper idea is the Remo Muff'l system. Muff'ls consist of thin plastic circular trays that sit on the bearing edge of the drum and include a removable perimeter ring of foam. They work well on bass drum batters but are usually too severe for toms and snare drums.

Muff'ls are great, though, for damping down a kit for quiet practice. The drawback is you have to completely remove the heads to insert and remove them.

The most widespread approach to damping these days is to place some material on top of the batter head. A popular trick is to take a strip of duct tape or an inch wide strip of gaffer tape, maybe three or four inches long, and form it into a little hump-backed bridge, or a series of small ripples, stuck on top of the head. Alternatively, loop the tape into a circle with the sticky outside and just plonk it down near the edge of the drum. This is a light form of damping which is very effective. It's easy to adjust the length of tape or size of loop and to move it about on the head until you achieve the right effect.

Materials that stick to the head have the advantage that you can apply them to the bottom, resonant head as easily as to the batter head, although fewer drummers do this. Drums are usually miked from above and it's the overtones from the top head that the mikes (and the drummer) mostly hear.

For a more severe version of tape damping, drummers sometimes take a strip of tape and simply strap it flat over the head, usually across the far side and stretching over the top rim, thus damping the rim too. Drummers have even been known to tape right across the drum, just off centre, though this is considered sacrilegious in the modern climate. It's also very messy when you try to get the tape off a few days/weeks/years later.

> "I do sometimes use tape but it tends to be less. It's like finding a squeak and pouring a bucket of oil over it. Sometimes all it needs is a tiny piece rolled into a circle. These days I'm using Moon Gel but I tend to cut it into half or quarters – one piece right out on the edge will do it."
>
> *DAVE MATTACKS*

Much more satisfactory are ideas that don't involve sticky residues. The most popular of these are perimeter rings of plastic head material and a clever product called Moon Gel. Moon Gel is a rubbery gel which comes in a tub of reusable oblong pads just an inch or so long. You simply lay one or two of the gel pads on your batter head where they stay put until you peel them off. They're easy to move around and surprisingly effective. They can also be used on cymbals and other percussion instruments.

Perimeter plastic rings can be bought singly or in packs and include Noble and Cooley's 'Zero Rings', Evans 'E' Rings and Remo's 'RemOs'. They work a bit like an electronic 'gate' since when the head is struck the shock wave lifts the ring off a fraction, after which it comes back down to rest and has its damping effect. You can of course make your own 'O' rings, by taking an old, lightweight head (or a new one if you're flush) and cutting concentric one-inch rings out of it to make up a decreasing-diameter set for all your toms and snare. It's very often sufficient to use a section – maybe a third or a quarter – of a ring, in which case you will need to stick the ring down with a bit of tape at each end so it doesn't fly off.

There are various head designs with in-built perimeter damping rings. These are particularly effective for bass drumheads and were first introduced by Evans with its EQ System series, which has a double layer of Mylar all around the edge. The other companies have followed suit, so we have Remo's Powerstroke 3, Aquarian's Super Kick and Pearl's budget ProTone EQ amongst others. Remo's Pinstripes also have a bonded perimeter edge, but remember these are in any case double ply heads, which already have a more damped sound. Aquarian offers Impact and Super Kick bass drumheads with inbuilt felt damping rings, while its Regulator front heads have a 10.5″ felt muffling ring in the centre.

Evans has gone on to develop its EMAD (externally mounted adjustable damping) system with removable damping rings. EMAD was also first used on its bass drumheads, and the concept adapted to snare drum and toms as the Min-EMAD. This takes the form of a small fabric pad that attaches to the top rim and extends across the edge of the head to varying distances, thereby changing the degree of damping.

DAMPING SNARE DRUMS

Although snare drum notes tend to be shorter than tom tom notes, that doesn't mean you want the snare drum to be dead. Snare drums ring, particularly metal ones. It's true this can be disconcerting if every time you whack a rim shot it's like Big Ben chiming. If you dampen the batter head right down you'll lose a lot of projection and once the whole band is thrashing away you'll have to play twice as hard to be heard. Many drummers just throw on an '0' ring type perimeter damper, but this may be overdoing it.

Try just a third or a quarter of one again, lightly taped in place. That's probably enough to neutralise the offending clang while still leaving the snare drum lively. The problem in any case is often not so much the ring itself as the pitch. Metal drums, like heavy ride cymbals, can deliver a bell-like note that clashes with the tuning of the band.

So try adjusting your tuning a bit before damping all the spark out of your drum. Always remember that the sound of John Bonham's snare drum– which is as good it gets in rock – is a totally undamped 6.5″ deep Ludwig 'Ludalloy' shell Supraphonic 402. He mostly used a Remo twin ply Emperor or CS black dot batter: in other words, a hard-wearing batter that had a touch of in-built damping.

DAMPING BASS DRUMS

Back in the 1970s and 1980s, when bass drums either had no front heads, or front heads with large holes cut out of them, they were also stuffed with serious amounts of damping material. This consisted of pillows or blankets, etc, pushed up against the bottom of the batter head and weighed down with a cast-iron stage weight.

The drum itself provided little resonance, which is a pity when you consider this was the most expensive instrument in your set. But the resulting sound consisted of a satisfyingly dry thud, prefaced by a cracking impact that was a dream to mike up. Another variation, and even more destructive of the bass drum's resonance, was to line the entire inside of the shell with an inch or two thickness of foam. No chance of the highly crafted birch shell exerting its subtle timbre through that lot.

Over the past decade, the fashion has steadily moved towards the reinstatement of the front head, first with a smaller port hole and eventually with no cutaway at all. The result is that you now have a drum with much more resonance that requires rather more careful tuning. It also needs more subtle and considered damping. And finally it requires more careful playing. The more resonant the batter head the more you have to bounce the beater off the head rather than simply burying it like in the old days. This surely has to be a good thing. Imagine if every time you hit your snare drum you 'buried' the stick in the head…

Some drummers have gone back to 1960s practice, in which damping of the bass drum took the form of slipping a two-inch wide felt strip under the rim of the head and securing it by placing the wooden hoop over it and tightening down the tension rods. This is an effective method, and the degree of damping can be altered positioning the felt strip. If it is closer to the edge, the strip will be shorter and as it approaches the centre of the drum it elongates. Many drummers have a vertical felt strip a few inches in from the edge of the batter head and a horizontal strip towards the bottom of the front head.

With today's livelier bass drum sounds, a felt strip, or the modern equivalent – something like Evans' adjustable EMAD system – is often all you need. Older swing band drummers have told me that it was also common to put shredded newspapers inside the drum – a cheap and flexible solution. Shredded foam is a more modern version. However, when a bit more damping is required, it's still usual to put a rolled up or folded towel, a pillow, or even a blanket inside the bass drum. There are commercially available pillows that are just the right size to touch the front and back heads.

TUNING FOR THE ROOM

What sounds good to you behind the kit may not sound so good to your audience. You're hearing the sound of the batter heads, but the resonant bottom heads actually have a big say in the overall sound. This is one reason why it's important not to neglect your bottom heads when adjusting your tuning. The problem is much more noticeable from out front, so you need to get someone else to play your kit while you go out there and have a careful listen.

Get them to play one drum at a time, slowly, to see if you like what you hear. Basically, the pitch of a drum drops very quickly over distance. So drums that sound sharp and clear to you behind the kit can sound muddy and dull to your listeners. You may therefore have to tune the drums higher than your natural inclination. Jeff Ocheltree, the Californian drum maker who was a drum tech for Led Zeppelin's John Bonham in the 1970s, tells me that Bonzo had his bottom heads tighter than his top heads, and all his heads a lot tighter than people imagine. This seems to illustrate the point that if you use large drums (Bonzo had 14″ or 15″ mounted and 18″ or 20″ floor toms) you can tune them high for good stick response and still get a huge, deep and resonant sound.

Your bass drum sits on the floor facing away from you. So again, the sound from behind is unlikely to be exactly that which is projected. Many drummers, when sitting at the kit, feel there is not enough bottom end to their bass drum and are pleasantly surprised, when they go out front, to find it's deeper than they imagined. So in this instance the perceived drop in pitch over distance is welcome.

LIVE AND STUDIO

The drummer is the foundation of any band and this fact is acknowledged when you do a sound check or go into a studio. You will invariably be the one who is scrutinised first. You will be asked to play just your bass drum in isolation, then your snare drum, then your hi-hat and finally your toms, cymbals and all of the kit together.

If you're worried or embarrassed by the possibility of snare buzz, when it comes to playing your toms individually, turn your snares off. Then when they ask you to play the whole kit turn the snares back on and go round the kit slowly and clearly: any buzzing will hardly be noticed. They might not be hearing it at all and it's probable that nothing more will be said. Listening to any instrument in isolation is deceptive, and since the drums are usually the first there is a lot of pressure. Everyone's anxious to get on and drums can take a lot of time. So I want to reiterate at this point that you should never feel bad about having difficulties with your sound and tuning. It happens to the greatest drummers.

Unfortunately, bad experiences early on can mean it takes you years to feel confident about your sound. It's a fact that those bad experiences often happen during your early encounters with amateur PA or studio engineers. Because of their lack of experience and confidence they can easily unload their feelings of fear and inadequacy onto you. They will often question your tuning and ask you to dampen drums when you really don't want to.

It's also true that cheap studios with sectioned off drum booths are the worst places to try to get a decent sound. Your lovely kit, that sounded massive on the previous night's gig, now sounds lame and dreary in this artificial enclosure. Hardly surprising – the booth is designed to be acoustically dead. When one day you finally roll into a big studio with a great live room, hard wooden floors and stone walls, your kit sounds like the 1812 Overture. Usually by then the engineer is also cool and will happily work alongside you, offering useful tips to make your drums sound even better.

In the meantime don't be intimidated by the sneering of other musicians and engineers, and snide remarks about idiot drummers not knowing how to tune their instruments. But, equally, you must take your responsibility seriously. You have to do all you can to make your drums sound good, to get to know your equipment, its capabilities and limitations inside out. Practise tuning. Most top players and producers will tell you that the sound source has to be good: you can't make a silk purse out of a sow's ear. If the kit sounds good 'on the floor', it will sound good when miked up. (You hope.)

Top UK session drummer Dave Mattacks once explained to me there is little point in tuning the kit the day before a recording session, because you will always have to re-tune for the room. Damn. However, there is no reason why you shouldn't put new heads on and play them in a little the day before. Make sure they're seated properly and evenly tensioned. I was never a top studio player like Dave, but I have recorded in dozens of studios, including most of the major places in London, and one thing I have lately found to work well is to use a bit of positive psychology. You and the engineer will probably be the first to arrive, so this gives you the chance to make contact, get his/her name right and generally be friendly and co-operative. Set your kit up and as soon as you start to tap around the drums, come out with something like, "Wow, what a great sound – what a great sounding room." All the while your heart is sinking as you realise the room is awful, and your drums sound like a bunch of Tupperware containers. But by being bullish, the effect is to disarm the engineer, and it's amazing how a positive vibe can carry the day. Wars have been won with positive thinking.

> "I went into my first pro studio and I said to the engineer can you make me sound like [British jazz drummer] Kenny Clare? He said, 'If you play like him, I will.' I thought, 'Don't you just twiddle a knob?'"
> **DAVE MATTACKS**

At the very least this ploy will buy you a little time to start working out what you're going to do to make your kit sound half decent in this unhelpful environment. Seriously, if you start off with a long face, the engineer will be nervous and looking to pick holes. Go in with a smile and nine times out of ten, between the two of you, you'll be getting a good, workable sound before the rest of the band arrive. The start of any recording session is the most highly charged situation and anything you can do to get through, carrying everyone with you, will help you perform well. Most of the top session drummers I know are great characters, as well as great drummers. (But just make sure your kit's in perfect working order.)

LOSING YOUR HEADS

When the idea of screwing down drumheads was perfected in the 1930s, no one realised just how hard drummers would get to play after the rock revolution. In other words the sheer power used in walloping the batter heads – particularly the snare batter head when you use rim shots as well – causes the tension bolts to detune and eventually fall out.

I'm a big Ludwig 400 fan, and I used to regularly get half way through the gig and find a couple of bottom head screws lying on the floor. Meanwhile, between every song, I was frantically screwing up the top bolts next to where I made rim shots. And I'm by no means a hard hitter, compared with today's nutters. Many of today's drums now have lug bolts that are designed to overcome this problem. The drag is that you lose the ability when tuning to start the lugs off by screwing up to finger tight. They are just too stiff. You have to use a drum key almost immediately, and thereafter you lose the feeling of direct feedback, making the tuning process harder to gauge. This is a pity, but I can see the advantage.

If you do encounter problems with lugs working loose, there are several mechanical solutions. First of all, it's usual for there to be washers between the bolt and the rim to cushion the impact. Sometimes, however, taking the washers away improves matters. A better alternative, though, is to leave the washers in place and tie a bit of fine thread– cotton or dental floss– around the bolt thread. This can provide just enough friction to keep the bolt in place. Or, you can try a commercial solution such as Lug Locks. These are small nylon grippers that slip over the head of each bolt and press against the rim, preventing the bolt from turning once you have the drum tuned. There are also engineering products like Loctite, which are specifically designed to prevent screws coming loose through vibration. Just make sure you get the non-permanent formulation, or your bolts will be glued in forever.

CONCLUSION

I've devoted a lot of space to the ups and downs of tuning. But as I said at the beginning, this is the one subject that baffles and worries drummers the most. Great technique? Easy – you practice your butt off. Good cymbals and good drums? Easy – you spend more money. But tuning? It's a mystery, almost an art in itself.

Even when some saviour has come along with a brilliant idea to make the whole process simpler – I'm thinking of Arbiter's Advanced Tuning (AT) drums, which have a single tuning bolt, and Remo's Pre-Tuned (PTS) heads – drummers have largely elected to stick with the difficult traditional route. Ivor Arbiter is convinced the ancient method of tuning using dozens of individual lugs is madness. He's right of course, but drummers mostly seem to want that extra freedom so they can tune their drums 'wrong' if they so wish.

Although everyone agrees that the basic idea with tuning is to get the head to an even pitch all round, there are many drummers who do that and then tune one bolt down slightly, to take the 'edge' off, as it were. And the great British big-band and session drummer Kenny Clare is famous for his method of tuning his snare drum to a 'gradient', with the far side higher than the near side. Listen to any of Kenny's recordings and you'll hear a really fat sound, way before its time.

And that brings me to my final point. So long as tuning is a 'feel' thing there will always be an awful lot of 'cod' science going around. I hope I haven't added to all that. Don't take anything I've said as gospel. I also hope I haven't given the impression that tuning is always a struggle. Most often you just play the drums and they sound fine.

I love to hear a beautifully tuned set of drums. For example, Dave Weckl's drums always sound perfect to me, both on record and live. I've got nothing but respect for a guy who is so on top of his craft that he can achieve a consistent sound like that. But I also love drums when they sound decidedly 'iffy'. After all, just how much hi-tech science and manufacturing accuracy went into the making and tuning of all those African tribal drums? And yet think how exhilarating and magnificent they sound. And as someone who grew up listening to early Jamaican reggae drummers, whose feel and ideas are sublime, playing what I imagine were some of the tattiest drum kits with some of the most beat-up heads known to man… Well, I rest my case.

ON THE ROAD

Drummers have more bits to keep track of than anyone. Drum kits break down into hundreds of components– all crying out to be lost or broken. So how do you make sure you've got everything to do the job: what shouldn't you leave home without, what might you need during the gig, and what should you do to make sure you arrive home with nothing missing?

It's essential to have some routine, or sooner or later you'll face disaster. Turning up with a magnificent kit and no cymbals is not funny. Arriving without a snare drum stand (OK, I confess that happened to me just two years ago) presents an interesting problem which no one else fully appreciates. Playing a heavy gig with a snare drum on a chair is really not an option.

Start by counting the number of cases you carry. For instance, your regular kit might involve seven cases: two for stands, three toms, one snare, one cymbal, and one bass drum. You throw them in the car/truck and simply count them before driving home. Such is your state of mind at 2am following a phenomenal gig you can easily forget a small case. Now, hands up those who feel a slight unease at this point? You're right; I said seven cases and then listed eight. That's how easy it is to mislay one.

JUST SAY NO

Next, a word about people helping you in and out with gear. This is welcome, of course, but they invariably put your cases down in the middle of the stage exactly where you intend to set up. So now you have to move them all before you can get started. Ask them to leave everything at the side or out front of the stage.

Friends and fans helping you after the gig can be worse: even catastrophic. Let them loose on your stands and they will take everything completely apart. Turn your back and they'll be easing the springs off your kick pedal and sorting your memory locks into a neat pile. They may also have had one drink too many, and will seize the opportunity to roll your toms down the fire escape. Whoops, sorry.

Worse, they will leave your cymbal bag outside the back door by the truck – without telling you. Your cymbals will, of course, be stolen. When loading out, never leave anything unattended for a second. If it's a regular venue the local outlaws will be skulking in the darkness looking for just such easy pickings. You might do better to say no to any offers of help and buy yourself a small collapsible trolley, so you can cart your own gear in and out quickly with least effort. And use two hardware cases instead of one if you insist on carrying heavy double-braced stands. It makes sense to distribute the weight evenly.

While on the unsavoury topic of thieving, dressing rooms are notorious. Most small gigs still don't provide lockable rooms. So be careful what you leave around. Never leave wallets, car keys, phones or anything else of valuable in unlocked dressing rooms. Take them on stage. Slip your wallet and keys in your stick bag, perhaps, while you're playing. (Just don't forget that's where you've put them afterwards.)

Finally, take a roadie's tip and always do an 'idiot check' before leaving any dressing room, stage or hotel room. That is, once everyone's out, send a reliable person back to check every nook and cranny. However, that doesn't ensure everything's in the vehicle, which is where an item-count puts your mind at ease. Learn from PA company and road crew practice again and carry a complete inventory list. Gear left behind won't be seen again.

Keep that inventory taped inside the lid of the last case you close. Now I'm sure you have your own 'never leave home without' list, but a basic list might include the following. Aside from the obvious– your drums and cymbals– there are the cases with all the hardware, your stick bag and that essential square of carpet.

> "If you're touring quite heavily you have to be physically fit. It's not just the gigs, it's the late nights and travelling. I'm a runner – four miles a day – and I've got a super-fit lady trainer who's a tri-athlete."
>
> *DERRICK MCKENZIE (JAMIROQUAI)*

Keep a spare head in every drum case and a snare and batter head in your snare case. A spare snare drum is an even better idea, particularly if you're a hard player. Include maybe some damping O-rings or a tub of Moon Gel or the charmingly named Gorilla Snot for quick damping of your batter heads.

Next comes that most vital bit of gear: your drum key(s). You can't have enough of them. I conceal drum keys everywhere– in cymbal bag pockets, in stands cases, in every stick bag, in every gig bag. I always have a roll of gaffer tape on the floor by my feet at the kit, and in the centre of the roll … a drum key. You never know when you might need to give your snare a quick tweak between tunes.

Drum keys are easily mislaid. Evans makes a magnetised key, which is a great idea. You can leave it on one of your floor tom tension bolts and it won't rattle or get shaken off. Or you can stick a bit of Velcro on a key and on your bass drum hoop and marry the two together. Some old Gretsch snare drums had a special cavity that held the drum key. Tama has revived the idea so you can slip your key into its tom holder and Yamaha has something similar: a stand mount clip holder. Hardwear Inc makes wearable drum key jewellery in six hand-carved gothic antique finish designs that you put on a cord around your neck. Nice.

SPARES AND REPAIRS

Smart drummers carry a small box of tools and spare parts. Spares might include cymbal felts and sleeves, washers and wing nuts, spare bass drum spring and hi-hat clutch, snare tie cords and/or tapes, spare snare, tension bolts in the correct lengths for each drum and Lug Lube for lubricating tension bolts. You can buy various packs, such as Zildjian's Survival Kit, which the drum and cymbal manufacturers supply and which contain the most vital spares. Then for tools there are screwdrivers – flat and Phillips – pliers, tweezers, Allen keys. Even a hammer might come in useful. Roadies invariably carry a 'Leatherman', a professional quality multi-tool: like a glorified Swiss Army knife and guaranteed for life. It's got pliers, files, saws and so on, most tools you will ever need all in a single unit. It's a good idea also to keep some light machine oil and/or grease for squeak-free drumming. And, of course, gaffer tape. It has a hundred uses. Just don't let anyone 'borrow' your roll.

> **"I was listening to the ringing in my ears this morning, maybe I should wear ear plugs; I've got the monitor system of doom!"**
>
> *MATT SORUM (GUNS'N'ROSES, THE CULT)*

Every drummer builds up a collection of spare parts and tools like this, and maybe just throws them in the bottom of the stands case. This is OK, but it's better if you keep everything in a small tool or accessories box, even a hobby case with separate small compartments. It's no good having spare snare cord in the bottom of your stands case if it's piled up with all your other cases somewhere round the back of the kitchens while you're on stage struggling with a broken snare drum. Get a small case you can place by your floor tom when you're on stage. And don't forget to pick it up after your performance.

Other items you may need from a musical perspective include paper, pencils, pens – including large felt tips – ready for set lists and notes. If you ever have to go on stage with parts or notes, be wary of using coloured pens and markers. I once highlighted all the tricky bits with a red marker pen so I couldn't possibly miss them. Then I went on stage, the red lights came up and everything promptly disappeared. Other items a lot of drummers carry these days include counting in and tempo aids, such as Tama's Rhythm Watch. For any small electronic device like this, make sure you have spare batteries.

COMFORT

Now let's move on to your comfort and health. Many drummers who tour extensively like to create their own familiar space. The Rolling Stones' Charlie Watts has a coat hanger on his kit for his immaculate jacket. When you've spent as much of your life on stage as Charlie – much of it in pretty crazy circumstances – you want to make yourself at home and comfortable. Many drummers like to customise their kits with personal touches. Things like drinks holders or towel rails. I've even heard of mobile/cellphone holders – strictly for use during rehearsals, of course.

It gets very hot under stage lighting, so carry your own portable fan with an extension lead.

You'll still sweat buckets and it's easy to get dehydrated, so always have plenty of drinking water to hand. Make sure it's somewhere you can't knock it over. Attach a bicycle-style drinks holder to a convenient stand, perhaps. One thing you don't want is bottles of beer around your foot-pedals. You're sure to kick them over, and something you can really do without is sticky gunge all over your pedals. Sitting with a towel over your seat is not a bad idea. Sweaty underwear leads to piles (what a delightful image), sweaty vests to chills, backache and worse. When you come off stage– like an athlete– you need warm clothing. Changing into a dry vest is heaven. But then you need a fleece or something else cosy so you don't get a chill and a sore throat and the first stirrings of Spinal Tap style 'touring lip' (mouth and lip ulcers).

You should also get proper ear protection for all but the softest of gigs. Cotton wool is no use. Nor are cigarette butts (seriously, a female drummer once told me that's what she used). There is a whole range of far more hygienic earplugs widely available. Your drum store will carry various types and happily advise you. Trust me, these days no one's laughing. It's no longer considered weedy for drummers to use hearing protection. Playing levels are now insane and virtually every top player out there uses some sort of plugs.

Don't forget, an awful lot of top acts now use in-ear monitoring, which includes protection. You may want to carry two or three different types of earplug for different situations. For practising on your own you can just use simple foam swimmers' earplugs – which are really effective and very cheap – or fully enclosed headphones.

For rehearsing and gigging you will probably want something that doesn't attenuate all the high frequencies leaving you with a distorted picture of the music. This will mean investing in a custom, personally moulded pair that have even attenuation across all frequencies so that the effect is just like turning down the volume knob. They are quite expensive, but no more so than a good pair of prescription spectacles or absurdly priced designer shades. Don't think twice about it if you're going to be playing regularly anything above moderately loud. Cheaper alternatives such as Doc's Pro Plugs and Etymotic Research's Hi-Fi plugs are still pretty good and very affordable.

PERSONAL SURVIVAL KIT

Still on the subject of your health, it's worth carrying a small first-aid kit. I once had the spring on a bass drum pedal fly off and bury itself in the end of my thumb while I was setting up. Blood everywhere. Not wishing to sound like a complete wimp, there are a couple of extra items I'd add to the first-aid box. Bear with me. The first is lip-salve, especially if you have a tendency to go to sleep in the back of the bus on long journeys. Dribbling is a drummer's complaint, obviously.

The second is travel sickness pills. Unlike idyllic summer holiday trips, traveling with a band often takes place in the worst winter weather. Apart from when you're in the back of the bus and feeling the worse for a heavy night, this can mean bad ferry trips and bumpy flights. I can remember suddenly feeling the urge to barf on take-off just a few thousand feet after leaving Edinburgh for London, one dreadful December morning with the gales blowing off the Firth of Forth. I always carried travel sickness pills after that.

Last but not least, always carry towels, soap and toilet paper. And for any small-time gigging that involves journeying out of town and the prospect of a bleak afternoon's sound check and four hours of hanging about at some remote, deserted club, a flask of coffee is a lifesaver. I reckon a proper knife, fork and spoon are not a bad idea also in these days of plastic cutlery. If it's a one-off gig in a strange place, ask the venue to send you a map or at least directions. Alternatively, it's possible to print off a map of almost anywhere in the world now from the Internet. And, so that you can read that map, a Maglite torch is a useful item to keep in any vehicle and on stage. It will also prove useful when you drop your keys in some dark alleyway behind a particularly seedy gig.

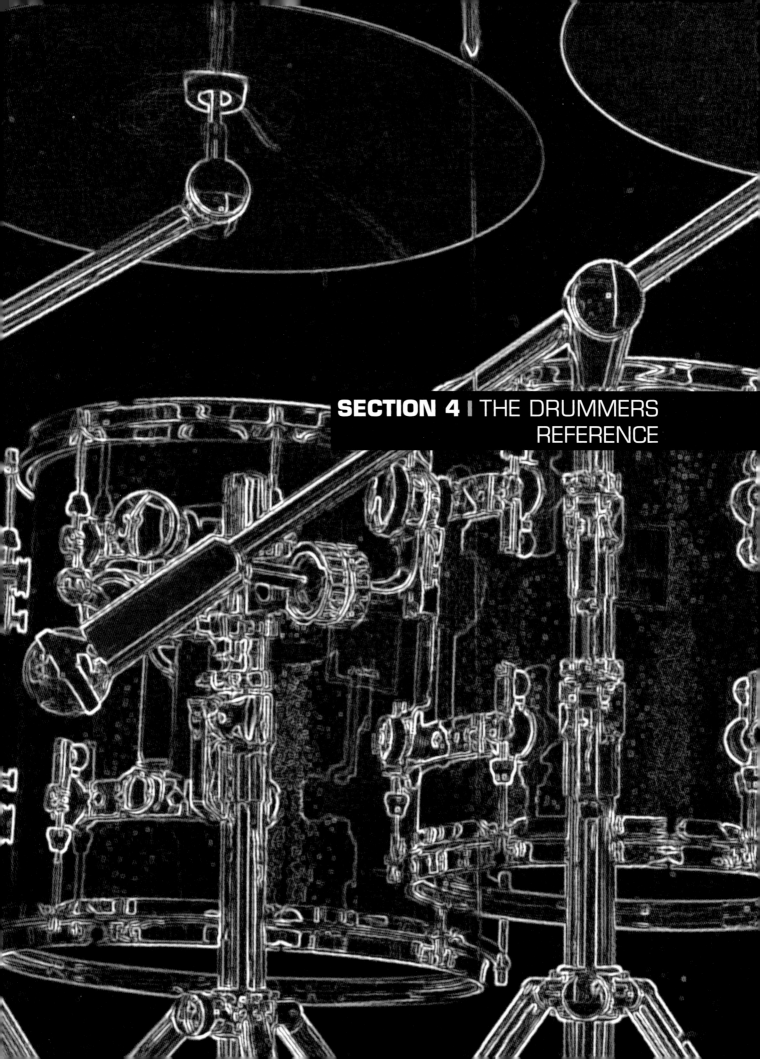

SECTION 4 I THE DRUMMERS
REFERENCE

INSTRUCTIONAL BOOKS AND VIDEOS

> "The best teacher I ever had was the record player, listening to how they get a sound. I had to guess at it. There were no videos – and there's something nice about that, 'cos whatever you do it's always going to be your version."
>
> *GARY HUSBAND (ALAN HOLDSWORTH, LEVEL 42)*

There is a vast amount of instructional material available to drummers today. The books and videos/DVDs recommended below are just those I've had the chance to check out over the years. I'm very aware that there are other terrific works I've simply not got round to, and to the authors of these I apologise. And to the reader, please accept this is a partial list to whet your appetite.

Just as the technique of today's top players is breathtaking, so the written and visual material now available is often staggering in its comprehensiveness and depth. A single book like Ed Uribe's encyclopaedic treatise on Afro-Cuban rhythms could occupy you for a lifetime. We've swiftly graduated from crying out for hip information to a modern era in which it's all too easy to be overwhelmed.

No one can possibly get to grips with every aspect of modern drumset playing. Despite the public's blissful ignorance, the drum kit is probably the fastest evolving instrument on the planet. Your best bet is to grab a couple of timeless classics, add no more than a sprinkling of modern books and videos covering your preferred styles, and stick with them. It's too easy to get distracted and flit around aimlessly, mouth open in awe.

It's wonderful that we can now see all our heroes close-up on video. But don't overlook material from the less glamorous teachers. They often have a better thought out methodology and a more feasible approach: that's their job. For example, probably the most informative clinic I ever attended was by the top educator Gary Chaffee, with barely 30 people in the room. For my money, his unassuming video is one of the best you can buy.

RECOMMENDED BOOKS

FOR BEGINNERS

Ironically, I find this the most difficult category. There are hundreds of books, and most drummers tend to use those that have been recommended by their teachers. Here are just a few examples of what's out there:

Drumset Essentials Volume 1, by Peter Erskine (Alfred Publishing). Classic/traditional style course from one of today's great players. Intelligent, well thought-out and challenging.
Graded Course For Drum Kit, by Dave Hassell (self-published). Excellent, proven material from one of Britain's most respected teachers.
Essential Styles for the Drummer and Bassist, Vol. 1, by Steve Houghton (Alfred Publishing).
The Drumset Crash Course, by Russ Miller (Warner Brothers Publications).
Ultimate Playalong For Drums, Vol. 1 Book 1, by Dave Weckl (Warner Brothers Publications).

> "I bought the Dave Weckl video (*Back to Basics*) and studied that for a while – holding the sticks and getting the kit positioned right so there's not too much effort."
>
> *DERRICK MCKENZIE (JAMIROQUAI)*

CLASSICS

Time-tested classics, essential for every serious student to check out.

Stick Control for the Snare Drummer and *Accents and Rebounds for the Snare Drummer*, by George Lawrence Stone (G B Stone and Son). These two books are the drummer's equivalent of those timeless classical music scales books. With a bit of lateral thinking they can also infuse every aspect of your kit drumming.

Advanced Techniques for the Modern Drummer, by Jim Chapin (Warner Bros Publications). Chapin is an amazing octogenarian who travels the world preaching the undeniable wisdom of his teacher, Sanford Moeller. This book really put the cat amongst the bebop pigeons on its first publication in 1946. It defines the basic approach to four-way jazz coordination.

Progressive Steps to Syncopation, by Ted Reed (Alfred Publishing). Another amazingly versatile classic.

Buddy Rich's Modern Interpretation of Snare Drum Rudiments (Music Sales). Written with Rich by his friend Henry Adler. A glimpse of the techniques used by the Mozart of the drum kit.

MODERN CLASSICS

The New Breed, and *The New Breed II*, by Gary Chester (Modern Drummer Publications). Unique approach from Chester, a session giant of the 1960s. A remarkable book that inspired the likes of Dave Weckl and even changed the drumset layout during the 1980s.

Patterns (a four book series), by Gary Chaffee (Warner Bros Publications). The Berklee College of Music professor has taught many of today's great players. Secrets of the 'linear' approach to playing, polyrhythms, four-way coordination and more.

Advanced Funk Studies, by Rick Latham (Carl Fischer/Hudson Music). The first book to reveal the cool beats of the post-Gadd generation. Thoughtfully graded, ending with ten solos of varying difficulty. Great fun.

Drum Wisdom, by Bob Moses (Modern Drummer Publications). Something completely different. A unique ideas and concepts book.

TECHNIQUE AND STROKES

Master Studies, by Joe Morello (Modern Drummer Publications). Loads of tricky stickings from the genius of the Dave Brubeck Quartet– the man with the silkiest pair of hands ever.

The Drummer's Complete Vocabulary, as taught by Alan Dawson, by John Ramsey (Warner Bros Publications). Pupil's respectful recreation of the teaching method of the great drummer and educator, Alan Dawson.

It's Your Move: Motions and Emotions, by Dom Famularo (Warner Bros Publications). Includes full exposition of the Moeller technique from the drum world's most enthusiastic educator (who is also a phenomenal technician).

READING NOTATION

Modern Reading Text in 4/4, by Louie Bellson and Gil Breines (Warner Bros Publications). Duke Ellington's legendary musician drummer shows you how.

Get Your Fills Together, by Sonny Igoe. Supremely logical treatise on every computation of big-band fills and set-ups. Whoever's got my copy, can I have it back?

FOR THE MATHEMATICALLY INCLINED

Rhythmic Illusions and *Rhythmic Perspectives*, by Gavin Harrison (Warner Publications). Exactly as the titles imply. Two to blow your mind. Mind-boggling exercises in beat displacement and rhythmic illusions. Destined to become modern classics.

Extreme Interdependence: Drumming Beyond Independence, by Marco Minneman (Warner Bros Publications). Frightening feats of physical and mental endurance but probably not for the faint hearted.

JAZZ

The Art of Bop Drumming and *Beyond Bebop Drumming*, by John Riley (Manhattan Music Publications). Beautifully thought out, challenging, non-patronising and always musical. Destined to become modern classics.

ROCK

The Updated Realistic Rock Drum Method, by Carmine Appice (Warner Bros Publications). Classic work by the progenitor of heavy rock and pioneer of rock education.

Monster Book Of Rock Drumming, by Joel Rothman (published by the author). Rothman has written more books than anyone else on every aspect of drumming you (or he) can think of. They follow a no-nonsense formula and many are well worth a look.

FUNK

Future Sounds and *The Funky Beat*, by David Garibaldi (Manhattan Publications). Tower Of Power's truly gifted and innovative star expounds his roots.

The Commandments of R&B Drumming, by Zoro (Warner Brothers Publications). Lots of personality and a cool history lesson from the clinic fave.

The Funkmasters: The Great James Brown Rhythm Sections 1960-1973, by Allan 'Dr Licks' Slutsky and Chuck Silverman (Warner Bros Publications). 'Funky Drummer', 'Cold Sweat', 'Sex Machine' and the rest, dissected before your eyes. Includes (essential) bass and guitar parts.

Give The Drummers Some: The Great Drummers of R&B, Funk and Soul, by Jim Payne (Warner Bros Publications). Chronology of fundamental grooves from the past 50 years. From simple to impossible.

DRUM'N'BASS

Jungle/Drum'n'Bass For The Acoustic Drumset, by Johnny Rabb (Warner Bros Publications). A welcome and thorough primer on the cutting edge of today's drumming.

FUSION

Contemporary Drummer Plus One, by Dave Weckl (Warner Bros Publications). Challenging, unpatronising and still very cool grooves from the hugely influential fusion hero.

In The Pocket, by Dennis Chambers (Warner Bros Publications). Includes the fiery virtuoso's interpretations of classic grooves from funk/fusion history.

LATIN

Afro-Cuban Rhythms for Drumset, by Frank Malabe and Bob Weiner (Warner Bros Publications).

Funkifying the Clave: Afro Cuban Grooves for Bass and Drums, by Lincoln Goines and Robbie Ameen (Warner Bros Publications). Groundbreaking treatises from pioneers of the genre.

The Essence of Afro-Cuban Percussion And Drum Set, by Ed Uribe (Warner Bros Publications). An absolutely monster piece of work that will last you a lifetime – and then some. Never less than exhaustive. Includes rhythm section parts for bass, piano, guitar, horns and strings. What a guy.

Conversations In Clavé, by Horacio 'El Negro' Hernandez (Warner Bros Publications). This guy has to be seen to be believed. King of the left foot clavé and so much more– and musical with it.

Brazilian Rhythms For Drumset, by Duduka Da Fonseca and Bob Weiner (Warner Bros Publications). Another indispensable primer.

NEW ORLEANS

New Orleans Jazz and Second Line Drumming, by Herlin Riley and Johnny Vidacovich (Warner Bros Publications). Includes revealing roots rhythms and feels, with unique historical perspective from Riley. You can sing all his solos. Fabulous.

AFRICAN

West African Rhythms for Drumset, by Royal Hartigan (Warner Bros Publications). Something different again and another humbling challenge.

BASS DRUMS

Bass Drum Control, by Colin Bailey (Hal Leonard). Classic work from a master player.
Double Bass Drumming, by Joe Franco (Warner Bros Publications). Faultless progressive approach from the rockin' double-kick veteran.
Double Trouble, by Peter Riley (Tindrum Productions). Definitive modern guide to double pedal concepts of the top players by the excellent English drum teacher and performer.
The Encyclopedia of Double Bass Drumming, by Bobby Rondinelli and Michael Lauren (Modern Drummer Publications). Exactly what it says. Exercises, tips, a discography and photos of famous double kick kits.

BRUSHES

Brush Artistry, by Philly Joe Jones (Premier Drum Company). Hard to find, but concise visual primer from the post-bop great.
The Sound of Brushes, by Ed Thigpen (CPP Belwin). The low-down from Ella Fitzgerald's elegant accompanist.

DRUM TUNING

Drum Tuning, by Larry Nolly (Drumstix Publications).
Drum Tuning: The Ultimate Guide, by Scott Schroedl (Hal Leonard)
See also www.drumtuner.com for online drum tuning advice.

VINTAGE DRUM AND CYMBAL HISTORY

All the books below are written by enthusiasts who have done lengthy research into the evolution of our beloved instrument. I recommend whichever takes your fancy. They all make fascinating reading.

Guide To Vintage Drums, by John Aldridge (Centerstream Publishing).
The Great American Drums And The Companies That Made Them 1920-1969, by Harry Cangany (Hal Leonard).
History of the Ludwig Drum Company, by Paul William Schmidt (Centerstream Publishing).
Ludwig, Yesterday and Today 1909-1999, by Paolo Sburlati (published by the author).
The Ludwig Book, by Rob Cook (Rebeats Publications).
The Rogers Book, by Rob Cook (Rebeats Publications).
The Slingerland Book, by Rob Cook (Rebeats Publications).
The Leedy Book, by Rob Cook (Rebeats Publications).
Gretsch Drums, by Chet Falzerano (Hal Leonard).
Star Sets, by John Cohan (Hal Leonard).
The Drum Book, A History Of The Rock Drum Kit, by Geoff Nicholls (Backbeat/Miller Freeman). This lavishly illustrated tome was described as 'drum pornography' by one ecstatic reviewer. If you only buy one book ….
The Cymbal Book, by Hugo Pinksterboer (Hal Leonard). An exhaustive and surprisingly engaging piece of research. Unique, revealing and valuable.
Zildjian, A History of the Legendary Cymbal Makers, by Jon Cohan (Hal Leonard).

DRUM MAGAZINES

Essential for keeping up. Take out long-term subscriptions: it's much cheaper and you'll never regret a penny:

Rhythm, Future Publications, UK
Modern Drummer, Modern Drummer Publications, USA
DRUM!, Phil Hood Publications, USA

VIDEOS AND DVDs

When it comes to videos and DVDs there are now so many and they are nearly all such good entertainment that I'm just going to name-check a few of my favourites. Thanks guys:

Herlin Riley, *Ragtime and Beyond: Evolution of a Style* (DCI). My favourite because it reminds me what drumming's really about.

David Garibaldi, *Tower of Groove* (DCI). Mesmerising control fromTower of Power's legendary Professor of Funk.

Rod Morgenstein, *Putting It All Together* (DCI). Early fusion leftie, an original and powerful voice.

Chad Smith, *Red Hot Rhythm Method* (DCI). Wacko Chado grooves hard with bassist Flea. Loud but funky.

Bernard Purdie, *Groove Master* (Rittor Music). Worth it just for the absurdly simple and joyous eighth-note groove at the beginning, which defies all known laws of physics. Each single tap on the hi-hat is worth a thousand drum machines.

Greg Bissonette, *Private Lesson* (DCI). Unbridled enthusiasm, great ideas and powerful technique.

Dave Weckl, *A Natural Evolution* (Carl Fischer). Typically comprehensive, thoughtful, musical and inspiring three video series from the master technician.

Yogi Horton, *A History of R'n'B/Funk Drumming* (Vintage DCI). Amateur quality footage but great feel from the sorely missed R 'n' B great.

Simon Phillips, and *Simon Phillips Returns* (two video set, DCI). Britain's own powerhouse super drummer in an excellent production. Makes yer proud....

Ian Paice, *Not For The Pros*. Great common sense and insight from the Deep Purple maestro with typically British aplomb.

Jason Bowld, *Drum-Rom* (Hudson Music). Interactive and innovative work from British rocker. The way forward?

Clayton Cameron, *The Living Art of Brushes* (DCI). Modern, inventive interpretation by crooner Tony Bennett's classy accompanist.

Johnny Rabb, *Rhythmsaw Techniques* (johnnyraBB publications). Yet more startling inventiveness. DJ turntable scratching on acoustic kit. Whatever next?

Steve Smith, *Drumset Technique* and *History of the US Beat* (Hudson Music). Much needed, authoritative historical perspective, plus definitive lessons in technique from one of today's premier league players.

> **"Videos are good for the student who needs to move on, as long as they contain the idea that you can use your imagination and wonder what that player's doing now. I see where he was then, now I'm looking at him again. And it's amazing, everything's changed again."**
>
> *BILLY COBHAM*

Gary Chaffee, **Sticking Time, Linear Time, Rhythm and Meter** (DCI). Totally engrossing material from a great teacher.

John Blackwell, **Technique, Grooving and Showmanship** (Hudson Music). Exactly what it says, from Prince's monster groove merchant. Pity those cymbals.

Horacio "El Negro" Hernandez at the Modern Drummer Festival (DCI). A performance which makes you (me, anyway) feel like starting all over again. A left foot with a mind its own.

Legends of Jazz Drumming (two parter from DCI). Revealing history lesson that should be seen by all.

Drum Tuning, Sound and Design, by Bob Gatzen (DCI). Thought-provoking and extremely useful.

FINALLY:
Any video/DVD featuring Buddy Rich or Steve Gadd.

ENDORSEMENT

We all have our heroes, and it's only natural to be influenced by what they play when it comes to choosing gear.

This is, of course, the rationale behind endorsement deals and advertising campaigns: if the world's top drummers play a certain brand of gear it must be good. To a large extent, this is a sound argument and a good reason for you to check out particular types of drums, cymbals, pedals, heads and sticks, etc. But you probably won't be surprised to hear that endorsement is not as simple as it might appear. Drummers endorse products for several reasons, some of which might include:

- **Because they absolutely believe it's the best gear available;**
- **To get a free – or cheap – supply of quality up-to-date gear;**
- **In order to have reliable back-up in any foreign territory they might be working;**
- **To increase their profile via advertising;**
- **To enable them to do clinic tours;**
- **To get their own product ideas manufactured, again increasing their standing and maybe providing them with royalty payments;**
- **Because they're paid to use the gear (which is rare today – drumming is not Formula One racing).**

To take the last and most controversial point first. Sponsorship is a major part of the modern commercial world, and that includes the music business.

However, without wishing to dampen your hopes/dreams too much, very few drummers (particularly in Great Britain) achieve sufficiently high profile to attract large cash handouts in exchange for their endorsement.

Major pop stars – singers, bands and the like – negotiate all sorts of sponsorship deals from commercial corporations, from soft drink firms to cosmetics companies. This is an essential part of the modern music business, helping acts to mount major tours and so on. But lowly drummers

> **"I'm not one of the guys who jumps around and looks for money. For me, with Sabian, Pearl and Vater, it's more the service I need. I've been with them a long time."**
>
> *CHAD SMITH (RED HOT CHILI PEPPERS)*

rarely get much from the drum and cymbal companies, beyond free gear and backup. There simply isn't that much spare cash any more.

The common exception is that drummers are, of course, paid negotiable fees for performing at clinics. The manufacturing companies need the endorsees in order to validate their equipment, to help them with product development and most of all to increase their sales.

When looking for an endorsement deal, drummers do not always go with their first choice company. The typical scenario is that a drummer has been playing Kit A for years and finally gets the big break, starts to get national exposure, and so on. At this point the drummer's management approaches Company A, saying he's always loved its gear, can a deal be worked out?

Companies are obviously more amenable to drummers who already use their gear, who come and say they've been using it for years, or have always wanted to use it but couldn't afford to. But it's quite possible the preferred company simply doesn't want this particular drummer at this time. It may be that company A has its books full and can't do anything. So the drummer inevitably turns to company B. It may be more important to the drummer to get an endorsement - any endorsement - even if the gear is not his or her first choice.

The truth is that all the major drum and cymbal companies make perfectly good gear, and, certainly so far as touring is concerned, most drummers can happily play virtually any make. When it comes to the studio… Well, no one is going to see the vintage kit, snare drums and cymbals that end up on the final cut.

Major companies have artist relations managers, who are swamped with requests for endorsements. They also act like record company A&R staff, and must constantly be on the lookout for new emerging talent.

But just because a drummer has some success does not mean he or she will automatically get a deal. The artist relations guy has to weigh up the chances of this year's sensation being around next year. Maybe the band will break up. Maybe the drummer will get the sack. It's a big commitment by the company, especially when it comes to supplying loads of cut-price or even free cymbals, sticks or heads for a very aggressive player to trash. Companies also have ideas about who they want to represent their name and whether that artist is likely to have a positive effect on their sales and standing. Companies have their own image to look after and they must look to the future.

Sometimes legends of the past get left behind, overtaken by the new *wunderkinder* as younger artist relations guys take over with new ideas. It's a cruel world, and fashions change. Then again, companies sometimes stand by older drummers long after they've passed their sell-by date, particularly if they've genuinely respected the company and worked for it without taking advantage by requesting excessive amounts of gear and selling it off to their pupils.

Drummers may also, from time to time, change their minds. A new or revitalised company may come along with ideas and equipment that the drummer prefers. Their own company may stop making a certain type of drum or cymbal and the drummer may simply not like the newer versions. The company will obviously want their endorsees to be seen with whatever is its latest product. Generally endorsees are happy to go along with this, to road test new gear and even have input in improving designs themselves. But not always. It's a mutual arrangement and sometimes it's time to move on.

Drummers may find the next generation of up-and-coming drummers taking their place in adverts and clinics. Then again, they might get 'poached' by another company that offers what seems to be a better deal – more clinics in new territories, or a new advertising campaign that looks cooler. That's business. Drumming is a career.

In return, drummers are expected to do their bit for the company by displaying company logos on their gear, always being seen live with the gear (although inevitably other equipment may get used in the studio) and by giving credits on albums and in interviews whenever possible. It's also important for endorsees to keep the company informed of how their careers are shaping up. The company may have dozens – if not hundreds – of drummers on its books and one artists representative in each major territory. The rep can't spend his whole time phoning artists' managements for updates. No, the smart drummer will keep in regular contact and send the company guy regular reports of progress and new projects.

In return, the company will keep an up to date inventory of the equipment used by each drummer and do its best to supply a service, particularly in foreign territories where, for example, an artist might be performing and cannot carry all his own gear. Or where the player needs a special set of gear (maybe some additional cymbals or snare drums), perhaps for a recording project. Or for when they are miming on a TV show.

A friend of mine runs the hire company that provides the drums for *Top Of The Pops* (the long standing British TV chart show). Every week, he phones the production office to find out who is appearing – often artists from the USA – and what kits are needed, whether they be Pearl, Yamaha, DW, Zildjian, Paiste, or whatever. He then selects appropriate kits and 'mute' cymbals (for realistic miming) from the stock he keeps from all the different companies, and takes them along to the television studio.

TYPES OF ENDORSEE

The drummers who get deals range from the living legends of the instrument to the latest kid on the block with a big selling album and plenty of TV exposure. Some endorsees are great technicians who win drumming polls; others are members of successful bands who are on MTV a lot. Some are esteemed jazz or session players and many are rock/commercial players. The big companies also supply gear on loan to establishments such as major drum teaching schools, etc.

Of course, the endorsees we mostly know about are the big name players who get their pictures in the adverts. But the big companies have many smaller name endorsees who do a useful job on a local or specialised level. An endorsee who is a respected teacher may have dozens of pupils – the up and coming stars of the next generation – and such a teacher can have a big effect on their product preferences. Similarly with clinicians. We all know the big names who can draw a thousand drummers into one room. But there are loads of smaller name players who might be more appropriate for small-scale promotions in local drum stores and educational arenas.

The companies have to keep their dealers sweet, too. Every drummer the company signs is a keen pro who is now taken out of the buying market: precisely the sort of committed customer who has spent all his cash on drums for the past half dozen years or more. That's less profit for the stores. If half the top guys in London, say, never buy their own cymbals or sticks, that's a lot of serious customers gone. There has to be a balance between the benefit of having those drummers advertising the products and the actual sales lost. And the money has to be made up somewhere. A lot of ordinary drummers wonder whether cymbals, say, are so expensive because the company is giving away so many to its endorsers.

One final thing to know about endorsement deals is that companies often operate different levels of deal. They might for example have three levels: silver, gold and platinum. Silver might be a sort of trial arrangement to see how the drummer's career progresses over a year or two. The drummer gets the opportunity to buy gear at reduced prices and gets some support and exposure thrown in. Gold would be full endorsement: a new kit or set of cymbals each year. Maybe a set for touring and a set for the studio. Platinum would be for the handful of really big name stars. These artists are ambassadors and figureheads for the company and get prestigious advertising, headline clinics and also have serious input into designs. They might well have signature models of their own and will get pretty much anything they ask for.

WEB DIRECTORY

Accessories

www.drumat.com Drumat drum carpet.

www.drumperfect.com Groove Guide digital tempo tachometer.

www.educationalmusicaccessories.com Metro Pad practice pad with built-in metronome.

www.extremeheadphones.com Drummers' headphones.

www.h3drumscience.com Drumstick grip wax.

www.luglock.com L.T. Lug Lock and Tempo REF.

www.puresoundpercussion.com Top class snare wires.

www.rtom.com Moongel damper pads.

www.sambarnard.net Drum Wrap stick tape and plastic recovering wrap, etc.

Cymbal companies

www.alchemycymbals.com Istanbul Turkish cymbals.

www.bosphoruscymbals.com Bosphorus Turkish cymbals.

www.istanbulcymbals.com Istanbul Agop Turkish cymbals.

www.istanbulmehmet.com Istanbul Mehmet Turkish cymbals.

www.meinl.de Meinl cymbals and percussion, Germany.

www.paiste.com Paiste cymbals, Switzerland.

www.sabian.com Sabian cymbals, Canada.

www.emdmusic.be Distributors of Stagg Chinese cymbals.

www.turkishcymbals.com Turkish cymbals.

www.ufip.com UFIP cymbals, Italy.

www.universalpercussion.com Distributors of Genuine Chinese Wuhan cymbals and gongs.

www.zildjian.com Zildjian cymbals.

Drum companies

www.arbiterdrums.com Arbiter drums, England.

www.ayottedrums.com Canadian hand made drums.

www.bradydrums.com.au Australian solid wood shell snare drums.

www.dwdrums.com Drum Workshop drums, USA.

www.gretsch.com Gretsch drums, USA.

www.ludwig-drums.com Ludwig drums, USA.

www.mapexdrums.com Mapex drums, Taiwan.

www.noblecooley.com Noble and Cooley drums, USA.

www.pacificdrums.com Pacific Drums by DW, USA.

www.pearldrum.com Pearl drums, Japan.

www.peavey.com Peavey Radial Pro drums, USA.

www.premier-drums.com Premier drums, UK.

www.remo.com Remo drums and drumheads, USA.

www.sonor.de Sonor drums, Germany.

www.slingerland.com Slingerland drums, USA.

www.tama.com Tama drums, Japan.

www.proelgroup.com Tamburo drums, Italy.

www.yamaha.com Yamaha drums, Japan.

Specialist and custom drum companies

www.allegradrums.com Allegra hand made maple drums, USA.

www.boomtheory.com Space Muffins maple kit with integrated triggering, USA.

www.cadesonmusic.com Cadeson maple finish Taiwanese drums.

www.candccustomdrums.com C and C Custom Drums, USA.

www.cledrums.com CLE custom built Maple drums, USA.

www.db-musical.com Large volume, bargain Taiwanese drums/percussion manufacturer.

www.drumsolo.cc Eco-friendly exotic hardwood snares, USA.

www.gmsdrums.com GMS maple drums, USA.

www.fibes.com Original fibreglass drums, USA.

www.groverpro.com Grover Percussion, USA.

www.headdrums.com Head stave construction snares, USA.

www.jalapenodrums.co.uk Jalapeno handmade drums, UK.

www.mrpdrums.com MRP custom maple drums, USA.

www.noonandrums.com Gary Noonan custom brass and solid wood shell drums, UK.

www.ocdrum.com Orange County drums, USA.

www.peacemusic.com.tw Peace Drums, Taiwan.

www.precisiondrum.com Precision Custom Drums and drum services, USA.

www.rocketshells.com Rocket carbon fibre drums, USA.

www.rmvdrums.com RMV Brazilian Bapeva wood shell kits.

www.sleishman.com Sleishman drums. Australian inventor of first twin bass drum pedal.

www.spaundrums.com Spaun maple drums with 45 degree V cut bearing edges, USA.

www.sunlitedrum.com Sunlite Industrial Corporation.

www.taye.com TAYE maple shell drums of Nashville, USA

www.trickdrums.com Trick aluminium shell drums; also drum and cymbal polishing products, USA.

www.westworld.com/~porkpie/ Pork Pie quality hand finished maple shell drums, USA.

www.worldmaxusa.com World Max drums, Taiwan.

www.zickosdrums.com Original acrylic drumsets, USA.

Electronic drum companies

www.edrums.com Pintech electronic pad kits and triggers.

www.alternatemode.com KAT percussion and drumKAT.

www.clavia.se ddrum electronic kits, Sweden.

www.hartdynamics.com Hart Dynamics Acupad electronic pads.

www.koby.co.uk Koby electronic pad kits and triggers, UK.

www.rolandus.com www.roland.co.jp www.roland.co.uk The Roland Corporation.

www.yamaha.com The Yamaha Corporation.

Hardware companies

www.axispercussion.com Hi-tech structural grade aircraft aluminium and steel kick pedals.

www.carbonlite.com Carbon fibre drum racks.

www.damicodrums.com D'Amico adjustable bass drum cradle.

www.drumframe.com Drum Frame complete mounting system.

www.dwdrums.com DW's class-leading pedals.

www.gibraltarhardware.com Broad range of hardware solutions.

www.hardcase.com Hardcase drum cases.

www.homestead.com/playsmart/pedals.html Smart heel-driven bass drum pedal.

www.humes-berg.com Enduro hard cases.

www.leatherman.com Leatherman multi-tools.

www.protectionracket.com Protection racket cases.

www.theduallist.com Award winning Scottish two-beats-for-one kick pedal.

www.vrukpedal.com Ingenious bass drum pedal modifier.

www.xlspec.com Protechtor cases.

Drumhead companies

www.aquariandrumheads.com Aquarian drumheads.

www.bearpercussion.com Three styles of Kevlar head.

www.earthtoneheads.com Pre-mounted and stretched calf skin heads on aluminium hoops.

www.evansdrumheads.com Evans drumheads.

www.remo.com Remo drumheads

www.universalpercussion.com Attack drumheads

Drumstick companies

www.agner-sticks.com Agner Swiss Drumsticks made from American hickory.

www.aquariandrumheads.com Aquarian synthetic sticks.

www.b-stick.com B-sticks sticks from Denmark finished with bees wax.

www.bigbangdist.com Ahead synthetic sticks.

www.cappelladrumsticks.com Wood sticks and aluminium practice sticks.

www.johnnyrabb.com JohnnyraBB sticks.

www.musicshipping.co.uk Pro-Orca sticks from France.

www.promark-stix.com Promark sticks.

www.regaltip.com Regal Tip: largest manufacturer of brushes.

www.shawstix.co.uk Leading manufacturer in Britain.

www.trueline.com Trueline sticks.

www.vicfirth.com Vic Firth sticks.

www.vater.com Vater sticks.

www.verisonicsticks.com Verisonic original aluminium sticks and brushes.

www.zildjian.com Zildjian sticks.

Further useful websites

www.pas.org PAS: The Percussive Arts Society.

www.moderndrummer.com *Modern Drummer* magazine.

www.futuremusic.co.uk *Rhythm* magazine.

www.notsomoderndrummer.com *Not So Modern Drummer* vintage magazine.

www.rebeats.com Vintage author Rob Cook's site.

www.foreverdrumming.com/books/g.html Contains an extensive list of drumming books.

Finishes and drum covering wraps

www.sambarnard.net/wrap_history.htm Drum wraps.

www.sambarnard.net/drum_wrap_video.htm Video on how to re-cover drums.

www.networkmusic.net Good selection of wraps and instructions for DIY covering.

www.drummaker.com Drum supplies, wraps, shells, finishes, advice, etc.

www.kellerproducts.com Keller drum shells.

Some Vintage Ludwig Vistalite sites (just for fun)

www.rcivistalite.com

www.angelfire.com/biz6/ludwigvistalites/index.html

www.vistalites.com

Hearing conservation

www.hei.org House Ear Institute's Sound Partners programme for hearing conservation.

www.hearnet.com Hearing Education and Awareness for Rockers.

www.hearos.com Graded foam ear plugs.

www.aearo.com E.A.R. earplugs, etc.

www.proplugs.com Doc's Pro Plugs.

www.etymotic.com Etymotic Research: moulded ear plugs for musicians.

www.bigbangdist.com Metrophones: musicians' enclosed headphones with optional built-in metronome.

GLOSSARY

acorn The tip of certain drumsticks, which have an acorn shape. See also 'bead' and 'tip'.

acousticon A synthetic material developed by the Remo drum company and used to make their drum shells.

action See 'snare action'.

air hole Most drums have a small hole, about 3/8" (10mm) in diameter, drilled though the shell, sometimes disguised within the company's nameplate. The hole is there to allow the escape of air when the drum is struck. Recently certain drums have been made with several air holes.

base plate The rectangular bottom plate used in some bass drum and hi-hat pedal designs to increase stability.

bass drum The biggest drum in the kit, which sits on the floor and is usually played with a foot pedal. Bass drums are sometimes referred to as 'kick' drums for brevity.

bass drum pedal The foot pedal that is used to play the bass drum.

bass drum spurs Spiked metal rods that keep the bass drum upright and prevent it creeping forward when played.

basket See 'snare basket'.

bass drum hoop See 'hoop'.

batter head The top membrane or 'skin' of the drum – the one you play on.

bead the tip of the drumstick, also called acorn or tip.

bead, centre bead The horizontal indentation(s) running around a metal shell snare drum that helps strengthen the shell and keep it round. On some drums, the centre bead also joins the upper and lower half of the shell together. Beads may be either convex or concave.

bearing edge The edge of the drum's shell over which the head is stretched. Often cut at an angle varying from 30 to 60 degrees.

beater This may be a felt beater stick as used by classical percussionists, or it may be the beater rod that is part of the bass drum pedal.

bell The central raised portion of a cymbal, often the thickest and heaviest section, with a bell-like tone. Also known as the cup.

boom stand A cymbal stand with an angled, extendable arm, bringing the cymbal into reach over the toms. Boom stands are particularly necessary with larger, extended kits.

bracket See 'tom tom holder'.

brushes Wire or plastic brushes, used instead of sticks to produce a lighter touch on drums and cymbals.

butt end The securing device for the snare at the opposite end to the snare strainer or throw-off. Also, the butt end of a stick is the thicker back end opposite to the tip.

butt joint A joint that meets flat, end-on, with no overlapping. This usually refers to the join in a wooden or metal shell.

cage See 'rack system'.

china (or chinese) type cymbal. As distinct from the Turkish/European/American type of cymbal, Chinese or China type cymbals have a trashier sound, upturned perimeter and often a squared bell.

chops Slang term for a musician's playing technique.

claves Paired short and thick hardwood sticks, played by cupping one stick in the palm of the hand and striking with the other.

claw hooks or **brackets** Before the advent of flanged metal rims, tuning was achieved by passing the tension bolts through metal claw brackets that hooked over the drum's wooden rims. These claw brackets are still retained on bass drums, which generally still have wooden rims. Modern retro-style drums with wooden rims also sometimes have claw hooks.

clutch The mechanical device that clamps the top hi-hat cymbal to the central hi-hat pull rod and thus causes the cymbal to go up and down with the motion of the foot pedal.

cocktail drum Cocktail kits were first seen in the 1950s in America and have been revived by Yamaha in the 1990s. The kit centres around a deep floor tom tom that is adapted to have a snare under the top head and a foot pedal beneath the bottom head. The pedal makes an upstroke so that the bottom head functions like a bass drum. In addition, there may be an attached cymbal, cowbell and sometimes a small snare drum.

coordination The technique of coordinating your limbs in order to play the drum kit. See also 'independence'.

concert tom tom A single headed tom tom in a group of toms, which may be tuned to melodic intervals.

counter hoop See 'rim'.

crash cymbal A cymbal whose primary function is to emphasize accents in the music. By 'crashing' the edge of the cymbal a more explosive accent is produced. Crash cymbals are usually thinner than ride cymbals.

cup See 'bell'.

cymbal The cymbal is a musical instrument described as an idiophone. It is usually a convex circular plate of highly worked bronze, although other metals/alloys are sometimes employed.

cymbal felt The thick circular felt washers which cushion the cymbal when tightened on to the cymbal stand or hi-hat clutch.

cymbal sleeve The short length of usually plastic or nylon tubing, which is slipped over the spindle on the top of the cymbal stand. The sleeve passes through the hole in the cymbal bell and prevents metal-to-metal contact.

damping or **dampening** The practice of reducing the excessive overtones and ring from a drumhead, usually by application of some external material. See also 'muffling'.

die-cast rim or hoop A type of metal drum rim, usually made by casting zinc alloy in a die mould. Die-cast rims are thicker and sturdier than flanged rims, which are usually made by bending strips of pressed steel or brass.

dot Central reinforcing circle of Mylar or other material that is stuck to the underside (or occasionally the top side) of a drum skin. See, for example, Remo's CS Black Dot heads.

double-braced Term used with reference to the tripod bases of drum kit hardware (cymbal or snare drum stands, etc), which may have single or double braced legs.

double (bass drum) pedal A device that allows two bass drum beaters to be played on a single bass drum. The main pedal is attached as normal to the bass drum hoop while an extension rod connects to the second 'slave' pedal.

double ended lug This is a lug box that is threaded at both ends and thus receives lug bolts from both the top and the bottom of the drum.

drop-clutch A special hi-hat clutch that, with the flick of a lever, allows the top hi-hat cymbal to drop on to the lower cymbal where it is clamped shut. This can be useful when playing a double bass pedal.

drum clinic Drum clinics are essentially master classes in which a leading drummer demonstrates technique and musicianship for other drummers and interested onlookers. The drummers are often endorsees of particular drum and cymbal companies, who sponsor the clinics to promote their products. Other sponsors might include store owners and magazines, etc.

drum key A special thumb key that is used to tension drumheads. Tension rods usually have a square end and require a square section key. Some

drum companies have in the past (Premier) and still today (Sonor) used conventional slotted screw ends on their tension rods. These can be tensioned with a normal screwdriver.

drum kit or drumset Interchangeable terms for the unified collection of percussion instruments that is the subject of this book. Note that drum kit is the usual British term whereas drumset is often used in the USA.

drum machine An analogue or digital device that allows the programming and playing back of electronically stored drum, cymbal and percussion sounds.

drum rack See 'rack system'.

drum tech A drum tech or technician is a member of a band's road crew whose specific job is to look after the drummer. This entails setting up the drum kit and maintaining it in good working order, particularly while on tour, but also during rehearsals and recording dates. The drumtech is also a personal assistant to the drummer when needed.

electronic drum kit A set of drum and cymbal pads that trigger percussive sounds via an accompanying electronic module.

european style cymbal This term is sometimes used to distinguish budget or mid-priced b8 bronze cymbals from so-called 'cast' Turkish-American style cymbals made from b20 bronze.

field drum, marching drum or **parade drum** The side drum of military origin, which is slung from the shoulder and played while marching. Field drums are specialist designs, usually deeper then kit snare drums and tuned to exceptionally high tensions.

flesh hoop Old fashioned term, used in connection with drum skins, for the hoop over which the skin, hide or vellum is shrunk.

floating head Some drums (for

example, those by Premier) have slightly undersized diameters so that that there is a small gap between the head and the rim.

floor tom tom The largest range of tom toms, which have their own three retractable legs.

flush base The base of a cymbal or other stand where the three legs fold out flat rather than in a pyramidal tripod.

flush bracing Single tension brace or lug which stretches the whole length of the shell, pioneered by Premier in the late 1940s. Also known as high tension lugs, and used in parade drums, which have to withstand extremely high tensions.

fulcrum With relation to stick control, this is the point where you grip the stick and about which the stick turns.

fusion set Marketing term used to describe a standard five piece drum kit with slightly smaller sized shells, usually 20", 10", 12" and 14" plus snare drum. The 14" tom is usually mounted on a floor stand rather than on its own legs.

gaffer tape All-purpose cloth-based sticky tape that comes in two-inch wide rolls and is universally used in the stage/entertainment industries. The tape has great strength and sticks to anything, but is easy to tear off in strips.

generic kits Drum kits, usually made in Taiwan or China, which follow a basic plan, derived originally from the early Pearl Export design. These kits continue to have many similarities, but have evolved into excellent starter kits. They are sold under numerous different brand names throughout the world.

glitter Classic plastic wrap used as a decorative finishing material on drum shells. Also known as sparkles, they are produced in several colours. Sparkles are also occasionally available in lacquered finishes.

glue ring A wooden hoop glued around

the inside upper and lower ends of a thin shell in order to strengthen and keep it in round. Also known as reinforcing ring or hoop.

gong drum A single headed bass drum, usually mounted upright on a floor stand like an orchestral bass drum. Introduced to the modern drum kit by Billy Cobham and Tama in the 1970s.

grommet A rubber ring lining a hole.

hanging toms Alternative term for the smaller toms that are mounted on the bass drum.

hardware All-encompassing term for the stands and pedals, etc, used to set up and play the drum kit.

head The modern term for drum skins, particularly those made from plastic or other synthetic materials.

hickory Hard wood commonly used for making drumsticks.

high-tension lugs See 'flush bracing'.

hi-hat, hi-hat pedal Hardware stand that is operated by a foot pedal connected by a pull rod to two horizontally mounted cymbals. The cymbals, which are normally of the same diameter, are clashed together by the action of the pedal.

hi-hat clutch (See 'clutch', above)

holder See 'tom tom bracket'.

hoop Drumheads are mounted on hoops. Drum skins used to be shrunk over flesh hoops, while today's plastic heads are mounted on hoops, usually made from aluminium or steel. There is some confusion between the terms **hoop** and **rim**. The metal tuning rims of the drums are also sometimes – confusingly – called hoops, while the rim of the bass drum, still made from wood, is normally called a hoop.

idiophone An instrument which produces sound from the material of an instrument itself without the assistance of reeds or strings, etc.

independence The art of playing the drum kit requires the drummer to play different rhythms with each limb. The limbs sometimes appear to be acting independently. In most cases, however, this is an illusion and the player is really practising coordination. Nonetheless, there is no doubt that in the case of the great players a sort of independence is achieved: the ability to improvise complex rhythms with two or three limbs, while maintaining a set pattern (ostinato) with the fourth. Steve Smith, one of today's leading players, suggests the term 'inter-dependence', while the phrase 'coordinated independence', made famous by Jim Chapin, also sums up the technique well. See also 'coordination'.

isolation mount or **resonance isolation mount** A mounting system for tom toms or snare drums that maximises the drum's resonance by 'isolating' the shell from the mounting hardware, usually by rubber grommets, etc. See also 'RIMS mount'.

jazz kit or set Modern term for a four piece drumset consisting of 20", 12" and traditional 14" floor tom (on legs), plus a snare drum.

jungle kit drum kit with under-sized drums, originally intended for playing super-fast jungle or drum'n'bass beats.

Kevlar A woven synthetic fabric most often used in the manufacture of extremely high tension marching band drums. The same material is famously used for bullet proof vests.

key (See 'drum key' above)

kit Drum kit and drumset are interchangeable terms.

lacquered finish Lacquered outer finishes are often applied to natural wood shells to enhance the grain and to seal and protect the wood.

lathed Cymbals are often lathed with concentric grooves, or 'tone rings',

around their top surface and sometimes underneath also.

lug bolt Also known as tension bolt or screw. Threaded bolts that are passed through the rim of the drum and screwed into the receiving lug box and thereby used to adjust the tension of the drumhead.

lug box, lug casing Lug boxes are fitted to the shell to accept the lug bolts which tension the heads. Lugs may be single or double ended. They may be hollow castings or they may be solid and tubular.

Melinex A polyester film which the Premier drum company used to employ for making its own Everplay drumheads. Today Melinex is used by Remo for its smooth white heads. Melinex is very similar to Mylar.

melodic tom toms See also 'concert toms'.

memory locks Specially designed small clamps, used between the sections of stands and other hardware with the dual purpose of extra stability and 'memorising' the set up height/angle, etc. First seen in the Rogers Memriloc hardware of the 1970s.

metric sizes See 'pre-international'.

metronome A mechanical or electronic device that marks exact time via a regular repeating click, tone, blip or flashing light.

MIDI Musical Instrument Digital Interface. The computer digital interface, devised in 1983 as the standard protocol allowing digital electronic instruments of all types to work together.

muffling See 'damping'.

multi-clamp A versatile multi-angled clamp that allows the mounting of add-on equipment, perhaps a splash cymbal or cowbell, to your existing hardware set-up.

Mylar The synthetic polyester film used

in the manufacture of most modern drumheads.

nap The slightly hairy/downy surface of animal skin, mimicked by the coating on synthetic heads, the purpose being to create friction for brush playing.

natural finish A wood shell that may be lacquered, oiled or otherwise sealed but not stained, painted or covered: ie, it displays the natural grain colour of the timber beneath.

nodal point A point of minimum resonance on a drum's shell. The term has been registered as a trademark by the Noble and Cooley drum company and it and subsequent manufacturers have identified the nodal points as the best places to position mounting brackets.

nut box The bracket on a shell's surface into which the tension rods are screwed. See also 'lug box'.

nylon tip Some drumsticks have a nylon cap glued on over the tip of the wood in place of the normal bead. Nylon tips last longer and produce a pingier sound.

o-ring A perimeter ring of Mylar or imilar material, laid on the surface of a drumhead to effect damping/muffling.

pad (See 'practice pad').

parallel action snare / parallel action A sophisticated snare straining mechanism that holds the snare under tension whether in the 'on' or 'off' position.

pearl Classic-style plastic wrap used as a decorative finishing material on drum shells. Pearls include many different patterns and colours.

port The hole in the front bass drumhead that allows the escape of air and is often used for miking.

powder coating Sometimes used on hardware instead of chrome plating. Powder coating is a sprayed and baked

finish with a similar appearance to textured paint, but with greater durability and stability, and more resistance to scratching and chipping.

power tom toms Tom toms that are deeper than standard size.

practice pad A pad of wood or rubber, etc, used for stick practice and warm-up exercises.

pre-international European drums before the late 1960s sometimes had metric diameters, which means that today's American-size drumheads may not fit. In particular, Premier tom toms made before 1969 suffer from this problem. It is still possible to get replacement plastic heads from Remo, although they are no longer made by Premier itself.

pull rod The metal connecting spindle that runs down the centre of the hi-hat pedal between the cymbals at the top and the foot pedal at the bottom.

rack, rack system A system of mounting tom toms, cymbals and other items of the kit on a rack, which usually consists of horizontal tubular or square section bars clamped to vertical feet posts. Also known as a cage.

rack tom tom, rack mount tom These are traditionally the small toms mounted on the bass drum via a standard tom mount. Since the advent of rack systems the terms also apply to toms mounted on racks.

ratchet A joint in any stand or piece of mounting hardware that has geared teeth enabling it to be fixed in place at different angles.

reinforcing hoop or ring See 'glue ring'.

remote hi-hat, remote bass drum pedal A remote hi-hat is one that is mounted elsewhere on the kit, away from the normal hi-hat stand, and worked by a 'remote' pedal, often linked via a flexible cable. Remote bass drum pedals are similar, except that the

mechanism in this case is usually a fixed rod like that used for the slave pedal of a double bass drum pedal.

resonance The natural sound vibrations associated with a drumhead, shell, or a cymbal, etc.

resonant chamber The drum shell is a resonant chamber that amplifies, colours and directs the sound produced by striking the drumhead.

resonant head The bottom head of a tom tom or snare drum which responds with sympathetic resonance when the batter head is struck.

ride cymbal A usually quite large (18"-24") and relatively heavy cymbal which is used to play continuous rhythms or 'ride patterns'.

rim The metal hoop of a drum which holds the head in place and tensions it. See also 'counter hoop' and 'hoop'.

RIMS mount The American company Purecussion is renowned for pioneering this method of mounting tom toms via a curved metal bracket that attaches to the tension rods, affording minimum contact and maximising the freedom of the shell to resonate. The principle has since been adopted by every other major drum manufacturer.

rivet A flat headed metal pin that, in relation to the drum kit, is most commonly used in bass drum pedal or hi-hat pedal construction, etc. Rivets are also sometimes used in 'rivet cymbals' to create a sizzle effect.

rivet cymbal A cymbal with holes drilled in it for the inclusion of small rivets to produce a sizzling sound. Also called a 'sizzle cymbal'.

rope tension drum Before the advent of modern tension lugs, European-derived military drums were tensioned by a system of ropes, diagonally crossing the shell.

Roto-toms These are single headed tom toms that have cast alloy basket-design frames mounted on a central spindle, which, when rotated, increases or decreases the tension in the head. They are therefore tuneable to specific pitches. Roto-toms are made by Remo.

Scarf joint A woodworking term referring to the method of joining plies of wood via a graduated sloping cut. Each section of plywood is shaved gradually from full thickness to a point, over a length of several inches. Compare this to a butt joint, in which the ends of the wood are joined flat on.

seamless shell Term applied to metal shell drums (usually snare drums) that are spun from a single sheet of metal and so do not have a seam or joint.

seating When a head is placed on to a drum shell and tensioned, it then needs to experience a process of 'stretching' or 'seating'.

self-aligning lug Self-aligning cast lugs, each containing a swivel nut that allows some leeway in lining up the tension rod with the hole in the metal rim it passes through. The incidence of cross-threading is thus reduced. This was a problem with older style tube lugs, which were tapped directly and allowed no lateral flexibility.

set Drumset and drum kit are interchangeable terms.

shell The shell is the resonating body of the drum.

shell set Marketing term for a drumset that consists of the shells, with or without appropriate mounting hardware and spurs, but devoid of stands, pedals and cymbals, etc. A shell set may also not include a snare drum.

single lug A single lug or single ended lug is a lug box that is threaded at one end only and thus receives a single tension rod.

size Drum sizes have been standardised since early in the last century and are measured in Imperial rather than metric figures. This book follows suit. The measurements refer to the actual size of the shell and not to the overall size of the drum including the metal rims. To make life confusing, the American convention is to quote the shell depth first, followed by its diameter: thus a typical snare drum is 5"x14". In Britain, these figures are given in reverse order, ie, 14"x5". That is the system used in this book.

sizzle cymbal A cymbal drilled with small holes (around 3/16") for the inclusion of rivets or other metallic pins to create a sustained sizzling effect when played. Otherwise known as a rivet cymbal.

snares The wires or cords tensioned beneath the bottom and (occasionally) top head of a snare drum to give the drum its characteristic sharp, rasping sound. Today snares are usually made from coiled metal wires. Snares are also made from silk-covered wire, gut, wire cable and a variety of other materials.

snare action This usually refers to the type of snare strainer fitted to a drum, which may have one of several different types of mechanical action.

snare basket The part of the snare drum stand that directly supports the drum and usually comprises three fold-up arms.

snare bed The shallow grooves cut into the bottom bearing edge of the snare drum to facilitate attaching the snare so that it lies flat against the snare head. This helps to reduce the incidence of snare rattle and choking.

snare drum The central drum of the kit, which is placed on a stand between the player's legs and which has a snare stretched across the bottom head to produce the distinctive rasping snare drum sound.

snare-side head or snare head The bottom head of the snare drum. Also called the resonant head.

snare strainer and snare release The mechanism whereby the snares are held under tension against the bottom (snare) head. Usually includes a spring and thumb screw tensioner and a lever (or throw-off) that switches the strainer between the 'on' and 'off' positions.

snare string and snare tape The snare is attached to the strainer and butt end by means of strong cords or 'strings', or by two short strips of strong tape.

snare throw-off A lever, today usually incorporated in the snare strainer, which switches the snares between the 'on' and 'off' positions. Different designs include side lever or pull-away actions.

soprano and sopranino Terms used by Peter Erskine to describe his extra-small diameter (10" and 12") signature snare drums.

sparkle See 'glitter'.

split shell In the 1980s, Ludwig produced the classic slotted Coliseum snare drum, which had a shell split in two with a horizontal gap running around the centre. The Spaun drum company has also adopted this style recently with a one-inch gap between the top and bottom half of the shell.

spring tension Term used in reference to bass drum pedals and to a lesser extent hi-hat pedals. Altering the spring tension affects the amount of effort required in making each stroke.

spurs Bass drum spurs are short, fold-out or telescopic legs with pointed ends, which prevent the bass drum from rolling sideways or from creeping forward during performance.

square sizes Term used with reference to shells – usually tom toms – that have the same depth and diameter, ie, 8"x8" or 16"x16", etc.

staggered plies This refers to the shell making technique where different plies within the shell are arranged so that they join up at different places around the circumference, rather than all at the same spot. This greatly increases the strength of the shell and its tendency to remain cylindrical.

stands General term for all the mounting hardware on the kit, which might include cymbal stands, snare drum stands, floor tom stands, and even the hi-hat.

straight sided A straight sided drum shell is one which has no internal reinforcing rings: ie, it is straight up and down internally. Also known as unsupported or unobstructed.

straight stand A cymbal stand that has no boom arm attachment.

suspended cymbal A cymbal that is hung from an arm (human or metal.) rather than mounted on a stand.

swivel nut See 'self-aligning lug'.

tension bolt/screw/rod The tension bolt passes through the metal rim of the drum and is screwed into the lug, thus pulling down on the hoop of the drumhead. It is also known as the tuning rod.

tension bracket See 'lug'.

tension rod See 'tension bolt'.

throne The drummer's stool. The term applies particularly to the cylindrical stands case, covered in the same material as the drumset, which doubled as a seat and was popular in the big-band era of drumming rather than today. Today's stools are adjustable for height, which the old thrones were not.

throw-off See 'snare throw-off'.

thumb rod Timpani-style tension rods that have 'T' handles so that they can be tightened by hand (using thumb and first finger) without the need for a drum key. They were found on early tom toms, and persisted on bass drums until the 1990s.

tilter The mechanism fitted to the top section of a cymbal stand to allow the cymbal to be tilted to the required angle for playing.

tip The tip or normal playing end of a standard drumstick.

tom tom Single or double headed drums without snares, which usually range in diameter from 8″ to 20″. Often shortened to 'tom'.

tom tom holder Any clamping device used to mount tom toms on the bass drum or on a stand. Also known as tom bracket or mount.

tom tom, single-headed A tom tom that has a tunable head on the batter side only, meaning the bottom end is left open.

toys Slang term used for small items of percussion, such as woodblocks, cowbells and maracas, played by a drummer, percussionist or other members of a band.

traps Term used to describe the early drum kit and its multiple percussive effects or 'contraptions'.

trigger pad An electronic drum pad used as a switch to trigger electronically stored sounds.

triple-flanged rim or hoop The pressed metal – usually steel or brass – rim fitted to either end of the drum shell and tightened over the drumhead via the tension rods. The rim – also known as the counter hoop or rim – has a triple flanged cross section. Hoops were originally flat strips of metal which then had a single, followed by a double flange incorporated for strength and to allow the tension bolts to pass through them. The third flange was added in the top of the hoop to save on stick wear. Rims without the third flange are known as 'stick chopper' rims or hoops.

tuning The process of tightening the head on an individual drum, or on the whole kit, to produce a 'tuneful' pleasing sound. For most drummers the term is more correctly 'tensioning' since the drums are not required to achieve specific melodic pitches.

Turkish-American style cymbal A cymbal made from b20 bronze in the tradition brought to the USA from Turkey. See also 'European style cymbal'.

unsupported or unobstructed See 'straight sided'.

vent hole A small hole drilled in the side of the drum shell that allows air to escape when the drum is struck (see also 'air hole'). More recently Orange County has produced snare drums with much larger circular 'vent' holes in the shells. These are said to increase volume and sensitivity while decreasing shell resonance. The term vented is also used by head manufacturer Evans to describe the perimeter pinholes in its Genera Dry batter heads.

Vintage The term vintage drums used to refer loosely to those from the jazz and swing ages, before the 1960s. Nowadays, vintage refers to pretty much any drums that are out of production, including, for example, Ludwig Vistalite (plexiglas) drums from the 1970s. Similarly, with cymbals, it's not just Turkish made 'K' Zildjians from the 1940s that attract interest, but also such cymbals as early Paistes from the 1960 and 1970s.

wire brushes Wire brushes may be used instead of sticks for playing the drums, particularly on softer tunes and ballads. The strands of fine wire are fixed in a handle of wood or rubber and are sometimes retractable, which prevents them from getting bent. Wire brushes probably developed from bundles of twigs tied together. Today, brushes may have plastic or nylon strands rather than wire.

x-hat A secondary hi-hat, positioned in any convenient place around the kit. The x-hat is fixed closed and is mounted on a short stand, played by hand rather then operated by the foot.

INDEX

AUTHOR'S ACKNOWLEDGEMENTS

I'm indebted to the following publications – in particular, *Rhythm* and *Modern Drummer* magazines – for the vast amount of information I have gleaned from them over the past twenty-odd years:

Drum! www.drummagazine.com
Rhythm www.futurenet.co.uk
Modern Drummer www.moderndrummer.com
Not So Modern Drummer www.notsomoderndrummer.com
The Old Drummers' Club email: dave.seville@btinternet.com

I'm also indebted to the following good guys: John Aldridge (*Not So Modern Drummer*); Sir Alan Buckley (Classic Drum Museum); Rob Cook (Rebeats Publications); James Cumpsty (*Rhythm* magazine); Ronald Fry (Hudson Music); Bill Harrison; Bob Henrit (Arbiter UK); Nick Hudson (Premier Percussion); Louise King (*Rhythm* magazine); Kevin Lowery (*Rhythm* magazine); Gary Mann (Remo Europe); Jerome Marcus (Sabian); Dave Mattacks; Gary Noonan (Noonan Drums); David Phillips (Pearl UK); Dave Seville (*The Old Drummers' Club*); Steve Smith; Gavin Thomas (Yamaha UK); Mike U'Dell (Drumhire) and Steve White.

I'm also indebted to the following drum-techs for their tips: Dodge (Steve and Alan White); Yard Gavrilovic (Steve Gadd, Zak Starkey); Lance Mills (Andy Gangadeen, Vinnie Colaiuta); Chris Sobchack (Simon Phillips, Nigel Olssen); Sam O'Sullivan (Larry Mullen Jnr).

I've also drawn on quotes from interviews (mostly for *Making Music* and *Rhythm* magazines) that I have previously conducted with the following drummers:
Will Calhoun, Billy Cobham, Geoff Dugmore, Andy Gangadeen, Gary Husband, Kenney Jones, Dave Lombardo, John Marshall, Dave Mattacks, Derrick McKenzie, Andy Newmark, Gary Noonan, Simon Phillips, J R Robinson, Ralph Salmins, Chad Smith, Steve Smith, Matt Sorum, Frank Tontoh, Charlie Watts, Alan White and Steve White. My thanks to all of them.